Windows Annoyances

D0232786

Windows Annoyances

David A. Karp

O'REILLY™

Cambridge · *Köln* · *Paris* · *Sebastopol* · *Tokyo*

Windows Annoyances
by David Karp

Copyright © 1997 O'Reilly & Associates, Inc. All rights reserved.
Printed in the United States of America.

Editor: Andrew Schulman

Production Editor: Nancy Wolfe Kotary

Printing History:

April 1997:   First Edition.

This book is printed on acid-free paper with 85% recycled content, 15% post-consumer waste. O'Reilly & Associates is committed to using paper with the highest recycled content available consistent with high quality.

ISBN: 1-56592-266-2   [8/97]

Table of Contents

Preface

Microsoft has inflicted Windows 95 and (for the brave) Windows NT 4.0 upon millions of unsuspecting users. Your mission, should you decide to accept it, is to create a usable operating system from what you've been provided. This book is an essential tool you can use to help you overcome all of the annoyances that plague your Windows PC.

Whether you're trying to speed up your connection to the Internet, figure out why your hard drive keeps crashing, or finally dump that useless MSN icon, *Windows Annoyances* is for you. This book includes solutions that enable you to both customize and troubleshoot Windows. This is an important distinction, as many times solving a problem requires that you know whether it's a bug or a feature of the software, and the dividing line isn't always clear. A bug is an action of some software that wasn't intended by the programmer. It's important to realize that if software doesn't respond in a way that you think it should, it should be regarded as poor design. You shouldn't be required to adjust the way you think in order to complete a task on a computer; rather you should learn how to adjust the computer to work in a way that makes sense to you. This is what this book is about.

Organization of This Book

Chapter 1, *So You're Stuck with Windows,* discusses the differences between Windows 95 and Windows NT 4.0 and describes the new features found in both products.

Chapter 2, *Customizing Your System,* starts by examining Windows' user interface (or lack thereof) and how to overcome its limitations. What follows is a discussion of the way you work with Windows and how it can be improved. The basics include some of the more arcane keyboard shortcuts, advanced tips for getting the most out of Explorer, and undocumented security and multiple-user settings. Replacing the awful Windows startup screen and customizing certain interface components is only the beginning; in this book, editing the **Start Menu** has a whole new meaning.

Chapter 3, *The Registry,* covers the Registry and the Registry Editor. This is important, because most of the solutions thereafter make use of this knowledge. Again, instead of simply including portions of the flimsy user's manual, this section covers some useful advanced techniques and solutions.

Chapter 4, *Advanced Customization Techniques,* continues with customization and problem-solving topics that take advantage of the Registry techniques discussed earlier.

Chapter 5, *Maximizing Performance,* and Chapter 6, *Troubleshooting,* cover improving performance and troubleshooting, respectively. These two subjects are closely related, and you'll find that the two chapters are structured similarly. The goal here is to improve your system without spending a load of money on new software and hardware.

Chapter 7, *Networking,* levels the playing field by covering many aspects of networking, including hooking up a simple local area network and dialing into the Internet.

Four appendixes are included as references written for humans, because we know that most references are designed for those who don't need them in the first place.

Getting the Most out of This Book

While this book is arranged as a reference and is not intended to be read cover to cover, it is structured so that you'll progress easily from one topic to the next, expanding your knowledge and experience as you go. You should be able to jump to any topic as needed, as long as you have the technical background. If not, don't worry, as it will be covered elsewhere in the book. The material in this book covers a wide range of issues and is divided into specific topics, most of which generally state a problem of some sort and one or more solutions to that problem. While most topics are arranged from simplest to most advanced, this isn't always the case.

We used some style conventions to assist you in reading this book. Each topic will begin with one or more introductory paragraphs explaining the problem or situation, and a series of steps to carry out the solution. The names of menu items or tabs to select and the buttons to click are **bold**:

Select **Options** from Explorer's **View** menu, and choose the **File Types** tab.

When any typing is involved, the text will be in a `monospaced` font. Most of the solutions are followed by a section called "Notes and other issues." Make sure to review these notes before proceeding with any solutions, as they may contain important warnings or considerations. Usually when quotation marks are used in examples, you should include them, unless otherwise specified. Filenames and commands are in *italic*.

Windows 95 or Windows NT 4.0?

Some of the procedures described in this book are valid for either Windows 95 or Windows NT 4.0 only. Where this is true, we've used the folowing icons:

● Windows 95

■ Windows NT 4.0

Software and the Internet

Some suggestions and solutions involve acquiring third-party software and utilities; some are freely available on the Internet, while others are commercial products available at your local vendor. Whenever possible, a solution or procedure will require the minimum investment of both time and money. If a problem can be solved without any additional software, such a solution will be presented first, followed by any utilities that can perform the same task.

Support for this book is available on the World Wide Web at both the Creative Element home page at *http://www.creativelement.com/*, as well as at the O'Reilly & Associates home page at *http://www.ora.com/*. Since some of the material in this book is based on content found at the Windows95 Annoyances web site at *http://www.creativelement.com/win95ann/*, you'll find updates to this book, frequently asked questions, and all the freely available software mentioned throughout the book at this site. Due to the constantly expanding, evolving, and changing nature of the Internet, any Internet addresses to resources other than the ones mentioned above will be listed at *http://www.creativelement.com/win95ann/*, rather than in this material.

We'd Like to Hear from You

We have tested and verified all the information in this book to the best of our ability, but you may find that features have changed (or even that we have made mistakes!). Please let us know about any errors you find, as well as your suggestions for future editions, by writing to:

> O'Reilly & Associates, Inc.
> 101 Morris Street
> Sebastopol, CA 95472
> 1-800-998-9938 (in the U.S. or Canada)
> 1-707-829-0515 (international/local)
> 1-707-829-0104 (FAX)

You can also send us messages electronically. To be put on our mailing list or request a catalog, send email to:

> *nuts@ora.com* (via the Internet)
> *uunet!ora!info* (via UUCP)

To ask technical questions or comment on the book, send email to:

> *bookquestions@ora.com* (via the Internet)

Acknowledgments

As you may know, this book is based on a web site entitled Windows95 Annoyances. If it weren't for the more than 1.6 million visitors to the site, or the one visitor who happened to be an editor for O'Reilly & Associates (or even Bill Gates, for annoying us all so much), this book would have been awfully boring. While you may have noticed that the Internet seems to get a lot of attention in this book, you may not know it's not that way for marketing reasons, but rather because the entire book was assembled *entirely* over email (with fewer than 150 messages).

Anyway, at the risk of sounding like I've just won an Oscar, I'd like to thank the following folks: my dad, my mom, the staff at O'Reilly & Associates (Andrew Schulman, Tim O'Reilly, Troy Mott, Andy Oram, Eric Pearce, and countless others), Ruth Kampmann (my book agent), and my friends and family who never got tired of asking, "Isn't it done yet?" Finally, this book would have never been written without the immense emotional and spiritual support, not to mention the uncanny timeliness, of Torey Bookstein.

Thanks also to everyone who worked on production of this book. Nancy Wolfe Kotary was the project manager and production editor; Frank Willison provided editorial review; Seth Maislin created the index; and Sheryl Avrach provided quality control. Production was handled by Editorial Services of New England (ESNE); thanks especially to Penny Stratton, Sarah Kimnach, and Peter Whitmer, as well as everyone else who worked on this book.

Thank you for your time with this book; I hope it's helpful in alleviating some of those Windows annoyances.

1

So You're Stuck with Windows

Chances are you've installed Microsoft's new operating system on your machine, and you're asking yourself, Now what? You've probably spent an hour or so watching the setup program copy files to your hard disk, and another few hours getting it to work with your old modem. An afternoon of exploring and tinkering has enabled you to choose your favorite screensaver, select *just* the right colors, and rearrange the entries in your **Start Menu**. While you were at it, you probably upgraded your word processor so you could use long filenames, added some more memory to help things run smoother, and got yourself hooked up to the Internet because the thought of not having instantaneous access to *One-hundred-and-one of Newt Gingrich's Favorite Cookie Recipes* bothers you to no end.

You're not an idiot. You *know* there's more to it. Microsoft has made lots of promises about this new software, but you're not quite satisfied with the features or the performance. This is where the ability to customize comes in handy. Customization is much more than choosing screen fonts or changing the name of My Computer to anything less precious. By learning how to customize Windows and the way you use it, you can not only improve your understanding of the software but increase your productivity and the efficiency with which you complete your work.

This book gives you solutions that enable you to both customize and troubleshoot Windows. This is an important distinction, as many times solving a problem requires that you know whether it's a bug or a feature of the software, and the dividing line isn't always clear. A bug is an action of some software that wasn't intended by the programmer. It's important to realize that if software doesn't respond in a way that *you* think it should, it should be regarded as poor design. You shouldn't be required to adjust the way you think in order to complete a task on a computer; rather, you should learn how to adjust the computer to work in a way that makes sense to *you*. This is what this book is about.

This book is probably quite different from that to which you're accustomed. Information is presented as the solutions to a series of problems, most of which are common among users of Windows 95 and Windows NT 4.0. This provides an extensive collection of tips, tricks, and workarounds geared for intermediate to advanced users of both products. This is not an advertisement for Microsoft or a beginner's guide for Windows 95. Don't look for instructions detailing how to edit the **Start Menu** or customize the color of the Desktop. Learning the basic Windows interface is pretty simple, and surely doesn't make for a very interesting book. We assume you've installed the software and used it for a little while. You don't have to be a programmer or a network administrator to take full advantage of the information here, although advanced users will not be disappointed.

Getting Up to Speed

Just in case you've been living in a cave for the past few years, Microsoft released Windows 95 on August 24, 1995, along with a $200 million advertising budget. Suffice it to say that it was blown a little out of proportion. However, this new class of operating system, in the form of Windows 95, Windows NT 4.0, and Windows CE (for palmtop computers), represents the direction of home computing for the next several years.

My first impression of Windows 95 was how much of an improvement it was over Windows 3.x. I was using a prerelease (beta version) of the software on my machine, and within a few hours after installation, the extent by which the previous version of Windows had *stunted* my machine became readily apparent. However, there were several "features" in the new product that were irritating rather than helpful. This book began in the form of a resource on the World Wide Web during the summer of 1995, entitled Windows95 Annoyances, containing an exhaustive collection of tips and tricks for getting around these irritating quirks. The content evolved into a more general question-and-answer forum and support center for Windows 95, before being expanded into this book. Throughout this book, we'll try to make the most of the good features of both Windows 95 and Windows NT 4.0 while trying to eliminate many of the irritations and problems.

Although most of you will be using Windows 95, this book also covers the more recently released version 4.0 of Microsoft Windows NT. Refer to the following section, "Windows Basics," for more information about NT and an examination of its similarities and differences with Windows 95. Since both operating systems implement the same user interface and share many new features, most of the content of this book will apply to both products. Refer to "Getting the Most Out of This Book" in the Preface for details on applying the material to your platform. Some of the new features found in both of these products include:

The Registry

One of the new features of Windows 95 and Windows NT 4.0 is the Registry, a central database containing all of the settings for Windows and most of the applications you run. Although the Registry was found in earlier versions of both Windows and Windows NT, it was used for little more than registering OLE-aware applications. The Registry is involved with many of the settings we'll be changing, and is discussed extensively throughout the book. Chapter 3 concentrates on the Registry itself, its structure, and how to make the most of the limited Registry Editor. Methods of backing up, repairing, compressing, and transferring portions of the Registry are laid out in plain English.

Plug & Play

Most of your hardware (more than you think) will be automatically detected and set up when Windows 95 is installed. For example, if you plug a CD-ROM drive into a Windows 95 system, the drive will show up in My Computer (the window providing access to all your drives) automatically when the machine is powered up. IRQs and IO addresses are switched for you on devices that use them (on newer PNP-compatible devices only) and the drivers are installed with virtually no work at all. As more vendors come out with cooperating devices, this feature will become more useful. Taking advantage of this technology involves more than plugging in new devices. Understanding the way it works can save you time and improve the way you work with your computer. Currently, this technology, along with its support for older Windows software, makes Windows 95 the most compatible operating system there is.

The new interface

A new interface, first sported by Windows 95, determines how you interact with your computer. Throughout the entire book, I will be critically examining this user interface and providing an exhaustive collection of tips and tricks for using it to its full potential.

Drivers and 32-bit software

Does Windows 95 currently support every card, drive, printer, pointing device, and so forth, that you have? If even one device is not yet explicitly supported in Windows 95, it may not work at all. In Chapter 6, *Troubleshooting*, you'll find plenty of advice for getting all your old (and new) hardware working properly. Additionally, the availability of new 32-bit software and hardware drivers, supporting such features as improved multitasking and long filenames, is making it difficult to be satisfied with your old 16-bit programs. We'll explore which programs and drivers need upgrading, and which don't.

Performance

If you have a fast computer (486 100-MHZ or faster), Windows 95 will provide better overall speed, disk access (up to 300%), and especially multitasking. Although Windows NT 4.0 has much stiffer hardware requirements, it is still possible to use it in less than ideal conditions. Finally, depending on the support of the manufacturer of your video subsystem, you may or may not see an increase in video performance. Chapter 5, *Maximizing Performance*, deals with methods for making the most of what you've got.

Windows Basics

In an effort to ensure you can follow most of the material in this book, here's a crash course in Windows. Refer to Appendix C, *Glossary*, for explanations of terms used here and throughout the book.

First-time users

If you've never used a Windows PC before, the first thing you should do is start Solitaire—yes, the card game. Don't laugh; it's fun and easy, and it's a great way to familiarize yourself with the major mouse functions, including clicking, dragging and dropping, and double-clicking. Besides, it's a good way to kill time while you're on the phone.

Files and folders

Your hard drive contains hundreds—perhaps thousands—of files. Your files make up your programs and hold your documents, letters, and spreadsheets. Files are organized into folders (sometimes called directories), and these files and folders live together in peace on your hard drive. Folders can contain files as well other folders. In Windows 95 and Windows NT 4.0, you can give your files long filenames. This probably means nothing to you unless you're used to DOS or Windows 3.x, and were forced to name your letter to your mom something like *LTR2MOM.DOC*. Get used to naming files like *A letter to my mom where I finally gain my independence.doc* from now on.

Objects

An object is something that you can expect to behave in predictable ways. In Windows 95 and Windows NT 4.0, for example, the icons on your screen are objects, whether they represent files, folders, drives, printers, or network connections. You can double-click on any of them to open them, or right-click on them to see what else they'll do. All objects behave similarly to your actions, and share many of the same properties. Most of them have a **Properties** entry in the context menu (the menu that pops up when you right-click on something). Learn to use this menu, because most of the good stuff is in there.

Mouse cursors

Your mouse cursor tells you what's happening. Look closely at your mouse cursor while you're moving it around; it's not always a plain, white arrow. For example, when you're dragging a file, Windows 95 gives you a clue as to what's going to happen when you drop it, depending on where you're dragging it and what's currently underneath the cursor.

Help is near

Pressing F1 in most situations will display detailed instructions or brief descriptions of the controls. The help has a search feature, too, allowing you to find desired information by typing in a keyword.

Explorer

Explorer is called Explorer for a reason. Don't be afraid to browse your hard disk. Look in all your folders, and try all the programs in the **Start Menu**. Explore!

Shortcuts

A shortcut is a little file that lets you open a program without having to find the actual executable on your hard disk. You can make a shortcut for any program, document, drive, or folder by dragging and dropping the icon onto the Desktop with the right mouse button. See "Edit your Start Menu," the next topic, for a good use for shortcuts.

Edit your Start Menu

You can fully customize your **Start Menu**. Don't bother with the Taskbar settings, though. Open Windows Explorer, and open the **Start Menu** folder located in your Windows folder. All the files and folders inside the **Start Menu** folder are mirrored (also appear) in the actual **Start Menu**. You can drag-drop program icons into the **Start**

Menu folder just as easily as making new **Start Menu** folders by using the right mouse button.

The Desktop is a folder

The Desktop is a folder (a.k.a. directory) on your hard disk, just like any other. It's located in your Windows folder (usually C:\Windows\Desktop\) and can contain files, folders, and shortcuts. The Desktop is a good place to store newly downloaded files from the Internet, email attachments, stuff from floppies, and other "recent" files.

Drivers

A driver is a software program that's used to help your computer work with a particular piece of hardware, such as a sound card or scanner. Many problems and errors in Windows are caused by buggy or outdated drivers. If you're having trouble, contact the manufacturer to see if there are any newer drivers for your hardware. See Chapter 6, *Troubleshooting*, for more information.

ZIP files

Many Internet sites allow you to download various types of software. More often than not, this software is squeezed into a ZIP file. A single ZIP file can contain an entire directory of files while occupying only a fraction of the disk space. This definitely helps to reduce download time, but you'll need to obtain the program used to extract the files—for example, PKZip for DOS (version 2.04g or later) or WinZIP for Windows 95.

✳ *Regular maintenance*

Windows 95 comes with two maintenance utilities, Scandisk and Disk Defragmenter. Scandisk is used to find and correct many types of errors on your hard disk, and Disk Defragmenter is used to optimize your files (rearrange them so they aren't broken up). Using each of these on a regular basis (such as once a week) will not only improve performance but reduce the likelihood of a disk crash or other loss of important stuff.

Windows 95 vs. Windows NT 4.0

Because these two platforms have nearly identical interfaces and share certain key features, the vast majority of topics explored in this book can cover both products. The interface is common between the two platforms because the main interface program, called the shell, is separate from the underlying operating system. While the operating system takes care of things like communicating with your printer and making sure your files get loaded quickly (things that both platforms do differently), the shell includes your **Start Menu**, the Desktop, and the Control Panel.

Windows 95 is Microsoft's major upgrade to Windows 3.1 and is designed to run the largest variety of software on the majority of home PCs. For most users, Windows 95 should yield better performance with less of an investment than Windows NT, but some users may require some of the added benefits that Windows NT provides.

Windows NT 4.0 has most of the features found in Windows 95, except—notably—for Plug & Play and Advanced Power Management. Windows 95 and Windows NT don't share drivers, so while nearly the entire industry offers support for Windows 95, Windows NT does not fare so well. While Windows 95 offers better support and a larger software and hardware base, Windows NT sports better multitasking, a more robust architecture (which makes it less susceptible to crashes), support for different processors as well multiple processors, and much better security than Windows 95.

Windows NT was born as version 3.1, which was nothing more than a lumbering version of Windows 3.1 that ran nonexistent 32-bit applications and had more extensive network support. Microsoft quickly developed this product into Windows NT 3.5, which won more support from software and hardware vendors. Not until the release of Windows 95 did substantial support surface for 32-bit Windows applications or Windows NT. Windows NT comes in two flavors, Workstation and Server, both available in version 4.0. The most obvious new feature of this version (from version 3.5) is the use of the Windows 95 interface, although there are many other improvements and enhancements (this book does not cover any release of Windows NT earlier than version 4.0). The workstation edition is positioned as a high-end "Desktop" alternative to Windows 95, and the server edition is intended to run small local area networks and Internet sites.

The Future of Windows

You may have heard Windows 95 referred to as "Chicago" before its release, or Windows NT 4.0 called "Daytona." These code names are used by Microsoft to denote the various editions of the Windows operating system. Some have become shipping products, while others represent combinations of features from current and future products. It all started several years ago with Chicago, which became Windows 95 in August 1995. Concurrently, Daytona was slated to be the next version of Windows NT, now known as release 4.0. Some of the features of

Daytona, such as Plug & Play and Advanced Power Management, didn't make it into Windows NT 4.0 but are slated for Windows NT 5.0.

Some users who have received Windows 95 with new computers after the middle of 1996 got a slightly improved version, known as Windows 95 OSR2 (OEM Service Release 2). OSR2 isn't available at local software stores, but it is shipping with many new PCs. This release is similar to Windows 95, except that it fixes some bugs and adds DriveSpace 3 (a new disk compression utility), FAT32 (a more robust and reliable file system), support for Universal Serial Bus peripherals, and support for Intel's new MMX processors. Internet Explorer 4.0, also known as Nashville, is tentatively planned for inclusion in Windows 98. Internet Explorer 4.0 puts Microsoft's desire to combine the Internet and the home PC into action by attempting to blend the World Wide Web and the Windows Explorer. In essence, this means you'll have what they call a "Web view of your Desktop." (Just what the world needs. If Microsoft wants to jump on the Internet bandwagon, that's fine—as long as they allow us to turn it off.)

Finally, there are Memphis and Cairo. Memphis is the code name for Windows 98, the replacement for Windows 95. Cairo is the intermediary product that will soon be developed into Windows NT 5.0, and is expected to enable Windows NT to catch up to Windows 98 in terms of features and industry support.

Supposedly, Microsoft plans to eventually merge Windows NT and Windows 98 into a single product, much as it merged Windows 2.x with Windows 386 and Windows 3.1 with Windows for Workgroups. This should give users the power, security, and stability of Windows NT and the compatibility, industry support, and low entry cost of Windows 95.

Note that the solutions in this book assume that you have the original shipping versions of either Windows 95 or Windows NT 4.0. Some of the information may differ for other releases, although not substantially.

2

Customizing Your System

Windows can be annoying. So much of your time on a computer is spent in Windows: starting programs, finding files, copying folders, configuring the interface. The first steps in dealing with the annoyances are to learn how to accomplish common tasks more easily and how to adjust various aspects of the Windows interface, making it easier to use, more pleasant to look at, and less irritating to work with. The ideal user interface should adapt to you rather than the other way around—but this isn't a perfect world, and the Windows interface is far from ideal.

This chapter starts by focusing on customizing your work habits— learning the basic tips and tricks to mastering the finer points of Explorer. The next bag of tricks, under "Customizing the Interface," begins to cover some advanced topics, such as customizing icons for your drives, changing the startup logo, and using shortcuts to improve the Control Panel and Device Manager. Finally, the chapter is rounded off with "System Enhancements," which will introduce some tips for the command prompt and multiple users.

Many of the topics discussed throughout this book require knowledge of the Windows Registry, with the exception of this chapter—I figured you'd want to jump right in. When you're ready, read through Chapter 3, *The Registry*. This should prepare you for the rest of the material in this book.

Coping with Explorer

Explorer is the all-encompassing term describing the program used to manage the files and folders on your hard drive. The Desktop, the My

Computer window, the folder windows, the Exploring tree-view window, and the **Start Menu** are all part of Explorer. Files are copied, moved, opened, closed, and deleted in the same way in all of these places. If you learn how to combine mouse movements with keystrokes effectively, for example, you'll see how much easier it is to use Explorer to accomplish everyday management tasks.

Forcing Windows to Remember Explorer Settings ● ■

For most users, the most irritating behavior is Windows' inability not only to save the settings for folder windows, but also to set defaults for new, unopened folder windows. Settings like position, size, sort order, auto-arrange, and icon size are almost always reset to the Windows default when folders are opened. The Explorer window (tree view) is a little better behaved, although it's not perfect, either. A similar limitation that plagued the DOS command *dir* was fixed no sooner than *13 years* after the first version of DOS was released (let's hope Microsoft figures this one out a bit sooner).

Other than a vague "memory" of the 29 most recently opened windows, there doesn't seem to be any way to save settings or configure defaults for new windows. The problem is that these settings are stored in the Registry, instead of with the folders; this design flaw will never allow Windows to remember settings for more than a limited number of windows. The following tips should help, however:

- If you hold either the Shift or Ctrl key while closing a folder window, it may force Windows to remember the settings for the window.

- Use Explorer instead of folder windows. Explorer remembers its window position and the widths of the various columns in the details view. Unfortunately, the sort order is reset to Name whenever the window is closed.

- If you're using folder windows, select **Options** from the **View** menu, and choose the **Folder** tab. Select the second option, **Browse folders by using a single window**, and press **OK**. This way, the same window will be used for all folders. Although the size and position of the window will remain unchanged, the sort order and icon size will be reset as you move from one folder to another.

Notes and other issues

See the next section, "Learning to Explore with Folders" for more infomation. See "How do I set the default sort order for use with DOS dir command?" in Appendix A, *Frequently Asked Questions*, for more information.

If you've taken steps to get rid of the unwanted Explorer windows at startup, as discussed in Chapter 4, *Advanced Customization Techniques*, the setting may be preventing Windows from saving your Explorer settings.

Learning to Explore with Folders ● ■

Here are some tips for controlling the way folders and files behave. Although selecting **Options** from the **View** menu in a folder window (such as My Computer) lets you choose whether to open each new folder as a new window or reuse the same window, there is a way to pick and choose this behavior on the fly. Additionally, there are several other keystrokes that will help you explore.

Setting 1

- Select **Options** from the **View** menu in a folder window, and choose **Browse folders using a separate window for each folder** .

- From now on, when double-clicking on folders, they will open up in new windows by default. Hold the Ctrl key while double-clicking to reuse the current window instead of opening a new one (be careful when using this, as Ctrl is also used to select multiple files).

Setting 2

- Select **Options** from the **View** menu in a folder window, and choose **Browse folders by using a single window** .

- From now on, when double-clicking on folders, they will use the same window by default. Now, one would expect that if one holds the Ctrl key while double-clicking, the opposite of what happened in Setting 1 would happen, and a new window would be created. Although a new window *is* displayed, the **View** setting is set to **List**, and the toolbar is turned on. There is no compelling explanation for the strange behavior.

Other keys that work with either setting

- Hold the Alt key while double-clicking on a file or folder to view the Properties window for that object.

- Hold the Shift key while double-clicking on a folder to open Explorer at that location (careful when using this, as Shift is also used to select multiple files).

- Press Backspace in an open folder to go to the parent folder—whether or not a new window appears depends on the setting described above.

- Hold the Shift key while clicking on the close button [X] to close all open folders that were used to get to that folder.

- You can right-click on any folder icon to present all of the exploring options, such as **Open** (folder view) and **Explore** (tree view).

Keystrokes for use with files only

- A quick way to choose a new program to be used with a certain file type is to hold the Shift key while right-clicking on a file, and select **Open with...** from the list.

- Hold the Ctrl key to select multiple files, one by one. Hold the Shift key to select a range of files. As long as we're at it, you can drag a rubber band around multiple files to select them. Just start in a blank portion of a folder window, and drag the mouse to the opposite corner to select everything in the rectangle.

- Press Ctrl-A to quickly select all of the contents of a folder—both files and folders.

Notes and other issues

For more information, see "Forcing Windows to Remember Explorer Settings" earlier in this chapter, and "Moving or Copying Files at Will" in the next section.

Moving or Copying Files at Will ● ■

Intuitively, when you drag a file from one place on the screen to another, it would seem reasonable that the file will be moved instead of duplicated (copied). That is, when you see an object disappear from a location, it shouldn't still be there the next time you look. One of the worst inconsistencies in Windows 95 is what actually happens to files when they're dragged. Dragging from one place to another on the same disk ends up moving the files, while dragging from one disk to another copies them. If you're just dragging .EXE files, however, only a shortcut to the file is created, and the file is neither copied nor moved. The only consistency here is that this same design flaw is duplicated on other operating systems, such as the Macintosh and IBM's OS/2. To help cope with this, follow these instructions:

- To *copy* a file under any situation, hold the Ctrl key *while* dragging. If you press Ctrl before you click, Windows assumes you're still selecting files.

- To *move* a file under any situation, hold the Shift key while dragging. Accordingly, if you press Shift before you click, Windows assumes you're still selecting files.

- To choose what happens to dragged files each time without pressing keys, drag your files with the right mouse button, and a special menu will appear when the files are dropped (see Figure 2-1). This context menu is helpful, as it will display only appropriate options, depending on the type of objects you're dragging and where you've dropped them.

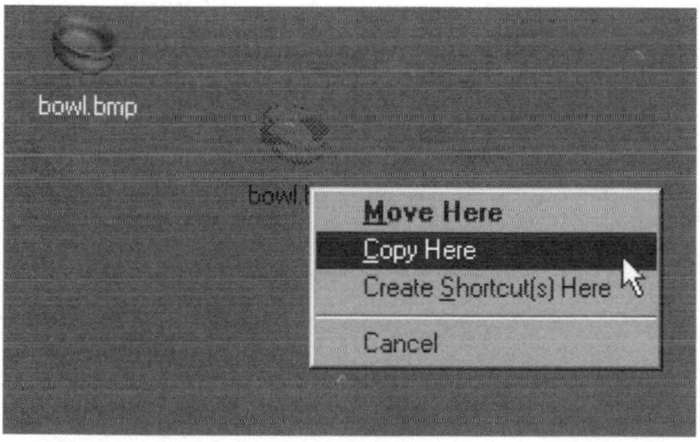

Figure 2-1: Drag files with the right mouse button for more control

- To aid you in learning the keystrokes, the mouse cursor changes depending on the action being taken. A small plus sign appears when copying, and a curved arrow appears when creating a shortcut.

- Using the Ctrl and Shift keys as described above will also work when dragging a file from one part of a folder to another part of the same folder. See "Making a Duplicate of a File" later in this chapter for more information.

Notes and other issues

There is no way to set the default action when dragging files—a glaring omission.

If you use ZIP files, you may find WinZIP useful—(see "Software and the Internet" in the Preface)—it uses the right-drag menu described previously to ZIP and unZIP files.

Renaming Files Without a Hassle ● ■

If you have Windows configured to display your registered file extensions and have ever tried to rename a file and change the extension, you'll see that Windows doesn't let you do it without a stern warning. Since Windows can't sense whether you know what you're doing, it assumes you're an idiot, and displays this useless message every time. Although there is no way to disable this message, there are other ways to rename files that don't use the message.

Solution 1—Use the command prompt

* Open the command prompt, change to the directory containing the file you want to rename, and use the *ren* command. For example, to rename *myfile.doc* to *myfile.txt*, type the following command:

```
ren myfile.doc myfile.txt
```

* The *ren* command also has the definite advantage of allowing you to rename multiple files simultaneously. For example, to rename all the files in a folder with the extension .DOC to .TXT, type the following command:

```
ren *.doc *.txt
```

Solution 2—Use the File Manager

If you can bear it, fire up the old Windows 3.x-style File Manager (*winfile.exe*). Not only will it not display the warning message, it will allow you to rename multiple files as described for the *ren* command above. You might also be pleased to learn that File Manager won't display the flying paper animation when you move or copy files—an added bonus.

Solution 3—Use the Send To menu

If you find yourself renaming files to the same extension all the time, you can set up an entry in your **Send To** menu to do it for you, without any typing, and without the useless warning message.

* Open a text editor, such as Notepad, and type the following:

```
ren %1 *.txt
```

* Here, %1 represents the file being selected with the mouse. Of course, you'll probably want to change *.txt to whatever extension you need; just remember the asterisk.

* Save the file in a folder on your hard disk, and call the file something like *Rename to TXT.bat* (make sure you use the .BAT extension at the

end, so that Windows knows this is a DOS batch file). Then make a shortcut to the batch file in your Send To folder (it's in your Windows folder), and call it something like *Rename to TXT*.

- From now on, you can right-click on a file in Explorer or a folder window, select **Send To**, and then **Rename to TXT** (or whatever you've called it), and the file will be renamed automatically.

Notes and other issues

If using a batch file as described in Solution 3, you can configure the DOS window to close automatically by right-clicking on the batch file, selecting **Properties**, choosing the **Program** tab, and turning on the **Close on exit** option.

Making a Duplicate of a File ● ■

Windows lets you copy and move files from one folder to another by dragging them with different combinations of keystrokes (see "Moving or Copying Files at Will" earlier in this chapter). You can also rename a file by clicking on its name or pressing F2. However, if you want to make a duplicate of a file in the same directory, but with a different name, the process might not be as obvious. Here's how you do it.

On the Desktop or in an open folder window

- Hold the Ctrl key while dragging a file from one part of the window to another part of the same window.

In Explorer

- Explorer won't let you drag a file from one part of the right pane to another part, but if you drag a file, while holding down the Ctrl key, from the right pane onto the name of the open folder on the tree in the left pane, the file will be duplicated.

In either case

- You can also use the right mouse button to drag the file from one part of the window to another part of the same window, and then select **Copy Here**.

- The duplicate of a file called *myfile.txt* would be automatically named *Copy of myfile.txt*.

- For keyboard enthusiasts, press Ctrl-C and then Ctrl-V to create a duplicate of a file using the clipboard.

Turning Off Delete Confirmation ● ■

One of the most annoying features of the Recycle Bin is the inability to configure it to delete a file immediately without several nag windows. You may have had a response to such nag windows similar to, "If I didn't want to delete the file, I wouldn't have dropped it in the Recycle Bin." What's strange is that Windows displays an additional prompt if you try to delete one or more .EXE files; Windows doesn't prompt you to delete .DLL files, even though they are just as necessary to applications as .EXE files. If you're not getting these "confirmation" screens, it's likely that any files you're deleting aren't really being deleted, but are rather being stored in the Recycle Bin, eating away at your precious disk space. Use the following steps to delete files immediately after they are dropped:

Solution 1

- Right-click on the Recycle Bin, and select **Properties**.
- Under the **Global** tab, select **Use one setting for all drives**.
- Turn on the option labeled **Do not move files to the Recycle Bin**. (For some reason, decreasing the **Maximum size of Recycle Bin** option to 0% doesn't do the trick.)

Notice that the option labeled **Display delete confirmation dialog** is grayed out at this point, meaning that there is no way to truly delete files in Windows without a confirmation dialog. Microsoft's attempt at a safety feature may have gone too far here.

Note that if you change this setting and have files sitting in the Recycle Bin, they may not be deleted automatically until you do so manually.

Solution 2

- Create a shortcut to the Recycle Bin in your Send To folder. To delete files, right-click, and choose **Recycle Bin** from the **Send To** menu.

Solution 3

- Obtain and install RtvReco (see "Software and the Internet" in the Preface), which can be configured to bypass many useless, repetitive screens

Notes and other issues

If you have configured the Recycle Bin to store files instead of deleting them, you can hold the `Shift` key to delete dropped files on the spot.

The old Windows 3.x-style File Manager (*winfile.exe*) will also allow you to delete files without confirmation and without storing them in the Recycle Bin.

Copying or Moving to Specified Path ● ■

To copy or move a file in Windows, both the source folder and the destination folder must be open and visible to drag-drop a file. There is no provision for specifying a destination folder with the keyboard when copying or moving a file, making this task nearly impossible without a mouse. To add this functionality, making file management far less awkward, follow these steps:

Solution 1—Use the Send To menu

- Obtain and install the OtherFolder utility, one of Microsoft's Power-Toys (see "Software and the Internet" in the Preface). Using the Send To command. It enables the user to specify a destination with the keyboard.

- If you're using the OtherFolder utility, see "Clear Unwanted Entries from the Start Menu's Run Command History" in Chapter 6, *Troubleshooting*, to clear the OtherFolder history.

Solution 2—Use Copy and Paste

- Select the file you want to copy, right-click on it, and select **Copy** to copy the file, or **Cut** to move the file (intuitive, huh?).

- Then open the destination folder, right-click on an empty area, and select **Paste**.

No, it's not exactly convenient or intuitive, but it comes in handy if you don't have a mouse. It's also not very consistent with drag-drop in other applications, as you can't paste a file into a document (even when you can drag-drop a file into the same document). Additionally, if you cut a file, it will still appear in the old location with a semi-transparent icon until you paste it. If you never paste it, it won't be deleted as you would expect.

Refreshing the Desktop Without Restarting Windows ● ■

The results of some of the procedures explained throughout this book will not take effect until you either restart Windows or refresh the Desktop. These include any changes to the Registry or any system folders. However, restarting Windows can take several minutes, and, for example, if you're using Dial-Up Networking, you'll be forced to disconnect. To refresh the Desktop without restarting Windows, follow these directions. Whether any of these solutions will cause any changes you've made to take effect depends on the type of setting you've changed.

Solution 1

- Click on any empty area of your Desktop or any icon on your Desktop with the left mouse button, and press the F5 key to refresh the Desktop.

Solution 2

In such cases where Solution 1 is not sufficient to implement your changes, you can still try to refresh Explorer without restarting.

- Press Ctrl-Alt-Del, and select **Explorer** from the list (don't select **Exploring...**, though). If you're using Window NT 4.0, click the **Task List** button first to see the list of running tasks. Don't worry; this shouldn't affect your other running applications.

- Click **End Task**. When the window asking if you wish to shut down Windows appears, click **No**.

- Wait about 10 seconds until another window appears confirming that you wish to close Explorer, and click **End Task** here.

- The taskbar and all Desktop icons will disappear temporarily, but then will reappear in a few seconds when Explorer is reloaded.

Solution 3

- If you have any network components installed, you can select **Shut Down** from the **Start Menu**, and then choose **Close all programs and log on as a different user**.

Notes and other issues

If you have the resource meter running, make sure to close it before using Solution 2.

Customizing the Interface

You should already know how to change your Desktop wallpaper or specify screen colors. The material in this section covers more specific changes to the taskbar, the tray, and Desktop icons. Pay close attention to the first two topics, as they can help with customization down the road and throughout the rest of the book by forcing Windows to effect changes you've made. The rest of this section should help you tame the tray, the Control Panel, and the **Start Menu**—stuff you won't find in the manual. You may want to skip down to "Replacing the Startup and Shut-down Screens" right away if you can't stand to look at the clouds another minute.

Restarting Windows Without Restarting Your Computer •

Choosing **Shut Down** from the **Start Menu** gives you several choices, including restarting your computer. However, to restart Windows 95 *without* restarting your computer, saving time, aggravation, and your hard disk, follow these steps. Although this procedure won't work in Windows NT 4.0, you can choose **Close all programs and log off as a different user** from the **Shut Down** list. This should refresh many NT settings.

Solution 1—Using keystrokes

- Select **Shut Down** from the **Start Menu**, select **Restart the computer**, and hold down the **Shift** key while pressing **OK**.

Solution 2—Make a restart icon on your Desktop

- Using a text editor, such as Notepad, type the following by itself:

  ```
  @EXIT
  ```

- Save the one-line file somewhere on your hard disk, and call it whatever you like, as long as it has the .BAT extension.

- Place a shortcut to the batch file on your Desktop or **Start Menu**, and name it *Restart Windows*.

- Right-click on the shortcut, select **Properties**, choose the **Program** tab, and make sure the **Close on Exit** option is turned on.

- Then, click **Advanced**, and make sure the **MS-DOS mode** option is selected and the **Warn before entering MS-DOS mode** option is turned off.

- Click **OK** twice, and then double-click on the icon to use it.

Notes and other issues

This functionality is also available in the Windows interface enhancement, Route 1 Pro, which is available for download on the Internet from the web site *http://www.creativelement.com/software/route1.html*.

See "Refreshing the Desktop Without Restarting Windows" earlier in this chapter for a few alternatives to restarting Windows.

Saving Your Desktop Layout ● ■

Many of you, after meticulously arranging all the icons on your Desktop, have been frustrated when Windows 95 randomly rearranges them or simply forgets their positions. Sometimes restarting Windows is all it takes to lose the Desktop layout, while other users may experience this only after a system crash. In fact, on some systems, the Desktop layout is lost whenever Explorer is opened. Here are two workarounds:

Solution 1

- If you're also losing other settings, such as taskbar settings or display colors, it may be that you're not logged in. Windows saves some of these settings only for configured users of the system, and if it thinks that there's no current user, it won't save the settings.

- Try selecting **Shut Down** from the **Start Menu**, choosing the **Close all programs and log on as a different user** option if it's there, and clicking **OK**. If it's not there, you probably don't have any networking components installed. If this is the case, double-click on the Passwords icon in Control Panel; choosing a new password should convince Windows that you're a user.

If this sounds ridiculous to you, you're not alone.

Solution 2

- Obtain and install the EzDesk utility. See "Software and the Internet" in the Preface for more information.

Notes and other issues

✱ If you're simply unable to move the icons on your Desktop, right-click on an empty portion of the Desktop, click **Arrange Icons**, and turn off the **Auto-Arrange** option.

Windows seems to refresh the Desktop under certain situations, such as when files are copied to or deleted from the Desktop, or when settings are changed in Explorer. There's no way to completely predict or control this behavior.

Customizing the Tray ● ■

The tray is the little box (usually in the lower right-hand corner of your screen, at the end of your taskbar) that, by default, contains the clock and the little yellow speaker (see Figure 2-2). You'll notice some other icons appearing in the tray, used either to start a program or show the options for a program that is already running. What's irritating is that there doesn't seem to be any sort of consistency or standards for items in the tray. Some icons get double-clicked, some require a single right or left click, and some don't get clicked at all. However, it's possible to remove most of the icons that appear in the tray, as well as to add your own icons.

Figure 2-2: The tray contains several icons as well as the clock

Add your own programs to the tray

- Obtain and install the Tray applet. See "Software and the Internet" in the Preface for more information.

- Run *tray.exe*, right click on the New icon in the tray, and select **Help** for instructions.

Hide the tray entirely (without manually removing all of its contents)

- Obtain and run TrayHide. (See "Software and the Internet" in the Preface for more information.) Run it again to restore the tray.

Get rid of the little yellow speaker

- Open the Control Panel by selecting **Settings** from the **Start Menu**.

- Double-click on the Multimedia icon.

- Under the **Audio** tab, in the Playback section, turn off the **Show volume control on the taskbar** option.

- Click **OK**.

Get rid of the little flashing modem icon (for use with dial-up networking)

- Double-click on the My Computer icon and then on the Dial-Up Networking icon. (For some unknown reason, this setting cannot be found in the Modems applet in Control Panel.)

- Right-click on one of the connections in this window, and select **Properties** (if you have more than one connection, you'll need to repeat these steps for each one).

- In the Connect using section, click on **Configure**... (this will display a box similar but not identical to the modem settings in Control Panel).

- Click on the **Options** tab, and turn off **Display modem status** in the Status control section.

- Click **OK**, then click **OK** again.

Get rid of the little flashing modem icon (for use with HyperTerminal)

- Click on the **Properties** button on HyperTerminal's toolbar (far right), or choose **Properties** from HyperTerminal's **File** menu.

- Click **Configure**, choose the **Options** tab, and turn off **Display modem status** in the Status control section.

- Click **OK**, then click **OK** again, and select **Save** from the **File** menu.

Notes and other issues

If you remove the yellow speaker, you can still adjust the volume with the Volume Control utility included with Windows. Removing the flashing modem icon will not have any effect on modem performance or functionality.

Forcing Explorer to Start with the Folder You Want ● ■

As you've undoubtedly discovered, the Windows Explorer always opens at the root folder of the drive on which Windows is installed. Since there are several ways to start Explorer, there are several ways to specify where it opens.

Launch Explorer from a shortcut

- Open Explorer, and go to your **Start Menu** folder.

- Find the shortcut for Explorer (or create one if it doesn't exist), right-click on it, and select **Properties**.

- Click on the **Shortcut** tab, and change the text in the **Target** field so it reads:

```
Explorer.exe /n, /e, d:\myfolder
```

where d:\myfolder is the folder where you want Explorer to start.

- If you want Explorer to start at the top level, My Computer, so no drive branches are initially expanded, type the following:

```
Explorer.exe /n, /e, /select, c:\
```

- Right-click on the **Start Menu** button and select **Explore** (see Figure 2-3). This will always open Explorer pointed at your **Start Menu** folder. This action assumes that the **Start Menu** is an object; right-clicking on that object and selecting (in this case) **Explore** will carry out that action on that object. In other words, there's no way to change this particular incarnation so that Explorer points where you want.

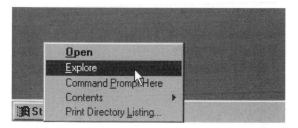

Figure 2-3: Right-click on the Start Menu button to explore the Start Menu folder quickly

Explore from a folder

- You can right-click on any folder icon and select **Explore**. This will open Explorer expanded to that folder. This works in the same way as the previous example. Although there's no equivalent command for the Desktop, the Desktop folder is located at the top of the Explorer tree, so it's always easy to get to.

Customizing Drive Icons ● ■

At this point, you should know that you can create shortcuts to all your drive icons in My Computer, place them in a folder or on the Desktop, and then change the icons of the shortcuts to something other than the default generic hard disk and floppy drive icons (see Figure 2-4). This solution, while relatively easy, is quite limited, especially since the icons aren't reflected in Explorer, and you can't customize your own icons for floppy and removable drives. Using the functionality built into the CD-ROM Autorun feature, there's a simple way to customize your drive icons (for hard, floppy, and removable drives):

- Using a text editor, such as Notepad, type the following:

```
[autorun]
icon=filename, number
```

  where *filename* is the name of the file containing the icon (either an .EXE, .DLL, .ICO, or .BMP file), and *number* is the index of the icon to use. (Leave this blank or specify 0 (zero) to use the first icon in the file, 1 for the second, and so on.)

Figure 2-4: The My Computer window may be a little more inviting with customized icons

- Save the file as *autorun.inf* in the root folder of the hard disk, floppy, or removable disk you wish to change.

- Double-click on the My Computer icon or open Explorer and press F5 to refresh the display and read the new icons.

Notes and other issues

This will work even if you've turned off CD-ROM Autorun.

This will also work for removable drives (floppies, Syquest cartridges, Zip drives, optical disks), but since Windows 95 isn't able to determine when you insert and remove removable media (as it can for CD-ROMs), you need to manually refresh the My Computer or Explorer window by pressing F5.

To turn on or off the **Display Certain Drive** icons in the My Computer window, use the My Computer tab in TweakUI, one of Microsoft's Power-Toys. See "Software and the Internet" in the Preface for more information.

Replacing the Startup and Shutdown Screens ● ■

The screens that tell you to "Please wait while Windows is shutting down" and that "It is now safe to turn off your computer" are pretty ugly, especially considering the artistic talent that a company as large as Microsoft should be able to afford. The three screens are simply bitmaps on your hard disk and can be replaced with your own designs.

For Windows 95

- The two shutdown screen files are stored in your Windows folder. *Logow.sys* is the one that reads "Please wait while your computer shuts down," and *logos.sys* is the one that reads "It is now safe to turn off your computer."

- The startup logo (the blue clouds with the pulsating lights at the bottom) is stored in *logos.sys*, located in the root folder of drive C. However, don't look for it because it won't be there. If you save your file with that name, it will be used instead of the default.

- Make duplicates of the file or files you wish to change in another folder, as it's never a good idea to fiddle with original files.

- These files are just standard bitmaps, so rename the extensions of these duplicates to .BMP. You can use any graphics editor to edit these files, such as MS Paint or Adobe Photoshop. Double-click on a file to run the associated program.

- The files are 256-color (8-bit) Windows bitmaps (RGB, Windows-encoded, but *not* RGB mode for you Photoshop users), and 320 × 400 pixels in size. Since the aspect ratio (width/height) of these files is not standard 4:3, like most computer screens, the bitmaps will appear vertically elongated in your graphics program.

- To make your new design conform to this strange aspect ratio, begin with a bitmap size of 534 × 400 while you're working on it, or resize an existing image to those dimensions.

- When you're done making your screens, resize them to 320 × 400 pixels, and save. If the dimensions are incorrect or you're not using the correct number of colors, the screens won't work.

- Once you're done, rename the extensions of your new files from .BMP back to .SYS.

- Last, copy the new files back to their original locations. It might be smart to back up your original files.

For Windows NT 4.0

- Windows NT 4.0 has no shutdown screens but does have a simple startup bitmap. There are two versions, *winnt.bmp* (for 16-color systems) and *winnt256.bmp* (for 256-color systems and higher), both located in the Windows folder. You can replace either of these two files with any bitmap of any size or color depth. Simply delete the files to disable the startup screen.

Notes and other issues

If you're using a disk compression program, such as Stacker or DriveSpace, and have compressed drive C, your boot drive may not be drive C. If this applies to you, consult your settings for the particular program you're using to find which letter is your host drive for C, and place the *logo.sys* file in the root directory of that drive instead.

See "Software and the Internet" in the Preface for information on some sample Windows 95 screens you can download.

If you're using Windows 95, you can remove the startup logo altogether by editing the file *MSDOS.SYS* (usually located in C:\), and adding the line LOGO=0 to the end of the Options section. However, this will only work if you have a custom startup screen in your root folder. For more information, see Appendix D, *Contents of MSDOS.SYS File*. This setting can also be changed with TweakUI, one of Microsoft's PowerToys. See "Software and the Internet" in the Preface for more information.

In Windows 95, if you delete *Logow.sys* and *Logos.sys* altogether, and have followed the instructions in "How to Exit to DOS" in Chapter 4, *Advanced Customization Tricks*, Windows 95 will exit to DOS automatically instead of shutting down.

If your machine reboots instead of shutting down when these logos are replaced, make sure the bitmaps are not corrupted and are using no more than 256 colors.

Making Control Panel Applets More Accessible ● ■

When you open the Control Panel, you are presented with a few dozen icons, allowing you to control many aspects of the Windows environment. Here is a tip that not only makes these Control Panel applets more quickly accessible, but allows you to exclude the ones you don't want and add your own custom icons. The first solution takes advantage of the fact that Windows shortcuts can be used with system objects (such as Control Panel applets) as well as files, folders, drives, and programs. The second solution shows you how to exploit one of the properties of *virtual folders*, the folders in windows that aren't actually on your hard disk, like the Control Panel and Dial-Up Networking.

Solution 1

• Open both the Control Panel and Explorer, and place them side by side.

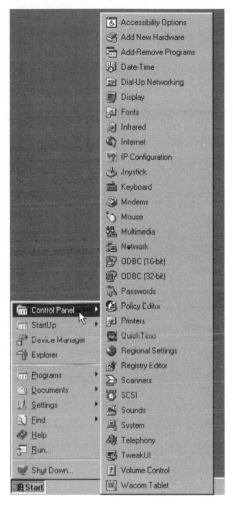

Figure 2-5: Putting the contents of the Control Panel in the Start Menu can make it much easier to use

- In Explorer, make a new folder inside the **Start Menu** folder, and call it *Control Panel*.

- Select some or all of the icons in Control Panel, and drag them into this new folder. Windows will display a message stating that "You cannot move or copy this item to this location." Select **Yes** to confirm that you "want to create a shortcut to the item instead."

Windows will make a shortcut to each icon you drop into the folder, forming new menu items accessible right off the **Start Menu**. Not only can you rename or remove any of the entries you wish, but you can add non–Control Panel items to the list, such as the Volume Control, the

System Policy Editor, and Dial-Up Networking (which should have been in the Control Panel in the first place). Note that any items that are installed into the Control Panel hereafter will have to be added to your custom Control Panel menu manually.

Solution 2

- In Explorer, make a new folder inside the **Start Menu** folder, and call it *Control Panel.{21EC2020-3AEA-1069-A2DD-08002B30309D}*. (See Example 2-1.) Make sure to include the period between the Control Panel and the code in brackets. When you press Enter, the code will disappear, and the icon will change to the standard Control Panel icon.

- This will create a menu right off the **Start Menu** (similar to Solution 1), although you can't change its contents. A benefit is that this process is automatic, and newly added Control Panel items will automatically show up in this menu.

- You can apply this solution to other system folders as well, by using the following codes:

Example 2-1. Duplicate Windows' virtual folders in the Start Menu for easy access

```
Dial-Up Networking.{992CFFA0-F557-101A-88EC-00DD010CCC48}
Printers.{2227A280-3AEA-1069-A2DE-08002B30309D}
Inbox.{00020D75-0000-0000-C000-000000000046}
My Computer.{20D04FE0-3AEA-1069-A2D8-08002B30309D}
Recycle Bin.{645FF040-5081-101B-9F08-00AA002F954E}
Network Neighborhood.{208D2C60-3AEA-1069-A2D7-08002B30309D}
Desktop.{00021400-0000-0000-C000-000000000046}
Briefcase.{85BBD920-42A0-1069-A2E4-08002B30309D}
Fonts.{BD84B380-8CA2-1069-AB1D-08000948F534}
Control Panel.{21EC2020-3AEA-1069-A2DD-08002B30309D}
```

Notes and other issues

These system objects (virtual folders) are also discussed in "Changing the Icons of System Objects" in Chapter 4. The codes that follow the names are called Class IDs, and are referenced in the Registry under HKEY_CLASSES_ROOT\CLSID\.

The process described in Solution 1 can also be applied to other parts of Windows 95, such as the drive icons in My Computer. Just drag them all into the **Start Menu** folder in Explorer to provide quick access to all your drives.

You can also use TweakUI (one of Microsoft's PowerToys)—see "Software and the Internet" in the Preface for more information—to create duplicates of virtual icons and virtual folders for use in your **Start Menu** and other places. Just use the **Create As File** button in the **Desktop** tab.

Going Directly to Device Manager •

The Device Manager is one of the most useful additions in Windows 95. It provides a list of all the devices attached to your computer, allows you to examine and change the resources they use, and refresh that list without restarting Windows. The Device Manager is just a tab in the System Properties Control Panel applet; you can access it by double-clicking on the System icon in Control Panel, and choosing the **Device Manager** tab. It's also accessible by right-clicking on the My Computer icon, selecting **Properties**, and choosing the **Device Manager** tab. Getting to the Device Manager this way can require up to six mouse clicks, but if you use it often, you might as well make it more accessible.

- Open Explorer, and go to your **Start Menu** folder. You can also just right-click on the **Start Menu** button and select **Explore**.

- Select **New** and then **Shortcut** from the **File** menu.

- In the field labeled **Command Line**, type:

  ```
  C:\Windows\Control.exe Sysdm.cpl, System, 1
  ```

  replacing C:\Windows\ with your Windows folder, if different.

- Click **Next**, type Device Manager for the name of this shortcut, and click **Finish** when you're done.

- There will now be a shortcut that will take you directly to Device Manager in your **Start Menu**. You can, of course, place this shortcut anywhere else, change its icon, or call it something different.

Notes and other issues

If you examine the command line above, you'll see what makes it work. *control.exe* is the program filename for Control Panel, *sysdm.cpl* is the filename for the System Properties applet, and System is the caption underneath the icon in the Control Panel. The last parameter (note that they're all separated by commas) specifies the tab to open, where 0 is the first tab and 1 is the second tab. In this case, Device Manager is the second tab in this dialog.

While it's easier to drag-drop the System icon from Control Panel into the **Start Menu**, the resulting shortcut doesn't have the flexibility to allow you to specify the tab to use.

As with any other shortcut, if you right-click on our new shortcut and select **Properties**, you can change the icon or any of the command line options, and even specify a hotkey.

Getting Rid of WinHelp's Contents Screen ● ■

The new help system used in Windows 95 and Windows NT 4.0 has some great new features, such as the ability to search a help file for text and the ability to stay on top of other windows. However, one of the worst new designs is the Contents window—an outline of the help file, which forces users to hunt for information by double-clicking on tiny icons of books and paper. Instead of seeing a friendly and familiar introductory page and being presented with an option to view the outline, users are forced to mess with this ridiculous hierarchy. This counterintuitive and counterproductive design is available only on applications that specifically support it. Thankfully, not all applications use this new window. To disable this window, follow these directions.

Along with an application's help file (*.HLP*), there can be up to three other files:

.GID

> This file is created the first time the help file is opened and helps Windows find the help file next time. It can be deleted as long as the help file isn't currently open.

.FTS

> This file is created when the file is indexed. The first time you choose the **Find** tab in the Help Topics window of a particular help file, the .FTS file is created. It can also be deleted to save disk space as along as the help file isn't open.

.CNT

> This file may be included with an application's help file but is not created on the fly. If the help file isn't open, you can delete this file, and the Contents screen will never appear again. If you delete the file and select **Contents** from the application's **Help** menu, the **Index** tab will be selected instead of the **Contents** tab. However, if you double-click on the .HLP file after deleting the .CNT file, the help file's main, introductory page will be displayed instead.

Notes and other issues

There may not be a .CNT file for every help file on your hard disk, and deleting a single .CNT file will only disable the Contents window for that particular help file.

Go ahead and use Windows' search feature to find all of the .CNT files on your system. You'll be pleasantly surprised at the hard drive space you'll retrieve as a result of deleting these files.

System Enhancements

This section rounds off the chapter with some final topics, including tips for the command prompt and multiple users. Note that throughout the book, the command prompt is not only mentioned but extensively utilized. See Appendix B, *MS-DOS Crash Course* for some details on some of the commands used here.

What to Do If You Hate the Start Menu ● ■

Nobody liked Program Manager, the shell that came with Windows 3.x. If you dislike the **Start Menu** as well, you have a few options:

Use the Desktop

- Since the Macintosh has no formal menu system, Mac users have been doing this for years. Just place icons for your applications directly on your Desktop, and forget about the **Start Menu**.

Use another program (Windows 95 only)

- The **Start Menu** and the **Desktop** are part of the **Explorer.exe** program. To configure Windows 95 to use another program as the system "Shell," first open a text editor such as Notepad.

- Open *System.ini* in your Windows folder. In the [Boot] section, which should be first, look for a line that begins with shell=. If it doesn't exist, add it to the end of the [Boot] section.

- Change the line so it reads shell=progman.exe, where *progman.exe* is the program filename for Program Manager. Since it's unlikely that anyone would prefer Program Manager to anything else, you can replace this with the full path and program filename of the application you wish. If you use your computer only for word processing, you can put your word processor here.

Obtain and install an alternate shell

- Route 1 Pro 2.0, an interface enhancement for Windows 95 and Windows NT 4.0, implements a simple row of buttons providing quick access to your programs and files. It also includes several features not found in Windows 95, such as a scheduler, a scripting language, security, better support for multiple users, and nested submenus to organize your files and programs the way you want. You can download a fully functional evaluation version of the software for free on the Internet at *http://www.creativelement.com/software/route1.html*.

Notes and other issues

If you replace Explorer as the system shell (using the second solution above), you'll also lose all your Desktop icons, the **Start Menu**, and the taskbar. Any minimized programs will be reduced to small rectangles instead of taskbar items. Make sure the new program you choose is able to launch programs, or you may get stuck. Additionally, the program should be able to shut down your system if you exit the software, which isn't always the case.

Using the Command Prompt ● ■

The command prompt has been improved over previous versions for Windows 95 and Windows NT 4.0. You can now execute Windows programs by typing their names at the command prompt, just as though you had double-clicked them (if Windows is currently running, that is). Following are a few tidbits that should help you accomplish nearly all command prompt tasks. Some familiarity with DOS is assumed but not required.

Use long filenames

- When using the *dir* command in DOS, the names of files or folders in the current directory with long filenames will appear truncated. That is, a file with the name *My List of Things.TXT* will appear as *MYLIST~1.TXT* in the left column. Look to the right, and you'll see the long filenames; you can type `dir /b` to view only the long filenames.

- If the name of a file or folder doesn't contain a space, you should be able to type it normally. That is, you can type the name of an .EXE file to run the program, and include the name of a document file after a command (such as *del*).

- Say you want to use the `cd` command to change the current working directory to C:\Program Files. If you type `CD Program Files`, it obviously won't work, since DOS will look only for a folder named Program. To get around this, you can use the short version:

```
CD PROGRA~1
```

or enclose the folder name in quotation marks:

```
CD "Program Files"
```

Run a shortcut from the command prompt

- While shortcuts linked to files, folders, applications, and other system objects can be opened from Windows, they aren't recognized by

DOS. However, by using the **Start** command prompt utility, either from the command prompt or from a batch file, you can run any Windows shortcut. Note the use of quotation marks from the previous tip.

- Type the following:

```
start "c:\directory\Shortcut to Someprog.exe.lnk"
```

where `c:\directory` is the full path containing the shortcut, and `Shortcut to Someprog.exe.lnk` is the filename of the shortcut.

Notes and other issues

When using long filenames, you can drop the closing quotation mark in most situations.

Using quotation marks to accommodate long filenames should work in most circumstances. If not, you'll have to use the short version (with the ~1).

Dealing with Multiple Users ●

The use of multiple users on a Windows system falls into two categories. Both Windows 95 and Windows NT 4.0 can be configured to have multiple users; that is, each user has a username and password and a specific collection of settings. The other type of multiple user support is when the system is used as a network server, which usually applies to Windows NT, and those users are allowed to log in from other machines. This section deals with the first category. The second category is covered in Chapter 7, *Networking*.

Save settings for multiple users

If you've configured Windows to be used with more than one user and want each user's Desktop settings to be saved individually, this section is for you. While Windows NT is built for this, it's sort of an add-on to Windows 95 and still may not work too well.

- Double-click on the Passwords icon in Control Panel and choose the **User Profiles** tab.

- Select **Users can customize their preferences**, turn on both options below, and click **OK**.

- You'll have to restart Windows for this change to take effect.

Prevent new users from logging in (Windows 95 only)

Anyone can simply log in to Windows 95 by choosing a new username and password, regardless of whether the administrator has attempted to restrict access. Clearly, Windows 95 isn't nearly as secure as Windows NT. To patch this hole in security, obtain and install the Shutdown utility. See "Software and the Internet" in the Preface for more information.

Use multiple languages on a single system

Although Windows 95 comes in several different languages, there doesn't seem to be any way to configure a single installation to use more than one language. This would be especially useful if the computer were used by more than one user, each using a different language. It would be nice if you could switch languages as easily as keyboard mappings, but this doesn't seem to be the case. However, if you have enough disk space, here's a way to do it.

- Configure your computer so you can boot directly into DOS, as described in Chapter 4.

- Install each version of Windows 95 into separate directories or drives, each with a different language.

- To get into either copy of Windows 95, change to the appropriate directory, and type win. To automate this step, you'll want to make a DOS startup menu, as described in Chapter 5.

3

The Registry

Whenever you change system colors, install an application, or change a setting in Control Panel, the relevant information is stored in your Registry. The Registry is a database of all the settings for Windows 95 and Windows NT 4.0, as well as the applications installed on your system. It existed in a simpler form in earlier versions of Windows but was used only to register object linking and embedding (OLE) applications. Knowing how to use the Registry is important for the advanced operation of Windows, as well as for the troubleshooting and extended customizing techniques discussed in this book.

All of your file types (see "Customizing Context Menus" in Chapter 4, *Advanced Customizing Techniques*) are stored in the Registry as well as all of the network, hardware, and software settings for Windows and all of the particular configuration options for most of the software you've installed. While the particular settings for each of your applications and Windows components can differ substantially, there are some techniques you can use to figure out undocumented settings and uncover hidden functionality. What's especially helpful is that most of the settings stored in the Registry are named in plain English rather than obscure codes and acronyms. You shouldn't take this fact for granted, but it does help quite a bit in finding settings and troubleshooting problems.

For a more in-depth look at the Windows 95 Registry, as well as programming tips and advanced techniques and tips, check out *Inside the Windows 95 Registry* by Ron Petrusha. Check out Appendix C, *Glossary*, for definitions of any of the technical terms used here as well as in the rest of the book.

WARNING   You can irreversibly disable certain components of Windows by changing settings in the Registry, so do so with caution. However, if you take the simple precaution of backing up the Registry, (described later in this chapter) you'll virtually eliminate the possibility of disaster. Furthermore, backing up your entire system, a more involved process than just backing up the Registry, will ensure that none of your valuable data or programs are compromised and undoubtedly will save you hours of hard work and a painful headache.

Getting to Know the Registry

While the Registry is stored in multiple files on your hard disk, it is represented in a single hierarchical structure, like the directories on your hard disk. The Registry Editor (*regedit.exe*, located in your Windows folder) is included with Windows 95 and Windows NT 4.0 to enable you to view and edit the contents of the Registry. Windows NT also comes with an older version of the Registry Editor (*regedt32.exe*, located in the Winnt\System32 folder), which is included only for compatibility. There's no reason to use this program other than nostalgia.

When you open the Registry Editor, you'll see a window divided into two panes (see Figure 3-1). The left side shows a tree with folders, and the right side shows the contents (values) of the currently selected folder.

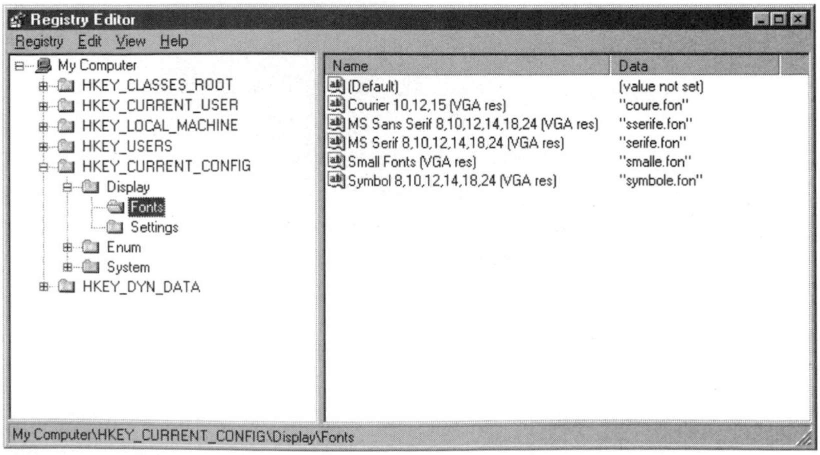

Figure 3-1: The Registry Editor enables you to view and change the contents of the Registry

Each branch (denoted by a folder icon in the Registry Editor) is called a **key**. Each key can contain other keys, as well as values. Each value contains the actual information stored in the Registry. There are three types of values: **String**, **Binary**, and **DWORD**. The use of these depends on the context in which they're used. To display the contents of a key (folder), click the desired key name on the left, and look at the values listed on the right side. To expand a certain branch to show the subkeys within, click on the plus sign [+] to the left of any folder, or just double-click on the folder.

You can add a new key or value by choosing the location for the new object and then selecting **New** from the **Edit Menu**. You can rename any existing value and almost any key with the same method used to rename files; right-click on an object and click **Rename**, click on it twice (slowly), or just press the F2 key. Lastly, you can delete a key or value by clicking on it, and pressing the Del key, or by right-clicking on it and selecting **Delete**.

You can search for text in the names of keys or values by selecting **Find** from the **Edit Menu**. Select **Refresh** from the **View** menu to refresh the displayed portion of the Registry, in case another running application has changed a setting. You can't, however, drag-drop any keys or values as you can with files in Explorer. Similar to Explorer, though, is the notion of a *path*. A Registry path is a location in the Registry, described by the series of subordinate keys in which a setting is located. For example, if a particular value is in the Microsoft key under SOFTWARE, which is under HKEY_LOCAL_MACHINE, the Registry path would be HKEY_LOCAL_MACHINE\SOFTWARE\Microsoft. Elsewhere in this book, when a setting is changed in the Registry, this type of Registry path is always given.

There are six primary branches, each containing a specific portion of the information stored in the Registry. These root keys can't be deleted, renamed, or moved, because they are the basis for the organization of the Registry.

HKEY_CLASSES_ROOT

This branch contains all of your file types, filename extensions, and OLE information for all your OLE-aware applications. See "Understanding File Types" later in this chapter for details on the structure of this branch. One special key here, called CLSID (short for Class ID), contains all of the OLE information, used for communication between different applications. While the contents of HKEY_CLASSES_ROOT are easy to edit, it's best not to mess with anything in the CLSID branch because almost none of it is in plain English.

This entire branch is a mirror of HKEY_LOCAL_MACHINE\SOFTWARE\ Classes but is displayed separately for clarity and easy access.

HKEY_USERS

This branch contains a sub-branch for each user on your computer. Although Windows 95 can be configured for multiple users, there is usually only one user, called *default*. In Windows NT 4.0, there are more built-in users, and the default user is Administrator.

In each user's branch are the settings for that user, such as Control Panel settings and Explorer preferences. Some applications store user-specific information here as well.

HKEY_CURRENT_USER

This branch points to a portion of HKEY_USERS, signifying the current user. This way, any application can read the settings for the current user without having to know which user is currently logged on.

The settings for the current user are divided into several categories; AppEvents, Control Panel, InstallLocationsMRU, Keyboard Layout, Network, RemoteAccess, and Software. The most useful of these branches, Software, contains a branch for almost every application installed on your computer, arranged by manufacturer. You'll find Windows settings under the Microsoft branch.

HKEY_LOCAL_MACHINE

This branch contains information about all of the hardware and software installed on your computer that isn't specific to the current user.

Be very careful when changing any information pertaining to installed hardware, as it can make certain devices unavailable. Most of the settings in the hardware key can be configured in the Device Manager.

The sub-branch of interest here is the Software branch, which contains all of the information specific to the applications installed on your computer. While there's also application-specific information stored in HKEY_CURRENT_USER\Software, this location is the first place to look for settings.

You'll also notice the Config branch. It contains one or more numbered Hardware Profiles. The current hardware profile is mirrored in HKEY_CURRENT_CONFIG.

HKEY_CURRENT_CONFIG

This branch points to the part of HKEY_LOCAL_MACHINE\Config appropriate for the current hardware configuration.

HKEY_DYN_DATA

> This is the only dynamic branch of the Registry. That is, while all other branches are static and stored on the hard disk, this branch is created every time you start Windows and is held in memory. Its contents represent the various VxDs (device drivers) and Plug & Play devices installed on your system, as reported by the Configuration Manager. This branch is not much use in completing the material discussed in this book.

HKEY_USERS and HKEY_LOCAL_MACHINE are the only two original root keys stored on the hard disk. Other than HKEY_DYN_DATA, the other root keys are simply mirrors of different portions of the first two. In Windows 95, these two keys are stored on the hard disk as *user.dat* and *System.dat*, respectively.

In Windows NT 4.0, HKEY_USERS is saved in *ntuser.dat*, a copy of which is saved in each user's directory. The information in HKEY_LOCAL_ MACHINE is stored in several files, called "hives," in your Windows/ System32\Config folder, none of which have extensions. Their filenames are listed in your Registry, in HKEY_LOCAL_MACHINE\System\ CurrentControlSet\Control\hivelist.

Knowing which files make up the Registry in each version of Windows is important only for backup and emergency recovery procedures (see "Backing Up the Registry" in the next section). In either version of Windows, the contents of the Registry are viewed and changed with the same Registry Editor, which works independently of the files used to make up the Registry.

Tips and Tricks

Once you're somewhat familiar with the Registry and the Registry Editor application, you can begin to use them to diagnose problems, implement new features, and customize the operating system and its software. The first topic, "Backing Up the Registry," is the most important, and can eliminate nearly all problems that can occur when changing settings in the Registry. The information in the other topics in this section should provide enough knowledge to complete any other procedure in this book regarding the Registry.

Backing Up the Registry ● ■

Since the Registry is stored in certain files on your hard disk, you can create a backup by copying the files to another location. In fact, the Registry is usually small enough to fit on a single floppy diskette. The files to copy depend on your version of Windows. Most backup software made for Windows 95 and Windows NT 4.0, such as the Backup utility that comes with Windows, includes a feature to back up the Registry. It's always a good idea to exploit this functionality.

When you start Windows, the information in the Registry is loaded into memory. While Windows is running, some changes may not be physically written to the Registry files until you shut down your computer, while others (such as those made by the Registry Editor) are written immediately. For this reason, if you've made any substantial changes to the contents of the Registry, you'll probably want to restart Windows before backing it up to ensure that the files on the disk reflect the most recent changes.

You should make a habit of backing up your Registry at least once a week, to save you hours of work if your system should fail. Here's how to back up your Registry.

For Windows 95

- In Windows 95, the Registry is stored in two hidden files in your Windows directory, *user.dat* and *system.dat*. You'll also find two files, *user.da0* and *system.da0*, which are backups created automatically every time you exit Windows. These files do not need to be backed up: they are simply older versions of the Registry.

- These files are all hidden, meaning that with Explorer's default settings, you won't be able to see or find them. To view hidden files, select **Options** from Explorer's **View** menu, select the **Show All Files** option, and click **OK**.

- Using Explorer or Windows' **Find** feature, locate and highlight *user.dat* and *system.dat*. If they're smaller than the capacity of a floppy disk (about 1.4 megabytes), drag both of the files onto the floppy drive icon. If they're larger and won't fit on a single floppy, you'll have to use a program like PKZip to compress them. If you have a tape drive or some other backup device, that's even better.

- There's also a command prompt utility on the CD-ROM that does this called Cfgback (*cfgback.exe*). Refer to the included documentation for details. If you don't have the CD version of Windows 95, see "Software and the Internet" in the Preface for more information.

For Windows NT 4.0

- In Windows NT 4.0, the Registry is in the form of several files, called "hives" in your Windows\System32\Config folder, none of which

with extensions. Their filenames are listed in your Registry, in `HKEY_`
`LOCAL_MACHINE\System\CurrentControlSet\Control\`
`hivelist`, but they're easily recognizable because they have no
extensions and are all dated the time you last shut down or restarted
your computer.

- You'll also see one or more files in the same folder with the .ALT
  extension. These are the backups automatically made by Windows
  NT when you shut down. These files do not need to be backed up;
  they are simply older versions of the Registry.

- Using Explorer or Windows' **Find** feature, locate and highlight the
  Registry files described earlier. If they're smaller than the capacity of
  a floppy disk (about 1.4 megabytes), just drag them all onto the
  floppy drive icon. If they're larger and won't fit on a single floppy,
  you'll have to use a program like PKZip (see "Support on the Internet" in the Preface) to compress them. If you have a tape drive or
  some other backup device, that's even better.

Restore a corrupted Registry

If either version of Windows finds that your Registry has become
corrupted, it will attempt to use the automatic backups (see your particular platform earlier). For this reason, don't make a habit of deleting the
backups to save disk space. It isn't worth it. If the backup files are
unavailable or corrupted as well, Windows will inform you that the
Registry is corrupted. You'll probably need to reinstall Windows to solve
the problem.

- The first step is to run the command prompt version of Scandisk
  (*scandisk.exe*) to fix any potential problems with your hard disk or
  files. To get into the command prompt, press the F8 key when Windows first begins to load, and select command prompt from the list.
  Then, just type `scandisk` at the prompt to start the program. If Windows is installed on a different drive from C, you'll need to change to
  that drive first.

- If you've made backups as described above, copy them over the damaged files and restart your computer. Since you're obviously not in
  Windows, this is accomplished with the *Copy* command. For example, type `copy a:user.dat c:\windows` if you wish to copy
  user.dat from your floppy drive (in this case, A) to your Windows
  folder (in this case, C:\windows).

- If you're using Windows 95, the Registry files are hidden. This
  shouldn't pose a problem, although if you use the *dir* command in

DOS, they won't be listed. Don't panic; just use the */ah* command line parameter to display hidden files. You won't need to unhide the files, nor will you need to hide them again if you've turned off the hidden attribute.

- If the damage is severe enough, you may still be required to reinstall Windows. Once you've done that, replace the Registry files with your previous backups, and most of your system should be restored. It may be a good idea to back up the *new* Registry files before replacing them, just in case your backups are damaged.

Automate the backup with a DOS batch file

Since the backup procedure is simply the copying of a few files to a floppy disk (or other safe location), it can be easily automated with a DOS batch file. The example is for Windows 95, but can be easily adapted for Windows NT by changing the filenames and names of the folders containing the Registry files.

- Using a text editor, such as Notepad, type the following:

```
copy c:\windows\user.dat a: /v
copy c:\windows\system.dat a: /v
```

This assumes that you wish to copy the files to drive A, and that Windows 95 is installed in C:\windows. The /v parameter tells DOS to verify the integrity of the copied files.

- Save the file as something like *regback.bat* (the .BAT extension is necessary), and place it in your Windows folder. Just double-click on the file to back up your Registry.

- If your Registry has gotten large, you may want to use a compression tool such as PKZip. Replace the lines shown above with the equivalent command, for use with the PKZip utility:

```
pkzip a:\reg.zip c:\windows\user.dat c:\windows\system.dat
```

This assumes that you wish to store the files in a file called *reg.zip* on drive A, and that Windows 95 is installed in C:\windows. The PKZip program should also be in your DOS path.

Notes and other issues

Backing up the Registry is easy, but it doesn't provide the level of protection achieved by a full system backup.

When you install Windows 95, a file named *system.1st* is placed in the root directory of your boot drive. This file is the *system.dat* file used when Windows 95 was first installed. If you ever reinstall Windows 95 over an existing installation, this file will be replaced with the last version of *system.dat* before you reinstalled. If you lose your backups and there's a problem with your Registry, you can try to use this file by renaming it to *system.dat* and copying it to your Windows folder. It won't have your most recent settings, it may allow you to start Windows 95 without reinstalling.

To back up certain portions of the Registry or to share certain settings in the Registry, see the next section.

Using Registry Patches ● ■

Although you can edit the Registry with the Registry Editor, you can also make changes by using Registry patches. A Registry patch is simply a text file with the .REG extension that contains one or more Registry keys or values. If you double-click on a .REG file, the patch is applied to the Registry, meaning that the contents of the patch are merged with the contents of the Registry. This is a good way to share or back up small portions of the Registry for use on your own computer or someone else's, because it's much simpler and less dangerous than manually editing the Registry. Since the Registry Editor is virtually identical in Windows 95 and Windows NT 4.0, the process of creating, editing, and using Registry patches is the same as well.

Create a Registry patch

- Open the Registry Editor, and select a branch you wish to use. The branch can be anywhere from one of the top-level branches to a branch a dozen layers deep. Registry patches include not only the branch you select, but all of the values and subkeys in the branch. Don't select any more than what you absolutely need.

- Select **Export Registry File** from the **Registry** menu, type a filename, and click **OK**. All of the values and subkeys in the selected branch will then be duplicated in the patch. Make sure the filename of the new Registry patch has the extension .REG.

Edit a Registry patch

Since the patch is a plain text file, you can edit it with any plain text editor, such as Notepad.

The contents of the Registry patch will look like the text shown in Example 3-1.

Example 3-1. The contents of a Registry path of HKEY_CLASSES_ROOT\.txt

```
REGEDIT4

[HKEY_CLASSES_ROOT\.txt]
"Content Type"="text/plain"
@="txtfile"

[HKEY_CLASSES_ROOT\.txt\ShellNew]
"FileName"="a.txt"
```

The first line, REGEDIT4, tells Windows that this file is a valid Registry patch. Don't remove this line. The rest of the Registry patch is a series of key names and values. The key names appear in brackets and are the full path of the key; the values contained within each key follow. The name of the value is given first, followed by an equals sign, and then the data stored in each value. The value names and value data are enclosed in quotation marks. A value name of @ tells the Registry Editor to place the value data in the (default) value.

If you are familiar with the information contained within a Registry patch you've just created, you can edit anything you wish and save the changes when you're done.

Apply a Registry patch

- When you apply a Registry patch, you are merging the keys and values stored in a patch with the Registry. Double-click on a Registry patch icon (as long as it has the .REG extension) in Explorer to apply it. Once you've applied the Registry, you'll see a message that looks something like "Information in registry_patch.reg has been successfully entered into the Registry."

- If you're in the Registry Editor, you can also select **Import Registry File** from the **Registry** menu, select the patch, and click **OK** to merge the file. Any keys or values in the patch that don't already exist will be added to the Registry. If a value already exists by the same name, the value will be changed to whatever is in the patch.

Notes and other issues

If you're creating a Registry patch on your computer for use on another, make sure any folder names or drive letters are corrected for the new computer. If, for example, your Registry patch tells Windows to open *C:\my_folder\wordpad.exe* whenever you double-click on a text file, you should make sure to change it to *D:\her_folder\wordpad.exe* if the Wordpad application happens to be in a different folder or drive on the other machine.

Although the Registry Editor has a search feature, it doesn't allow you to search and replace. If you have a branch of settings you wish to change—for example, if you've moved an application from one drive to another—you can use a Registry patch. Just create a patch of the branch in question, and use your favorite text editor's search-and-replace feature to change the values in the patch. When you apply the patch, all the settings will be changed for you. Note that you should use this with caution, as you can mess up many settings unwittingly. See the next section for more information.

Searching the Registry Effectively ● ■

The Registry Editor has a simple search feature, allowing you to search through all the keys and values for text. Just select **Find** from the Registry Editor's **Edit Menu**, type the desired text, and click **Find Next**. Since the Registry can become quite large and have a wide variety of settings and information, it is important to learn to search effectively, so you don't miss anything and don't waste time. Additionally, since the Registry Editor doesn't have a search-and-replace feature, doing something as simple as changing every occurrence of C:\windows to D:\windows can be a chore. Here are some tips that may help:

- Many folder names in the Registry are stored in both long and short versions. Say you want to move your Program Files folder from one drive to another (see "Cleaning Up and Customizing System Folders" in Chapter 4 for more information). When you install Windows, any settings pertaining to this folder may be stored in the Registry as \PROGRAM FILES or \PROGRA~1. Make sure you search for both.

- If you're searching the Registry for both PROGRAM FILES and PROGRA~1, you may want to just search for progra, which will trigger both variations. Since this will trip upon other uses of the word *program*, try placing a backslash in front of it to limit the search to directory names beginning with those letters.

- On certain occasions, you may search the Registry for an interface element, such as a new item added to a context menu or the text in a dialog box. If the text contains an underlined character, you'll need to add an ampersand to the search string. For example, say you've installed a program that creates ZIP files, and the program has added the command *Add to Zip* to the context menu of all files that you

wish to remove. You'll need to search for add to &zip to match
the text properly.

- While most settings you'll want to change will be the data (the contents
  of the values), you should be aware that some settings are also stored in
  the value names as well as the key names. When searching, turn on all
  of the options in the Look At box, so you don't miss anything, unless
  you're sure of what you're looking for. For the same reason, you probably don't want to be using "Match whole word only," which will skip
  over any settings where your text is part of a larger word.

- Searching begins at the currently selected key. If you want to be sure
  to search the entire Registry, make sure the My Computer entry at the
  top of the Registry tree is highlighted before you begin. However, if
  you know in which key the setting you want to change is, for example, HKEY_LOCAL_MACHINE, you should highlight that beforehand to
  reduce the search time.

- Although the Registry Editor has a search feature, it doesn't allow you
  to search and replace. If you have a branch of settings you wish to
  change—for example, if you've moved an application from one drive
  to another, you can use a Registry patch (see "Using Registry
  Patches" earlier in this chapter). Just create a patch of the branch in
  question, and use your favorite text editor's search-and-replace feature to change the values in the patch. When you apply the patch, all
  the settings will be changed for you. Use this with caution. You can
  mess up many settings unwittingly by searching and replacing common pieces of text.

- If you find yourself wanting to use search-and-replace more often
  and the Registry patch tip above isn't sufficient, you may want to try
  the Registry Search and Replace utility.

Compacting the Registry ●

As you may have noticed, your Registry can become quite large. As you
know, the Registry is a database. As with all other databases, when information is removed or added, the entire database file is *not* rewritten
entirely, in order to improve performance. Instead, new information is
simply appended to the end of the file, and gaps are left in the file where
information has been removed. After a lot of use, the files that make up
the Registry become enormous. The process of compacting a database
like the Registry involves reading all of the settings and then writing them
into a new file. This way, the empty space is eliminated, and the entries
are stored in order.

This is probably the only topic in this book you're *not* encouraged to try on your own, as it can be a painful experience and not quite worth the effort. However, for those of you who wish to give it a try, a solution has been included to provide the necessary information. Compacting the Registry can help reclaim some free disk space, marginally speed up the Windows startup process, and make Registry reads and writes slightly more efficient. If you have the time and have made a backup of your Registry, give it a try. Because of the nature of the solution, it's recommended that you try this with only Windows 95, not Windows NT 4.0.

Important: Back up your Registry before continuing (see "Backing up the Registry" earlier in this chapter).

- Open the Registry Editor.

- Highlight the HKEY_USERS and HKEY_LOCAL_MACHINE branches in the Registry, and select **Export Registry File** from the **Registry** menu to create Registry patches for each of them. Since the other branches are simply mirrors of portions of the first two branches, you don't need to export them. It's best not to export the root entry (usually called My Computer), as the Registry patch it creates can be too large and contains a lot of duplicate information.

- Save the Registry patches in a new folder on your hard disk, and make sure not to use long filenames, as you'll be using these files in DOS. The rest of the solution assumes that you've named the two files *user.reg* and *system.reg*, respectively, and that you've placed them in an otherwise empty directory called Newreg on drive C. If you've used other names, be sure to alter the following commands appropriately.

- Restart Windows in MS-DOS mode (or just exit to DOS, as described in Chapter 4).

- Change to the directory containing the new Registry patches by typing cd c:\newreg at the command prompt.

- The Registry Editor has a DOS counterpart that allows you to import and export Registry patches into the current Registry, as well as create a new Registry from a Registry patch—all from the command prompt. Start by creating a new Registry in this new folder from one of the Registry patches, by opening a DOS window and typing the following command:

```
regedit /l:.\system.dat /r:.\user.dat /c user.reg
```

The /c parameter tells the Registry Editor to create a new Registry with the patch, rather than appending the settings in the patch to the current Registry. The /l and /r parameters tell the Registry Editor where to create the two Registry files. (Note the periods before the backslashes, which specify that the files should be created in the current directory.)

- Next, use a similar command (without the /c parameter this time) to merge the other Registry patch:

```
regedit /l:.\system.dat /r:.\user.dat system.reg
```

If you get an error while importing either patch, such as "Cannot import user.reg: Error accessing the registry," refer to "Notes and other issues" at the end of this section.

- Once you've issued both commands, you should have two new files in the directory: *system.dat* and *user.dat*. Before these files can be copied over your old ones, unhide both the new and old Registry files. Type the following commands to accomplish this:

```
attrib -r -s -h system.dat
attrib -r -s -h user.dat
attrib -r -s -h c:\windows\system.dat
attrib -r -s -h c:\windows\user.dat
```

- Now replace the old versions with the new ones with the following commands:

```
copy .\system.dat c:\windows
copy .\user.dat c:\windows
```

assuming that your Windows directory is c:\windows.

- Restart your computer. You should now be able to use Windows with the newly compacted Registry files. If you notice anything strange, such as forgotten settings or error messages, proceed to the following step.

If you received an error

- First, don't panic. If you've backed up the your Registry files as instructed, you can recover them. However, you might still be able to start Windows in its current state. Again, don't worry if it appears as though Windows 95 has forgotten all your settings. For some reason, the command prompt version of the Registry Editor doesn't always work properly. It sometimes chokes on large Registry patches and doesn't complete the process. If you can get back into Windows 95, you can use the Windows version of the Registry Editor to complete the process.

- If Windows won't start in its current condition, try starting Windows 95 in safe mode by pressing F8 when your computer just begins to load Windows, and selecting **Safe Mode** from the **Start Menu**. If this still doesn't work, you'll need to restore your old Registry files and abandon the endeavor.

- Once you're able to get back into Windows 95, select **Run** from the **Start Menu**, type regedit, and press the Enter key.

- Once the Registry Editor appears, select **Import Registry File** from the **Registry** menu, find and select one of the Registry patches you created (either *user.reg* or *system.reg*), and click **OK**. Repeat the step for the other patch as well.

- The Registry Editor should successfully merge both files. If one of them fails, try again. It may work the second time. If you can't get it to work, you'll need to restore your old Registry files and abandon the endeavor.

- Once you've been successful in merging the entire contents of both files, restart your computer one more time. When Windows 95 loads, everything should be back to normal.

Notes and other issues

Any crashing that may occur when you try to reconstruct the Registry (see "If you received an error" previously in this chapter) is supposedly caused if some branches (like HKEY_CLASSES_ROOT) are too large. Microsoft is "working" on the problem. For some users, exporting from DOS instead of Windows may yield better results.

An alternative to the above method is to use the *System.1st* placed in the root directory of your boot drive by the initial installation of Windows 95. Take the file, rename it to *system.dat*, and copy it into your Windows directory (while Windows 95 is not running). When Windows starts, many aspects will appear as though you've just installed Windows. At this point, apply the two patches to the Registry Editor, as described in the "If you received an error" section. This should yield the desired results.

Understanding File Types •

The term *file types* describes the database of associations between applications and the files they use. The most apparent use of this feature is that Windows knows to run Notepad when you double-click on a file with the .TXT extension. The traditional method for configuring these associations to suit your needs is discussed in "Customizing Context Menus" in Chapter 4, but it goes quite a bit deeper than that.

It all starts with file extensions—the letters (usually three) that follow the period in most filenames. For example, the extension of the file, *readme.txt*, is .TXT, signifying a plain-text file; the extension of *resume.wpd* is .WPD, signifying a document created in WordPerfect. By default, Windows hides the extensions of registered file types in Explorer and on the Desktop, but it's best to have them displayed. File extensions not only allow you to determine easily what kind of file a certain file is (as icons are almost never descriptive enough), but allow you to change the type of a file by simply renaming the extension. To display your file extensions, select **Options** in Explorer's **View** menu, and turn off the **Hide MS-DOS file extensions for file types that are registered** option.

By hiding file extensions, Microsoft hoped to make Windows easier to use, a plan that backfired for several reasons. Since only the extensions of registered files are hidden, the extensions of files that aren't yet in the File Types database are still shown. What can be even more confusing is that when an application finally claims a certain file type, it can appear to the inexperienced user as though all of the old files of that type have been renamed. It also creates a knowledge gap between those who understand file types and those who don't. Try telling someone whose computer still has hidden extensions to find *readme.txt* in a directory full of files. Other problems have arisen, such as trying to differentiate *excel.exe* and *excel.xls* in Explorer when the extensions are hidden. One file is an application and the other is a document, but they may have the same icon. Sometimes applications like Wordpad take a file such as *Read.me* and try to save it as *Read.me.txt*—utterly useless.

The HKEY_CLASSES_ROOT branch of the Registry stores all your file types. File extensions (preceded by periods) are listed first, followed by the actual file types. If you look in a key named for a file extension, such as .TXT (note that the period is included), you'll notice that it contains only the (default) value, set to something like "txtfile." "Txtfile" is the actual file type, which is stored lower down in the branch (see Figure 3-2).

All of the details of the file type are stored in the txtfile branch, such as the formal name (in this case, "Text File"), the icon, and the program used to open the file. Since many different extension keys can point to this branch, a file type like txtfile can have several extensions associated with it. This is important; there's no way to assign more than one extension to any given file type in the File Types editor in Explorer.

There are several ways that file types are created. The structure shown in Figure 3-2 is what you'll usually get when an application claims a file type. In this case, Windows setup created the "Text File" file type when Windows was first installed. If you use the File Types editor in Explorer (see "Customizing Context Menus" in Chapter 4), you'll get something

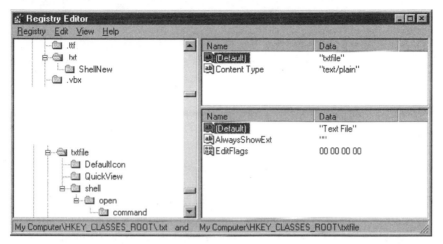

Figure 3-2: These two portions of the Registry make up a basic file type

similar. If you've ever double-clicked on an unregistered file type, you've seen the Open With window asking you which program you want to use with that type of file (also accessible by right-clicking on a file while holding the Shift key and selecting **Open With**). File types created in this way are recognized by "auto_file." For example, choosing a program for a file with the .DAT extension will create a file type called "dat_auto_file." The final way to create a file type is manually, by editing the Registry directly or by applying a Registry patch.

Regardless of the method by which a file type has been created, the structure in the Registry is virtually the same. All of the major components of a file type are shown in Figure 3-2. First, a key is created for each extension of the file type. The (default) value contains the name of the key containing the file type, not the name of the file type itself—for example, put `txtfile` here and not `Text File`. The `Content Type` value shown may appear for some file types but is not necessary for normal operation.

A key called `ShellNew` may also appear underneath the file extension key. This key tells Windows to include the extension in the **New** menu (found in Explorer's **File** menu), allowing one to create a new, empty file of that type right in Explorer, and without starting the associated application. The reason that the `ShellNew` key is located underneath the extension key and not the file type key is that a file type may have more than one extension, and Windows needs to know which extension to use when creating a new file. The `ShellNew` key is usually empty, although there may be a value called FileName, which points to a "template"—a file on your hard disk that Windows will use to create a new, blank document. In most cases, the FileName value is omitted, and Windows will create a zero-byte (empty) file with the appropriate extension.

Most of a file type's definition is located in the main file type key, the name of which is specified in each of the extension keys already listed. In Figure 3-3, the txtfile key is the main key containing all of the settings for the "Text File" file type. First of all, the (default) value here is the aesthetic name of the file type: the text that appears in the File Types editor in Explorer and in the Type column in Explorer's Details view. If the value named AlwaysShowExt is present (always empty), the extension for this file type will be displayed in Explorer, even if the user has elected to hide extensions for file types that are registered. You may also see a value entitled EditFlags. If this value is omitted or set to 00 00 00 00, you will be allowed to edit this file type in Explorer. If EditFlags is set to 01 00 00 00, the file type won't be visible in Explorer's File Types editor.

Underneath the file type key are three or four independent subkeys. DefaultIcon contains only the (default) value, set to the filename of the icon used for the file type. Icons are specified by filename and icon index, such as d:\path\filename,### where d:\path\filename is the full path and filename of an .EXE, .DLL, .ICO, or .BMP file containing one or more icons, and ### represents the number of the icon (you won't actually see pound signs). To use the first icon in the file, specify **0**; the second icon, 1; and so on. The easiest way to choose an icon is through Explorer, as the File Types editor will allow you to browse and choose icons without typing.

If a key entitled QuickView is present, the context menu for the file type will include QuickView. (See "Using QuickView with Any File" in Chapter 4 for more information.) This key normally has the (default) value set to an asterisk.

Most of the meat is stored in the Shell key. The keys here define what happens when the file of this type is double-clicked and which commands appear in the file type's context menu (see Figure 3-3). Underneath Shell is a separate key for each command in the file's context menu. That is, when you right-click on a file of this type, these are the items that will appear at the top of the list. Most file types have an **Open** command; you may also see **Edit**, **Print**, **PrintTo**, and **View** here. You can add, remove, or change any of these commands you wish. Underneath each one of *these* keys is a key called Command (now you see why a figure is so helpful). The Command key contains the (default) value set to the program filename used to carry out the command. For example, if

Notepad is associated with the **Open** command for text files, the contents of HKEY_CLASSES_ROOT\txtfile\shell\open\command will be "Notepad.exe %1". The "%1" is very important; %1 is what Windows substitutes in the application's command line, and the quotation marks are necessary in case there are any spaces in the filename of the clicked file. So if you were to right-click on any file with the .TXT extension (say, *c:\documents\my file.txt*), and select **Open** from the context menu that appears, Windows will carry out the command Notepad c:\ documents\my file.txt, which will launch Notepad and instruct it to open the document.

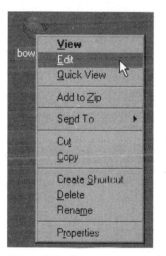

Figure 3-3: A context menu for the bitmap file type shows the default View option, as well as the extra Edit and Add to Zip options

If there is more than one command for a given file type, one of the commands will appear in bold (see the **View** command in Figure 3-3). This command is called the default and is the one that Windows uses when one double-clicks on a file instead of right-clicking. Usually, "open" is the default, but any command can be the default. To set the default to a different command, specify the name of the command in the **(default)** value in the Shell key. For example, if a file type contains **Open**, **Edit**, and **Print** and you type print in the (default) value, the **Print** command will appear bold in the file type's context menu. Note that the while the word *open* is often spelled with all lowercase letters, it still appears as **Open** in the context menu. Windows will preserve the case of all other commands but will automatically capitalize **Open**.

Finally, the Shellex key contains references to shell extensions; unless you're a programmer, these items will be of little use to you. You can remove some unwanted context menu commands and extra tabs in the property sheets of certain file types by removing the corresponding keys here; just be careful. You might also see CLSID and ddeexec keys scattered around the Registry. These also have special uses but are of little interest to most users.

Since there are so many parts to a standard file type, the easiest way to copy or save a file type is to create a Registry patch (see "Using Registry Patches" previously in this chapter). If you're creating an entirely new file type, it's easiest to start by exporting an existing file type and then changing the particulars. Here's a tip: Create individual registry patches for any file types that get commonly overwritten, such as .JPG, .GIF, .BMP, .TXT, .DOC, and .HTML. See "Preventing Programs from Changing Your File Types" in Chapter 4 for more information.

Notes and other issues

For more information on the File Types editor in Explorer, see "Customizing Context Menus" in Chapter 4. See "Change the Icons of System Objects" in Chapter 4 for another use of the DefaultIcon key.

Using .INI Files • ■

If you've been using a Windows PC for any length of time, you've probably come across .INI files. Initialization files (called *configuration files* in Windows 95) were used to store settings for many applications as well as previous versions of Windows before the Registry was implemented. These .INI files are simply text files (editable with any plain text editor, such as Notepad) that are specially formatted to store such settings. Since .INI files are limited in their maximum file size and are not as efficient as the Registry, application developers have been encouraged to abandon .INI files and instead store settings in the Registry. Since some older applications, written before the release of Windows 95, and even some newer ones still use .INI files to store certain settings, it may become necessary to look for and change settings in .INI files as well. Here are some tips on working with .INI files:

Edit an .INI file

*   Double-click on any .INI file to open it in Notepad. To configure another text editor to be used with .INI files, see "Customizing Context Menus" in Chapter 4.

The structure of .INI files is similar to that of Registry patches. See Example 4-2. Sections are specified in brackets, and individual settings in those sections are listed thereafter.

Search your .INI files for a setting

- Select **Find** and then **Files or Folders** from the **Start Menu**.

- Type *.ini for in the **Named** field, and then choose the **Advanced** tab.

- In the **Containing Text** field, type the text for which you want to search. This has essentially the same effect as searching through the Registry for a setting. It may be necessary to do this if you're tracking down an annoyance or another particular setting.

System.ini and win.ini

- The settings for previous versions of Windows were stored in *system.ini* and *win.ini*. Although these files are no longer used in Windows 95 for the most part, they are kept somewhat up to date to maintain compatibility with older applications that expect to find or store certain settings in them.

- In Windows 95, certain sections of *win.ini* are read and integrated into the Registry, just in case any application has saved something there that needs to be brought up to date. One of those sections, [Extensions], contains the Windows 3.x-equivalent of File Types. Anything you put in there will be integrated into the Registry every time you start Windows 95—a good idea if your favorite file type is constantly being overwritten.

- In the [Windows] section, at the top of the *win.ini* file, are two lines labeled Load= and Run=. These lines were used to list any programs to run when Windows was started, and there may still be something there. Try checking these out to see if something is being loaded of which you're not aware.

- Clearing out unneeded or outdated information from either of these files will marginally speed up Windows boot time as well as reduce the likelihood of certain conflicts. If you try to clean these out, do so with caution, and be sure to keep backup copies.

Registry Tools

The Registry Editor is included in Windows 95 and Windows NT 4.0 for viewing and changing the contents of the Registry. Unfortunately, this utility is quite limited, especially when compared with some of the other tools available. Following is a list of available software utilities for use with the Registry. You may want to take the precaution of backing up your Registry before using any of them. Unless otherwise specified, each of these tools is available for free download on the Internet. See "Software and the Internet" in the Preface for more information.

- Registry Search and Replace is a full-featured tool used to make a global search and replace in the Registry much easier and quicker. Registration of version 2.0 is $20.

- RegClean is a freely available Microsoft product used to correct problems with certain OLE entries in the Registry.

- Norton Utilities 95 version 2.0 is a commercial package that comes with an enhanced Registry Editor, as well as many other tools. It is not available on the Internet but it can be purchased at most computer stores.

- TweakUI, an innovative "PowerToy" is available for free download from Microsoft's home page. It allows you to make many changes discussed in this book *without* having to edit (and possibly mess up) the Registry.

Selected Topics

The following topics found elsewhere in this book demonstrate and take advantage of many settings and facets of the Windows Registry:

Chapter 4 ● ■

"Changing the Registered User Information"
"Turning Off the Documents Menu"
"Cleaning Up and Customizing System Folders"
"Clearing Unwanted Entries from Explorer's New Menu"
"Customizing My Computer"
"Renaming the Recycle Bin"
"Changing the Icons of System Objects"
"Turning Off the Bouncing 'Click Here to Begin' Arrow"
"Getting Rid of Shortcut Residue"
"Enabling Iconic Preview of Bitmaps"
"Customizing Context Menus"
"Clearing Unwanted Entries from Add/Remove Programs"
"Printing Out a Directory Listing"
"Using QuickView with Any File"
"Preventing Programs from Changing Your File Types"
"Getting Rid of Irritating Splash Screens"

Chapter 6 ● ■

"Clearing Unwanted Entries from the Start Menu's Run Command History"

Chapter 7 ● ■

"Changing the MTU and RWIN Settings in Dial-Up Networking"

4

In this chapter:
- *Cleaning Up the Desktop*
- *Resolving Annoyances*
- *Advanced Configuration*
- *Tips and Techniques*
- *System Administration*

Advanced Customization Techniques

The material in this chapter should satisfy anyone's desires for customizing Windows far beyond Microsoft's intentions. We'll start by clearing some of the clutter caused by the installation of Windows and move on to customizing whatever is left over to suit our needs. The "Resolving Annoyances" section starts with what I consider to be the three biggest annoyances: overwritten file types, splash screens, and CD-ROM Autorun. The chapter continues with "Advanced Configuration," where you'll learn to change some aspects of Windows that you're not supposed to, such as the previously unchangeable components of the **Start Menu**. "Tips and Techniques" follows with some configuration solutions to help you get your work done faster; "Customizing Context Menus" is an important one. The final section closes things up with advanced administrative duties, such as multiple users, security, and designating drive letters.

If you haven't reviewed Chapter 3, *Registry*, I suggest you do it at this point. It covers the Windows Registry and the Registry Editor, which are used extensively in many of the solutions in this chapter and later in the book. Many solutions require that you change a setting in the Registry and then restart Windows for the change to take effect. You'll learn from these examples how this whole system works and, hopefully, how to solve problems that aren't covered by the material here.

The variety of solutions presented here should be a testimony to the power and flexibility of Windows 95 and Windows NT 4.0. This flexibility is one of the primary reasons Microsoft's operating systems are so predominant among personal computers today. However, I'd also like to note the need for such solutions in the first place.

Cleaning Up the Desktop

When Windows 95 is first installed, the Desktop is littered with icons, some of which can be removed and some of which cannot. The problem here is that the Recycle Bin is intended as a means by which objects on the screen can be deleted by dragging and dropping them into it. But some items can't be deleted this way, and others can't be deleted at all (including the Recycle Bin itself).

Two types of objects reside on the Desktop (this doesn't include the taskbar, **Start Menu**, or tray). Those objects, the physical files and short-cuts to files, are stored in your Desktop folder (usually C:\Windows\Desktop); these items can almost always be thrown into the Recycle Bin. All other objects are virtual objects; they don't represent actual files on the hard disk. Virtual objects include My Computer, the Recycle Bin, and the Network Neighborhood. What follows should help you remove any unwanted icons from your Desktop.

Getting Rid of the
Network Neighborhood Icon ● ■

If you have installed Dial-Up Networking or any other networking compo-nents, you'll see the Network Neighborhood icon on your Desktop. If you're connected to one or more other computers on a local area network (see Chapter 7, *Networking*), this icon provides access to the shared files and other resources of those computers. However, if you've only installed Dial-Up Networking for use with, say, an Internet connec-tion, this icon is of absolutely no use and can be removed.

- Open the System Policy Editor (*poledit.exe*) on your Windows 95 CD-ROM (it's in the Admin\Apptools\Poledit folder). If you have the floppy disk version of Windows 95, see "Software and the Internet" in the Preface.

- If you are asked to "Open a Template File," choose *admin.adm* in the same folder, and click **OK**.

- Select **Open Registry** from the **File** menu.

- Double-click on the Local User icon.

- Expand the branches to LOCAL_USER\SHELL\RESTRICTIONS by clicking on the small plus signs to the left of the yellow folder icons.

- Turn on the **Hide Network Neighborhood** option. While you're at it, you can also turn off **No Entire Network In Network Neighborhood**, although it won't make much difference if you're not using the Network Neighborhood.

- Click **OK,** select **Save** from the **File** menu, and close the System Policy Editor.

You'll have to restart Windows for this change to take effect.

Notes and other issues

This setting can also be changed with TweakUI, one of Microsoft's Power-Toys. See "Software and the Internet" in the Preface for more information. See "Hide all Icons on the Desktop" later in this chapter for another solution.

If you've removed the Network Neighborhood icon yet still need the functionality it provides, you can create a movable version of the icon to place in your **Start Menu** or elsewhere on your hard disk with TweakUI as well.

A consequence of hiding the Network Neighborhood is that any resources previously available through the Network Neighborhood will be unavailable unless mapped to a drive letter (see "Setting Up a Workgroup" in Chapter 7 for more information). Since shell support for the Universal Naming Convention (UNC) notation is handled by the Network Neighborhood, hiding the Network Neighborhood icon will prevent Explorer from accessing resources via UNCs. If you don't use browsing features on your network, you won't have any use for this icon. Since it's just as easy to bring back the icon as it is to remove it, you can always bring it back if you find that you need it later. For example, hiding this icon will make it impossible to explore the shared drives and folders of other computers attached over a network or the direct-cable connection utility. See Chapter 7 for more information on networks and browsing shared resources.

Getting Rid of the Inbox Icon ● ■

The Inbox icon in Windows 95 provides a shortcut to Microsoft Exchange, the universal email and fax program that most users view as a complete failure. If you're using Windows NT 4.0 or have obtained the appropriate Windows 95 update from Microsoft, an improved version of Exchange, Windows Messaging, is used instead. Many users of Exchange and Messaging don't need the Inbox icon at all, but the only obvious way to remove it is to remove the Exchange/Messaging component altogether. Since it's another one of those virtual icons, it can't be dragged into the

Recycle Bin as one would expect. However, the following procedure should do the trick.

Solution 1

- Right-click on the Inbox icon on the Desktop, select **Delete**, and press **OK**.

Solution 2 (if your Inbox doesn't have a Delete option)

- Open the Registry Editor (*regedit.exe*). (If you're not familiar with the Registry Editor, see Chapter 3.)

- Expand the branches to HKEY_LOCAL_MACHINE\SOFTWARE\Microsoft\ Windows\CurrentVersion\explorer\Desktop\NameSpace\.

- Look for the key 00020D75-0000-0000-C000-000000000046, which should have a default value of Inbox.

- Delete the entire key (not just the default value), and close the Registry Editor.

- Click on the Desktop, and press F5 to refresh the Desktop so that this change will take effect.

Notes and other issues

Network administrators who wish to automate this process might be interested in Microsoft's INF Generator. See "Software and the Internet" in the Preface for more information.

The Inbox icon for Exchange can also be removed with TweakUI, one of Microsoft's PowerToys. However, users of Windows NT 4.0 will not be able to remove the icon for Messaging with TweakUI.

You don't need this icon to start Exchange. Just use the Exchange icon in the **Start Menu**, or double-click on *exchg32.exe* in the Microsoft Exchange folder.

See "Hiding All Icons on the Desktop" later in this chapter for another solution.

Getting Rid of the MSN Icon ● ■

Whether or not you installed the Microsoft Network (MSN), you'll see this useless icon on your Desktop. Although this is a virtual icon, it can be dragged into the Recycle Bin *most of the time*. If you've been successful in removing this icon, you've probably found out that it keeps reappearing whenever you use MSN. Aside from abstaining from using MSN altogether, it may not be possible to be rid of this silly icon forever. This mysterious behavior of the MSN icon varies, depending on what version of MSN you're using. However, Microsoft keeps making it more difficult to remove this icon, in a seemingly misguided attempt to increase the number of MSN users. To get rid of the MSN icon, follow these steps:

Solution 1

- Right-click on the MSN icon on the Desktop, select **Delete**, and press **OK**.

Solution 2

- If Solution 1 doesn't work or if the MSN icon doesn't have a **Delete** option, you can create a new folder, drag the MSN icon into that folder, and then drag the folder into the Recycle Bin.

Notes and other issues

Although you can use Add/Remove Programs in Control Panel to remove the MSN component from your system, doing so before deleting the icon as described in Solution 1 will cause the **Delete** option in the MSN icon's context menu to disappear. If you don't have MSN installed in the first place, the **Delete** option should be available.

Network administrators wishing to automate this process might be interested in Microsoft's INF Generator. See "Software and the Internet" in the Preface for more information.

This icon can be also removed and restored with TweakUI, one of Microsoft's PowerToys. See "Software and the Internet" in the Preface for more information.

See "Hiding All Icons on the Desktop" later in this chapter for another solution.

Getting Rid of the My Computer Icon ● ■

The My Computer icon provides access to all of your drives, Control Panel, your printers, and Dial-Up Networking. Since these resources are also accessible through Explorer and the **Start Menu**, the My Computer icon isn't strictly required. While there isn't a perfect solution for getting rid of this icon without clearing all the icons from the Desktop, the following suggestion should satisfy most users.

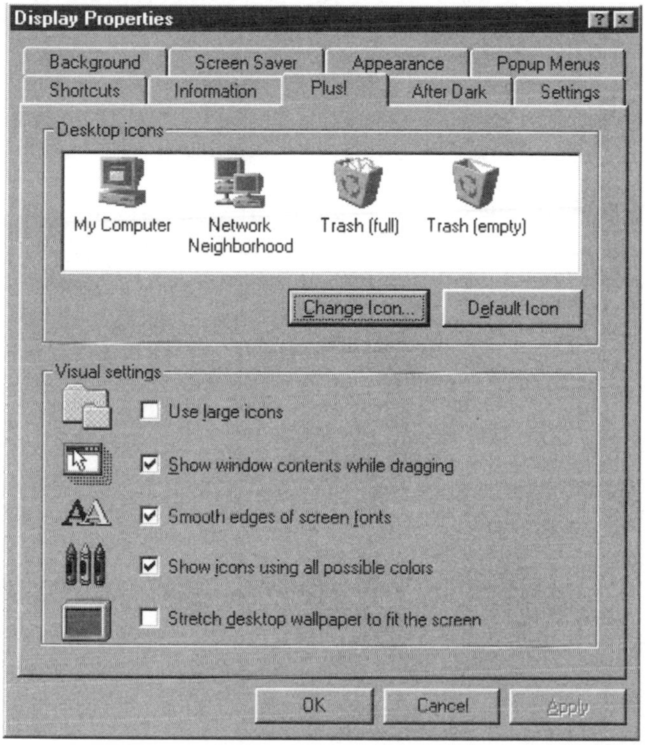

Figure 4-1: Use Display Properties to change the icon of My Computer

- If you're using Windows NT 4.0 or Windows 95 with the Microsoft Plus! Pack (a commercially available add-on from Microsoft), right-click on an empty portion of your Desktop, and click **Properties**. Click on the Plus! tab, select the My Computer icon in the Desktop Icons box, and click **Change Icon**.

- If you're using Windows 95 without the Microsoft Plus! Pack, refer to the topic later in this chapter entitled "Changing the Icons of System Objects" for information on changing the icon for My Computer.

- Choose a blank, clear icon to replace the one that's there. Don't look for one included with Windows; you'll probably have to create it using your favorite icon editor or MS Paint.

- If you're using **Plus!** press **OK** at this point. Then rename the icon to a single space (right-click on it and select **Rename**).

- This process doesn't actually remove the icon from the Desktop, although it does render it invisible while still allowing access if you know where to look.

Notes and other issues

See "Hiding All Icons on the Desktop" later in this chapter for another solution.

Getting Rid of the Recycle Bin ● ■

You can remove the Recycle Bin from your Desktop without losing the ability to delete files. You can still right-click on a file and select **Delete**, as well as using the Del key on your keyboard. Furthermore, there is still a Recycle Bin folder on every drive in Explorer that will delete files in the same way. To remove the Recycle Bin from the Desktop, you need to add a **Delete** option to the Recycle Bin's context menu. Here's how to do it:

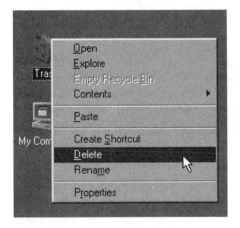

Figure 4-2: Add the Delete option to the Recycle Bin's context menu

- Open the Registry Editor (*regedit.exe*). (If you're not familiar with the Registry Editor, see Chapter 3.)

- Expand the branches to HKEY_CLASSES_ROOT\CLSID\{645FF040-5081-101B-9F08-00AA002F954E}\ShellFolder\.

- Double-click on the Attributes value, and replace the contents with 70 01 00 20.

- Close the Registry Editor. The change should take effect immediately.

- Right-click on the Recycle Bin, and select **Delete**.

Notes and other issues

This will also add the **Rename** option to the Recycle Bin's context menu. See "Renaming the Recycle Bin" later in this chapter for more information. See "Hiding All Icons on the Desktop," in the next section for another solution. This setting can also be changed with TweakUI, one of Microsoft's PowerToys. See "Software and the Internet" in the Preface for more information.

Hiding All Icons on the Desktop ● ■

The following solution will disable all icons on the Desktop, including any files in your Desktop folder as well as the virtual icons already discussed. (See Figure 4-3.)

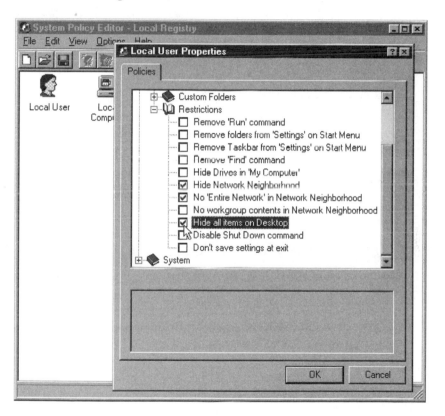

Figure 4-3: Use the Policy Editor to hide all Desktop icons

- Open the System Policy Editor (*poledit.exe*) on your Windows 95 CD-ROM (it's in the Admin\Apptools\Poledit folder). If you have the floppy disk version of Windows 95, see "Software and the Internet" in the Preface.

- If you are asked "Open a Template File," choose *admin.adm* in the same folder, and click **OK**.

- Select **Open Registry** from the **File** menu.

- Double-click on the Local User icon.

- Expand the branches to LOCAL_USER\SHELL\RESTRICTIONS by clicking on the small plus signs to the left of the yellow folder icons.

- Turn on the **Hide all items on the Desktop** option.

- Click **OK** and select **Save** from the **File** menu.

- Click on an empty area of the Desktop, and press the F5 key for this change to take effect.

Notes and other issues

This setting can also be controlled with the Desktop Control Center and HideIt utilities. See "Software and the Internet" in the Preface for more information. If you're using HideIt, configure it to hide Program Manager. This will hide all Desktop icons yet keep the taskbar intact.

If you're trying to remove a stubborn icon from the Desktop, other than the ones mentioned here, try opening the Registry Editor (see Chapter 3 for more information on the Registry) and deleting keys from HKEY_LOCAL_ MACHINE\SOFTWARE\Microsoft\Windows\CurrentVersion\explorer\ Desktop\NameSpace.

Refer to the previous topics in this chapter for information on removing individual icons from the Desktop.

Changing the Icons of System Objects ● ■

Although direct support isn't built into Windows for changing the icons used for the various system objects, such as the Control Panel and My Computer, it can be done. The icons discussed here are referred to as *shell icons* and are standard windows icons used for virtual objects, that is, objects other than drives, folders, files, and shortcuts. See the notes that follow for changing other icons.

Solution 1: Shell icons

- Open the Registry Editor (*regedit.exe*). (If you're not familiar with the Registry Editor, see Chapter 3.)

- Expand the branches to HKEY_LOCAL_MACHINE\Software\ Microsoft\Windows\CurrentVersion\explorer\ShellIcons\. To the right, you'll see a listing of numbered values. Each number represents a specific shell object, and the content of each value specifies the icon used with that object.

- Icons are specified by filename and icon index, as follows:

```
d:\path\filename, ###
```

where d:\path\filename is the full path and filename of an .EXE, .DLL, .ICO, or .BMP file containing one or more icons, and ### represent the number of the icon (you won't actually see pound signs). To use the first icon in the file, specify 0; the second icon, 1; and so on. To find out which number corresponds with which object, refer to Figure 4-4:

0 - default generic icon
1 - default document
2 - default executable
3 - closed folder
4 - open folder
5 - 5¼ floppy drive
6 - 3½ floppy drive

7 - removable drive
8 - hard drive
9 - network drive
10 - unusable network drive
11 - cd-rom drive
12 - ram drive
13 - entire network

14 - network connection
15 - network computer
16 - printer
17 - network neighborhood
18 - network workgroup
19 - start menu; programs
20 - start menu; documents

21 - start menu; settings
22 - start menu; find
23 - start menu; help
24 - start menu; run
25 - start menu; suspend
26 - docking station
27 - start menu; shut down

28 - shared resource
29 - shortcut arrow
30 - large arrow
31 - empty recycle bin
32 - full recycle bin
33 - dial-up networking
34 - desktop

35 - control panel
37 - printers folder
36 - program group
38 - fonts folder
39 - windows logo
40 - audio cd

Figure 4-4: Shell icons

While all of these icons appear to be specified in this section of the Registry, changes to some of these will not take effect. Those icons set elsewhere are discussed in the next solution.

Solution 2: Individual system objects

- Open the Registry Editor (*regedit.exe*). (If you're not familiar with the Registry Editor, see Chapter 3.)

- For each of the following, icons are specified in the (default) value of the Registry path shown. The syntax for specifying an icon filename is the same as in Solution 1.

Inbox

HKEY_CLASSES_ROOT\CLSID\{00020D75-0000-0000-C000-
000000000046}\DefaultIcon.

Network Neighborhood

HKEY_CLASSES_ROOT\CLSID\{208D2C60-3AEA-1069-A2D7
08002B30309D}\DefaultIcon.

My Computer

HKEY_CLASSES_ROOT\CLSID\{20D04FE0-3AEA-1069-A2D8-
08002B30309D}\DefaultIcon.

Empty Recycle Bin

HKEY_CLASSES_ROOT\CLSID\{645FF040-5081-101B-9F08-
00AA002F954E}\DefaultIcon.

Dial-Up Networking

HKEY_CLASSES_ROOT\CLSID\{992CFFA0-F557-101A-88EC-
00DD010CCC48}\DefaultIcon.

Printers

HKEY_CLASSES_ROOT\CLSID\{2227A280-3AEA-1069-A2DE-
08002B30309D}\DefaultIcon.

Desktop

HKEY_CLASSES_ROOT\CLSID\{00021400-0000-0000-C000-
000000000046}\DefaultIcon.

Briefcase

HKEY_CLASSES_ROOT\CLSID\{85BBD920-42A0-1069-A2E4-
08002B30309D}\DefaultIcon.

Fonts

HKEY_CLASSES_ROOT\CLSID\{BD84B380-8CA2-1069-AB1D-
08000948F534}\DefaultIcon.

Notes and other issues

Most icons and executables have only one file. Zero should be used in this case. For files containing more than one icon, you can find out the number of the icon you want by creating a "dummy" shortcut on your Desktop. Right-click on it, select **Properties**, choose the **Shortcut** tab, click **Change Icon**, specify the desired filename, and count from the left.

Most of the icons discussed here can be changed with the Microangelo Engineer utility. See "Software and the Internet" in the Preface.

Although you can change the single icon used for all folders, you can't change folder icons individually. To specify an icon for a specific folder on your hard disk, you can create a shortcut to that folder and then change the icon of the shortcut.

To change the icons for drives in My Computer, see "Customizing Drive Icons" in Chapter 2, *Customizing Your System*.

You can't change the icons for applications, but you can change the icons for shortcuts to those applications, such as those used in the **Start Menu** and on the Desktop. Just right-click on the desired shortcut, click **Properties**, choose the **Shortcut** tab, and click **Change Icon**. You can also change the default icon used for application documents (including icons 0 and 1 from Solution 1), such as the icon used for all text files with the .TXT extension. See "Customizing Context Menus" later in this chapter for more information.

Using True-Color Icons ● ■

Both Windows 95 and Windows NT 4.0 support true-color icons (16-bit per 65,000 colors or higher) for users with displays that support them. However, there are two obstacles to using them on your system. First, you need to turn on Windows 95's support for true-color icons. (Why it isn't already enabled is a mystery. Windows NT 4.0 has this enabled by default.) Second, you need to be able to create these icons (most icon editors support only 16 colors). Everything you need is here, except artistic talent; you'll need to supply that on your own. Here's what you need to do:

Step 1: Enable true-color icons (Windows 95 only)

- Set your display color depth to 16 bit or higher. Double-click on the Display icon in Control Panel, and click on the **Settings** tab. Adjust the Color Palette to your liking, as long as it's high color (16-bit) or better. Refer to the following notes section for display concerns.

- Next, open the Registry Editor (*regedit.exe*). (If you're not familiar with the Registry Editor, see Chapter 3.)

- Expand the branches to `HKEY_CURRENT_USER\Control Panel\ Desktop\WindowMetrics`, double-click on the `Shell Icon BPP` value (on the right side), and change the value to either 16 or 24 (for 16 or 24 bits, depending on your current settings; see the following Notes section for the meaning of different bit values).

- Close the Registry Editor when finished.

Step 2: Create true-color icons

- Using a bitmap editor, such as MS Paint (which comes with Windows), create a Windows Bitmap (.BMP), 32 pixels × 32 pixels, in 256 colors or 24-bit, and save it to a folder on your hard disk.

- To use the icon with a shortcut, right-click on the shortcut, and select **Properties**. Choose the **Shortcut** tab, click **Change Icon**, and specify your new bitmap file.

Notes and other issues

Your video card or monitor may not support the higher color depths necessary to use true-color icons. Additionally, increasing the color depth may slow performance and decrease the maximum resolution available. For example, if the current settings were 1024 × 768 in 256 colors, raising the color depth may decrease the resolution to only 800 × 600 if you don't have enough memory on your video card. You need at least high color (16-bit) to use true-color icons.

The number of colors used in an image or on a video card is often specified in bits. The maximum number of simultaneous colors is equal to $2x$, where x is the number of bits. So 4 bit is 16 colors, 8 bit is 256 colors, 16 bit is roughly 65,000 colors, and 24 bit is roughly 16 million colors. Higher color depths result in better image quality but also can decrease performance and maximum resolution. If you use a program like Adobe Photoshop, RGB mode is synonymous with 24-bit color, and Indexed color means 8-bit mode.

Step 1 can also be accomplished with Microangelo. See "Software and the Internet" in the Preface. Using Microangelo Engineer, turn on the **Show icons using all possible colors** option.

Step 1 can also be accomplished with the Microsoft Plus! Pack (sold separately) or if you have Windows NT 4.0. Right-click on an empty portion of your Desktop, select **Properties**, and choose the **Plus!** tab. In the Visual Settings section, turn on the **Show icons using all possible colors** option.

See "Changing the Icons of System Objects" earlier in this chapter to replace Desktop icons such as My Computer and the Recycle Bin.

Resolving Annoyances

I suppose every solution in this book can be thought of as a resolution of some annoyance. A common complaint is that it's annoying when your word processor crashes. True. It's also annoying that the computer you bought six months ago is now half the price and twice the speed. While there's nothing we can do about those annoyances, there are a few nasty ones built into Windows that we can deal with. The worst include over-written file types, splash screens, CD-ROM autorun, and the **Documents** menu. All of these topics are covered in the next few pages.

Turning Off the Documents Menu ● ■

The **Documents** menu is a clever idea. It displays a list of the last dozen-or-so programs and files opened from the Explorer. You can easily clear the menu temporarily (albeit using a long series of mouse clicks); the only problem is that there's no way to disable it permanently. This is not only a hole in security but a major irritation, and the lack of a simple method to turn this feature off is mysterious at best. Microsoft calls this a "feature" and claims that there is no way to disable it. We have neverthe-less come up with a few ways around it.

Solution 1: Clear the Documents menu temporarily

- Right-click on an empty portion of the taskbar and select **Properties** from the menu that appears, or select **Settings** and then **Taskbar** from the **Start Menu**.

- Choose the **Start Menu Programs** tab, and then click **Clear** to clean out the menu. This is only temporary and doesn't prevent new items from being added to this menu the next time you launch a file.

Solution 2: Clear the Documents menu quickly on demand

- Open a text editor such as Notepad, and type the contents of Example 4-1.

- Save this in a file called *clear.bat*, and place the file in any folder you wish.

- You can then place a shortcut to this batch file in your **Start Menu** or on the Desktop. Just double-click on it to clear the **Documents** menu at any time.

- To clear the **Documents** menu every time you start Windows, place a shortcut to *clear.bat* in your Startup folder.

Example 4-1. Use Clear.bat to clear the Documents menu quickly on demand

```
@ECHO OFF
IF EXIST C:\WINDOWS\RECENT\*.* GOTO CLEAR
GOTO ENDING
:CLEAR
DELTREE /Y C:\WINDOWS\RECENT\*.*
GOTO ENDING
:ENDING
```

Solution 3: Disable the Documents menu permanently
(may require changing Recycle Bin settings)

- Right-click on the Recycle Bin icon on the Desktop, and select **Properties**.

- Under the **Global** tab, select **Use one setting for all drives**.

- Turn on the **Do not move files to the Recycle Bin** option. This will ensure that any deleted files are erased from the disk instead of stored in the Recycle Bin—necessary for this solution to work.

- Next, open the Registry Editor (*regedit.exe*). (If you're not familiar with the Registry Editor, see Chapter 3.)

- Expand the branches to HKEY_CURRENT_USER\SOFTWARE\ Microsoft\Windows\CurrentVersion\explorer\Shell Folders.

- At the right side of the window, there should be a list containing one or more of the "special" system folders. If an entry named Recent doesn't already exist here, select **New** from the **Edit** menu, and then select **String Value**. Type in Recent for the name of the new item.

- Next, double-click on the new Recent entry in the Value Data field, and type c:\recycled. Press **OK** when finished.

- **Important**: In the key named User Shell Folders, just below the Shell Folders key we were just in, add the Recent entry here as well, duplicating the steps above.

- Close the Registry Editor when finished. You'll probably have to restart Windows for this change to take effect. At that time, you can safely delete the Recent folder from your hard disk, because Windows will now be using the Recycle Bin to store shortcuts to your recent files. Since the Recycle Bin is set to delete files instead of storing them, the **Documents** menu will always be empty. (See Figure 4-5.)

Notes and other issues

In order for Solution 3 to work, you must set the Recycle Bin so it deletes files instantly (as described earlier), or you'll have a bunch of deleted files in your **Documents** menu. If you still can't get this to work, you probably didn't add the new entries to both the Shell Folders and User Shell Folders keys.

If you use the *clear.bat* solution, you can configure the DOS window to close automatically by right-clicking on the *clear.bat*, selecting **Properties**, choosing the **Program** tab, and turning on the **Close on exit** option.

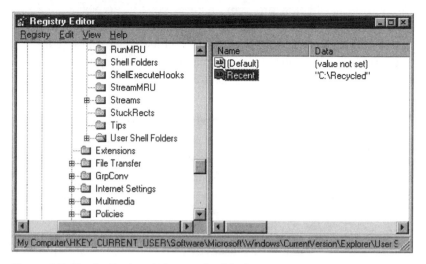

Figure 4-5: Use the Registry Editor to disable the Documents menu permanently

You can use the *clear.bat* solution in conjunction with the System Agent that comes with the Microsoft Plus! Pack (sold separately) to clear the menu, say, every five minutes.

The **Documents** menu can be automatically cleared every time you start Windows using TweakUI, one of Microsoft's PowerToys. See "Software and the Internet" in the Preface for more information. Just click on the aptly named **Paranoia** tab, and turn on the **Clear document history at logon** option.

See "Customizing Start Menu Components" later in this chapter for a solution that will allow you to remove the **Documents** menu from the **Start Menu** entirely (advanced users only).

If you're using multiple users in either Windows 95 or Windows NT, make sure to apply the solution you choose to each of the profiles.

Preventing Programs from Changing Your File Types ● ■

This annoying and troublesome problem has been around since the days of Windows 3.x. Some developers have set up their applications to change your Windows file types without asking, so that double-clicking on an associated file launches their program. The problem is that any file types that you had set up previously are ignored and overwritten. Say you had configured Windows to launch a certain graphics viewer every time you double-clicked on a .BMP file, or you want to use your favorite text editor with your .TXT files. Then you decide to install a new

program, and its installation program changes your file types so that the
new program is launched every time you double-click on that same .BMP
file. Or, worse yet, your file types may be changed every time some of
the more arrogant applications are opened. For some applications that
use proprietary file types (like .XLS for Microsoft Excel files), this isn't a
problem, but many applications use many common file types, and their
programmers should be more thoughtful of their users.

Your file types are stored in a portion of your Registry (see Chapter 3 for
more information). While there's no direct way to protect a portion of the
Registry, there are a few ways to help keep the file types that enable you
to get your work done.

Solution 1: Edit win.ini

- *Win.ini* is a configuration file used by earlier versions of Windows,
  before there was a Registry. In Windows 95 and Windows NT 4.0, it
  is kept for compatibility with older applications.

- Using a standard text editor, such as Notepad, open *win.ini* (it's in
  your Windows folder), and scroll down until you see [Exten-
  sions].

- These are what file types used to look like, and although they're no
  longer used directly by Windows, they are read into the Registry
  every time Windows is started. The syntax is as follows:

  ```
  TXT=C:\Windows\Notepad.exe  ^.TXT
  ```

  where .TXT can be replaced with whatever extension you wish to
  use, and C:\Windows\Notepad.exe can be replaced with the application that you wish to associate with that extension.

- If you're finding that some old application keeps reclaiming a file
  type even though you never use it, it may be listed here. Feel free to
  remove any unwanted entries from this section.

- Make any desired changes, and save the file when you're done. This
  isn't the easiest way to change file types, but it may accomplish what
  you need.

Solution 2: Save portions of your Registry

- Open the Registry Editor (*regedit.exe*). (If you're not familiar with the
  Registry Editor or Registry patches, see Chapter 3.)

- Expand the branches to HKEY_CLASSES_ROOT\. All of your file types
  are listed here, starting with the registered extensions (e.g., .TXT).

- Select any desired branches of this portion of the Registry, and use the Export feature to save them into Registry patches. Don't try to export the entire Registry; it will be too large.

- Once you've exported the desired branches, you can merge the Registry patches together into a single file with a plain text editor, such as Notepad.

- Double-click on one or more Registry patches to merge them back into the Registry. A benefit of this solution (as opposed to backing up and restoring the entire Registry) is that only those file types you've stored into Registry patches will be saved. Although these will overwrite any other settings in the same branches, they won't overwrite new branches.

Solution 3: Use File Manager

- If you can bear it, try using the old Windows 3.x File Manager (*WIN-FILE.EXE*) to associate your file types. Just select **Associations** from the **File** menu, and do it the old-fashioned way.

  This works because File Manager associates file types with *win.ini*, and not the Registry. Windows 95 updates the Registry when you boot up with any information it finds in *win.ini*. The downside is that not all of the new features of Windows 95's File Types are supported, so this isn't a perfect solution. It works in much the same way as Solution 1.

Example: Stop Netscape from changing file types

This is an example that builds on Solution 2. When you install Netscape Navigator 32-bit, versions 2.0 and later, it changes your file types so that double-clicking on any HTML file starts Netscape by default. If that isn't enough, if you change your file types to use another browser, text editor, or otherwise, Netscape may reassign itself to your .HTML file types *every time* it is restarted. Following these directions will stop this from happening.

- Open a plain text editor, such as Notepad, and type the following:

```
REGEDIT4
[HKEY_CLASSES_ROOT\HypertextMarkup]
@="Hypertext Markup File"
[HKEY_CLASSES_ROOT\HypertextMarkup\shell\Open\command]
@="c:\\netscape\\program\\netscape.exe %1"
[HKEY_CLASSES_ROOT\HypertextMarkup\shell\Edit\command]
@="c:\\windows\\notepad.exe %1"
[HKEY_CLASSES_ROOT\HypertextMarkup\DefaultIcon]
@="c:\\netscape\\program\\netscape.exe ,0"
```

```
[HKEY_CLASSES_ROOT\.htm]
@="HypertextMarkup"
[HKEY_CLASSES_ROOT\.html]
@="HypertextMarkup"
```

Make sure you replace c:\windows with your Windows folder (if different), and c:\netscape with your Netscape Navigator folder (if different). You can also replace *netscape.exe* with a different program, if you wish.

- After typing the above, save it into a file called *ns-fix.reg*. Find the file in Explorer, and double-click on it. It will create a new file type called Hypertext Markup File, which won't be changed by either Netscape or Microsoft Internet Explorer.

Notes and other issues

A shortcut for choosing a new program to be used with any given file type is to hold the Shift key while right-clicking on a file and then select **Open With**.

Windows 95 won't allow certain file types to be changed or removed. However, there's a way around this, and you don't have to mess around with the Registry. Simply start up the old File Manager, as described in Solution 3.

Getting Rid of Irritating Splash Screens ●.■

Applications these days are getting larger, fatter, and slower. One trick that's used is to display a *splash screen*, a large banner with the application's title, while the program loads. This supposedly helps to hide the fact that a program takes so long to load, but it often makes the program load more slowly. Even worse, some applications now display their splash screens when Windows starts. This is of absolutely no use to the user. What follows are some tips for disabling these screens, as well as a list of a few common applications' splash screens, and how to disable them:

A general solution

- First, don't underestimate the documentation. Search the help file for the words "splash screen," "startup logo," or whatever else comes to mind. Also, look for a readme file in the application directory and on the distribution disks for any other hints.

- Many applications have a settings window, and some let you turn off the splash screen.

- Look in the Registry. Do a search for the application name, and look for any suspicious keys or values. Be careful not to change any existing settings, however.

- Lastly, some applications (see "Norton Navigator 95 and Norton Utilities 95") come with Registry patches for disabling the splash screens. Look in the application directory and on the distribution disks for any suspicious .REG files.

Norton Navigator 95 and Norton Utilities 95

- Look in your various Norton directories and on the distribution disks (depending on the release of the software you've got) for *nns-plash.reg* and *nusplash.reg*. Double-click on them to remove the splash screens for Norton Navigator and Norton Utilities, respectively.

Norton AntiVirus 95

- If your version of Norton AntiVirus is dated before December 1, 1995, you'll need to obtain a patch from the Symantec home page at *http:// www.symantec.com/* to bring the software up to date.

- Once you have the more recent version, look for the Registry patch file *logo_off.reg* in the AntiVirus directory, which can be used to remove the splash screen by double-clicking on it.

Eudora (Pro and Light versions)

- Make sure Eudora isn't running, and open *eudora.ini* (in the Eudora directory) with a text editor, such as Notepad.

- In the [Settings] section, add the line NoSplashScreen=1. Save the file when finished, and start up Eudora. To Qualcomm's credit, this is mentioned in the included documentation.

McAfee VShield 95

- Make sure VShield isn't running, and open *default.vsh* (or whichever .vsh file you're using) with a text editor, such as Notepad.

- In the [General] section, change the line bNoSplash=0 so it reads bNoSplash=1. Save the file when finished.

WordPerfect, version 6.0 and later

- Right-click on the shortcut to WordPerfect, and select **Properties**.

- Choose the **Shortcut** tab, and add a space and then a colon after the text in the **Target** field. Click **OK** when you're finished.

WS_FTP

- Right-click on the shortcut to WS_FTP, and select **Properties**.

- Choose the **Shortcut** tab, add a space, and then type -quiet after the text in the **Target** field. Click **OK** when you're finished.

Clearing Unwanted Entries from Add/Remove Programs ● ■

In Add/Remove Programs in Control Panel, a list of installed applications is displayed for the purpose of easy removal. Only programs that are correctly designed for Windows 95 and Windows NT 4.0 will show up here, but there is no obvious method for removing these entries without uninstalling the programs. To remove an unwanted entry—for example, to prevent accidental removal—do the following:

- Open the Registry Editor (*regedit.exe*). (If you're not familiar with the Registry Editor, see Chapter 3.)

- Expand the branches to HKEY_LOCAL_MACHINE\SOFTWARE\Microsoft\ Windows\CurrentVersion\Uninstall, and remove any unwanted keys under this branch.

Notes and other issues

Uninstalling the actual program should also do it. If you removed it manually and have found that the entry is still here, use Solution 1. If you wanted to remove the application, you may want to reinstall it and then uninstall again to make sure all the components are properly removed.

This setting can also be changed with TweakUI, one of Microsoft's Power-Toys. See "Software and the Internet" in the Preface for more information.

Turning Off the CD-ROM Autorun ● ■

When a Windows 95–aware CD-ROM is inserted into a CD-ROM drive, Windows 95 automatically launches the program contained on the disk, whether you want it to or not. Similarly, the audio CD player pops up whenever you insert an audio CD and starts playing it immediately. This is cute the first or second time, but soon gets infuriating. What's worse, if you double-click on the CD icon in the My Computer window, the autorun program fires up instead of a folder window, as you would expect with any other drive icon. This is especially irritating on slower computers, where you have to wait for what seems like an eternity for it to load some useless welcome screen. The lack of a simple provision for turning this "feature" off is not exactly impressive. Follow these instructions to disable autorun:

Solution 1: Disable autorun (Windows 95 only)

- Right-click on the My Computer icon, and select **Properties** (this window is also available by double-clicking on the System icon in Control Panel).

- Choose the **Device Manager** tab.

- Expand the CD-ROM branch, and select the entry for your CD-ROM drive.

- Click **Properties**, and then choose the **Settings** tab.

- Turn off the **Auto insert notification** option.

- Click **OK**, and then **OK** again. You'll have to restart Windows for this change to take effect. From now on, your system won't know when you've inserted a CD and won't run it right away.

Solution 2: Bypass autorun one time

- If you hold down the Shift key when inserting a CD, autorun is ignored, although it's somewhat less than graceful trying to insert a CD while holding down keys on the keyboard.

Solution 3: Disable autorun (Windows 95 only)

- Open the Registry Editor (*regedit.exe*). (If you're not familiar with the Registry Editor, see Chapter 3.)

- Expand the branches to HKEY_CURRENT_USER\Software\Microsoft\ Windows\CurrentVersion\Policies\Explorer.

- Change the value of the NoDriveTypeAutoRun value from 95 00 00 00 to BD 00 00 00.

- You'll have to restart Windows for this change to take effect.

Solution 4: Make it easy to explore audio CDs

- Double-click on the My Computer icon, and select **Options** from the **View** menu.

- Select **AudioCD** from the list, and click **Properties**.

- Click **New...**, type Open in the **Action** field, and explorer.exe in the **Application used to perform action** field, and click **OK**.

- Next, select the new **Open** entry in the **Action** list, and click **Set Default** so the word **Open** now appears bold.

- Click **OK** when you're finished. The change should take effect immediately. When you double-click on the CD-ROM icon when an audio
  CD is inserted, it will open an Explorer window showing an icon for
  each track on the disk instead of playing it right away. You can also
  use this method to change the default CD player used for audio CDs.

Solution 5: Turn it off

- Obtain and install TweakUI, one of Microsoft's PowerToys. See "Software and the Internet" in the Preface for information. Autorun can be
  disabled by turning off the **Play audio CDs automatically** and **Play data
  CDs automatically** options under the aptly named **Paranoia** tab. Also,
  make sure that the **Auto Insert Notification** option discussed in Solution 1 is turned on.

Notes and other issues

Although none of these solutions will allow you to explore the contents
of an autorun-enabled CD-ROM by double-clicking on it in My Computer
(as you can with any other type of drive), you can still right-click on the
icon and select **Open**. Additionally, you can open Explorer to navigate
the CD-ROM.

To configure your CD player to appear automatically without playing an
audio CD automatically, edit the Play action in the AudioCD file type (see
Solution 4), and remove /Play from the command line.

Once you've followed the instructions in Solution 1, Windows will no
longer be notified when you insert a new CD. Not only will it not play a
CD when inserted, but it also won't display the CD's icon (if it has one)
or title in the My Computer window. To make sure the correct icon and
title for the current CD are displayed in My Computer and Explorer, press
F5 to refresh the window and force Windows to reread the disc.

If you're using a CD writer, disable auto-insert notification altogether;
simply turning off autorun (Solution 5) won't suffice. The "polling" of the
CD-ROM drive to determine if a new disk has been inserted will interrupt
the CD recording process.

Using the autorun functionality, you can create custom icons for use with
the other drives in your system. See "Customizing Drive Icons" in Chapter
2 for more information.

Stopping Menus from Following the Mouse ● ■

One of the new "improvements" to Windows 95 is how the menus seem to be magnetically attracted to the mouse pointer. Instead of reacting to a single click like almost every other operating system in the world, Windows menus will disappear if you accidentally let the mouse stray and hit another menu. This is especially irritating to users with sensitive pointing devices, such as notebook pointing devices, pens, and other digitizers. Here's how to disable this behavior:

Solution 1

- Obtain and install the Old Mouse Mode utility. See "Software and the Internet" in the Preface for more information.

- This utility will force the menus in Windows 95 and Windows NT 4.0 to behave exactly like Windows 3.x menus.

Solution 2

- Open the Registry Editor (*regedit.exe*). (If you're not familiar with the Registry Editor, see Chapter 3.)

- Expand the branches to HKEY_CURRENT_USER\Control Panel\ Desktop.

- Click on the string value in the right pane named MenuShowDelay (add it if it's not there by selecting **New** and then **String Value** from the **Edit** menu).

- Specify 65534 for its value, and close the Registry Editor when finished.

You'll probably have to restart Windows for this change to take effect. This will increase the delay that the menu is opened to its maximum setting, virtually disabling it. It will prevent submenus from opening automatically, but the main menus still follow the mouse like a starving alley cat.

This setting can also be changed with TweakUI, one of Microsoft's PowerToys.

Getting Rid of the Unwanted Explorer Windows at Startup ● ■

You may have noticed that any Explorer and folder windows left open when you exit Windows are reopened the next time you start. On some machines, these windows are opened regardless of whether they were left open. There are a few things that could be causing this:

- Make sure you close all Explorer and folder windows before shutting down.

- You might not be shutting down completely; make sure you see the screen that says, "It is now safe to turn off your computer before turning off the power."

- You may have Explorer specified in your StartUp folder, or in the RUN= or LOAD= lines of *win.ini*.

To stop Windows 95 from saving
Window locations when you exit

- Open the System Policy Editor (*poledit.exe*) on your Windows 95 CD-ROM (it's in the Admin\Apptools\Poledit folder). If you have the floppy disk version of Windows 95, see "Software and the Internet" in the Preface.

- If you are asked to "Open a Template File," choose *admin.adm* in the same folder, and click **OK**.

- Select **Open Registry** from the **File** menu.

- Double-click on the Local User icon.

- Expand the branches to `Local_User\Shell\Restrictions` by clicking on the small plus signs to the left of the yellow folder icons.

- Turn on the **Don't save settings at exit** option.

- Click **OK**, select **Save** from the **File** menu, and close the System Policy Editor.

- Click on an empty area of the Desktop, and press F5 to refresh the Desktop so that this change will take effect.

Notes and other issues

If you turn off this setting, Windows 95 will not remember any of your window positions or settings (icon sizes, sort order). See "Forcing Windows to Remember Explorer Settings" in Chapter 2.

This setting can also be changed with TweakUI, one of Microsoft's PowerToys.

You also might want to check out any other programs configured to start when Windows is started.

Advanced Configuration

Chapter 2 covered some basic configuration and tweaking of the Windows interface and Explorer. This section expands on this with some extreme cases of customization, such as changing the previously unchangeable **Start Menu** components, getting rid of the silly yellow "Click Here to Begin" arrow, and cleaning up all of those nonremovable folders that Microsoft applications create. These topics rely heavily on the Registry Editor. Make sure you read through Chapter 3 to familiarize yourself with the concepts of the Registry.

Customizing My Computer ● ■

Double-clicking on the My Computer icon allows you to do file management with separate drives, folders, and file icons rather than with the condensed tree view found in Explorer. It also provides access to Control Panel, the system printers, and Dial-Up Networking. Since all of these resources are also available in Explorer and the **Start Menu**, you may prefer to connect another program to the My Computer icon. For example, if you prefer Explorer's hierarchical tree view to My Computer's Macintosh-style navigation, you can configure My Computer to launch Explorer (see Figure 4-6):

- Open the Registry Editor (*regedit.exe*). (If you're not familiar with the Registry Editor, see Chapter 3.)

- Expand the branches to HKEY_CLASSES_ROOT\CLSID\.

- Select **Find** from the **Edit** menu, and search for "My Computer." If you can't find it, open the key named {20D04FE0-3AEA-1069-A2D8-08002B30309D}.

- Right-click on the Shell key, select **New** and then **Key**. Type Open and press Enter.

- Right-click on the new Open key, select **New** again and then **Key**. Type Command and press Enter.

- Click once on the new Command key, double-click on (default), type explorer.exe in the box, and press Enter.

- Close the Registry Editor when you're finished.

- Click on an empty area of the Desktop, and press F5 to refresh the Desktop so that this change will take effect.

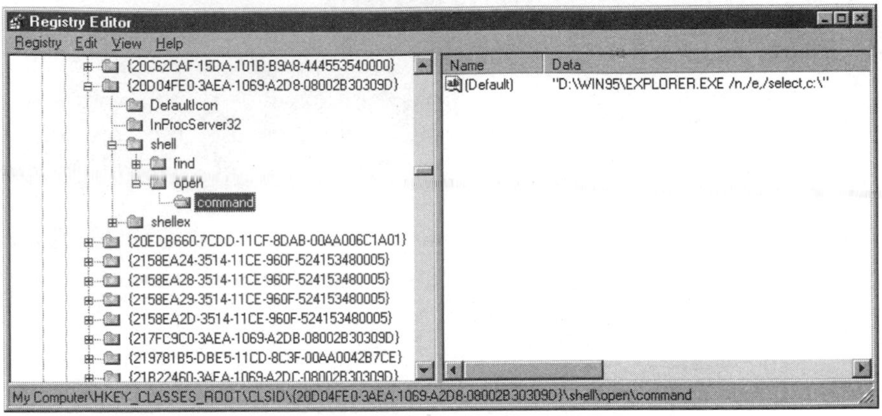

Figure 4-6: Use the Registry Editor to customize the My Computer icon

Notes and other issues

If you can't find the key specified above and have renamed My Computer to something else, try searching for the new name.

To configure My Computer to launch another application, simply replace *explorer.exe* in the instructions above with the full path and filename of the program you wish to use.

To make the contents of My Computer more accessible (for example, while an application is covering the Desktop), you can create a folder inside your **Start Menu**, and drag shortcuts for all of the desired items into the new folder.

To customize the icons of the drives in the My Computer window, see "Customizing Drive Icons" in Chapter 2.

To turn on or off the display certain drive icons in the My Computer window, use the My Computer tab in TweakUI, one of Microsoft's Power-Toys. See "Software and the Internet" in the Preface for more information.

Renaming the Recycle Bin ● ■

Although you can rename any file on your hard disk, as well as almost any virtual icon on your Desktop, Windows won't allow you to rename the Recycle Bin by default. To rename the Recycle Bin to something more compelling, such as "Garbage," "Trash," or "My Aching Stomach," follow either of the following procedures:

Solution 1: Add the Rename option to the Recycle Bin's context menu

* Open the Registry Editor (*regedit.exe*). (If you're not familiar with the Registry Editor, see Chapter 3.)

- Expand the branches to HKEY_CLASSES_ROOT\CLSID\{645FF04 0-5081-101B-9F08-00AA002F954E}\ShellFolder\.

- Double-click on the Attributes value, and replace the contents with 50 01 00 20.

- Close the Registry Editor. The change should take effect immediately.

- Right-click on the Recycle Bin, select **Rename**, and type in any new name you wish.

Solution 2: *Manually rename the Recycle Bin*

- Open the Registry Editor (*regedit.exe*). (If you're not familiar with the Registry Editor, see Chapter 3.)

- Expand the branches to HKEY_CLASSES_ROOT\CLSID\.

- Select **Find** from the **Edit** menu, and search for "Recycle Bin." If you can't find it, open the key named {645FF040-5081-101B-9F08-00AA002F954E}.

- Double-click on (Default), and type in any new name you wish.

- Press **OK** and then close the Registry Editor.

- Click on an empty area of the Desktop, and press F5 to refresh the Desktop so that this change will take effect.

Notes and other issues

A process similar to Solution 1 adds the **Delete** option to the Recycle Bin's context menu. See "Getting Rid of the Recycle Bin" earlier in this chapter for more information.

If you have Norton Utilities for Windows 95, right-click on the Recycle Bin, select **Properties**, and choose the **Desktop Item** tab to rename the Recycle Bin.

Turning Off the Bouncing *"Click Here to Begin" Arrow* ● ■

The little yellow "Click Here to Begin" arrow that bounces off the **Start Menu** when you first start Windows 95 was irritating right off the bat. I suppose it's useful for those folks who can't figure out what "Start" means, but for the rest of us, there's a way to get rid of it. (See Figure 4-7.)

- Open the Registry Editor (*regedit.exe*). (If you're not familiar with the Registry Editor, see Chapter 3.)

- Expand the branches to HKEY_CURRENT_USER\Software\ Microsoft\Windows\CurrentVersion\Policies\Explorer.

- If it's not already there, create a binary value called NoStartBanner. To do this, right-click on the Explorer key, select **New** and then **Binary Value**. Type NoStartBanner for the name.

- Double-click on the NoStartBanner value, enter the value 01 00 00 00, and press **OK**. This type of value is not a text value. You won't be able to erase the numbers. Instead, either highlight a digit with the mouse cursor and type over it, or type and then erase so that there are still four pairs of digits. This may take a little practice.

- Repeat these same steps for HKEY_USERS\.Default\Software\ Microsoft\Windows\CurrentVersion\Policies\Explorer.

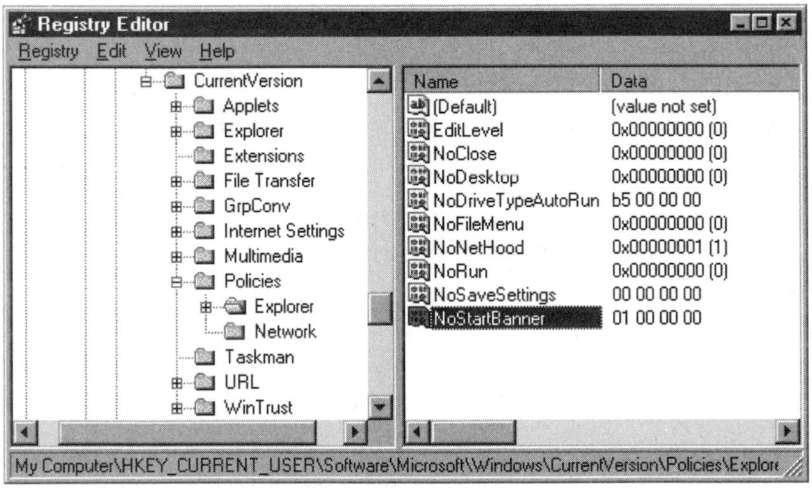

Figure 4-7: Use the Registry Editor to get rid of the "Click Here to Begin" arrow

Notes and other issues

If you don't see the "Click Here to Begin" arrow, it's likely that a **taskbar** button for an open window is blocking it. When Windows starts, this arrow appears on the taskbar to the right of the **Start Menu** button, unless a window is open. Having any window appear when Windows starts is another solution to this problem.

This setting can also be changed with TweakUI, one of Microsoft's Power-Toys. See "Software and the Internet" in the Preface for more information.

Customizing the Start Menu Button ● ■

NOTE   A hex editor and an icon editor are additional requirements for this process.

The button on the taskbar used to open the **Start Menu** consists of a small
Windows logo and the word **Start**. The **Start Menu** button was a tough
nut to crack. There is no built-in method for customizing the text or the
icon that appears here. However, advanced users with the correct tools
will be able to accomplish this in only a few minutes. Anyone not familiar
with a hex editor should not attempt this procedure. If you're smart,
you'll make sure to back up all files before editing them. Here's how to
edit the various aspects of the **Start Menu** button (see Figure 4-8).

Change the word "Start"

● Copy the file *explorer.exe* from your Windows folder to a temporary
working folder. You won't be able to edit the original file, as it will
be in use by Windows.

● Using a hex editor (like UltraEdit-32; see "Software and the Internet'
in the Preface), open the *copy* of *explorer.exe*.

● At the hex address 0002DF0Eh, you will see 53 00 74 00 61 00 72 00
74, which are the letters in the word "Start," separated by null characters (# 00). If these characters aren't at this address, you may have a
different build of Windows 95. Just do a search for the hex code specified above. The address of these characters in Windows NT 4.0 will
also be different.

● You can replace any of the five characters here, *but do not change
the null characters*. Although you can't use a word longer than five
characters, you can have shorter words by including spaces (#20) for
the remaining places. These numbers are in hex and represent characters' positions in the ASCII table. For example, the capital letter S is
ASCII character 83, hex code 53.

● You'll need to search and replace all occurrences of "Start" in the
file; just editing this one won't do it.

● Save the changes, and exit to DOS (or restart in MS-DOS mode if necessary). *Back up the original file*, and then replace it with your modified
version. When you restart Windows, the change should take effect.

Figure 4-8: The Start Menu button after slight alteration

Change the icon

- Copy the file *user.exe* from your Windows\System folder to a temporary working folder.

- Using an icon editor that can read executables (like Microangelo. See "Software and the Internet" in the Preface), open the *copy* of *user.exe*.

- The **Start Menu** uses the flag logo, the first icon in this file. Be aware that there are several versions of this icon in the file, each a different size. Depending on what font size you have your **Start Menu** font configured (using Control Panel, Display Properties, Appearance), Windows may be using the 16 × 16 or the 22 × 22 variations. Your best bet is to edit them all.

- Save the changes, and exit to DOS (or restart in MS-DOS mode if necessary). *Back up the original file*, and then replace it with your modified version. When you restart Windows, the change should take effect.

Notes and other issues

You can permanently disable Windows if you don't know what you're doing. Make sure to back up any files in a safe place before proceeding.

To change or remove any of the standard components of the **Start Menu** itself, see the next section.

Customizing Start Menu Components ●

NOTE   A hex editor is an additional requirement for this process.

We know that the **Start Menu** is just a folder on your hard disk and that you can customize most of the items in the **Programs** menu by simply moving, renaming, creating, or deleting shortcuts in that folder. However, what about the items that can't be changed, such as Help and Find? It's possible, but only for advanced users who are familiar with using a hex editor. If you're smart, you'll make sure to back up all files before editing them. Here's how it's done:

Customize the Start Menu labels

- Copy the file *explorer.exe* from your Windows folder to a temporary working folder. You won't be able to edit the original file because it will be in use by Windows.

- Using a hex editor (like UltraEdit-32; see "Software and the Internet" in the Preface), open the *copy* of *explorer.exe*.

- At the hex address 0002C2A0h, you'll see & P r o g r a m s (the characters are separated by null characters (#00), and not spaces—similar to the solution for "Customize the Start Menu Button" earlier in this chapter). If these characters aren't at this address, you may have a different build of Windows 95. Just do a search for the hex code specified. The address of these characters in Windows NT 4.0 will also be different.

- The other **Start Menu** items (**Documents**, **Settings**, **Find**, **Help**, **Run**, and **Shut Down**) are also stored in this way. Just do a search for the hex code to edit a specific entry.

- You can replace the existing characters with different letters, as long as the interstitial null characters aren't disturbed and the new name isn't any longer than the original counterpart. Include spaces at the end of words to eliminate unused letters.

- If you replace all of the characters with spaces (hex 20), the labels will disappear *entirely* (see the next solution for this concept taken to an extreme).

- Save the changes, and exit to DOS (or restart in MS-DOS mode if necessary). *Back up the original file*, and then replace it with your modified version. When you restart Windows, the change should take effect.

Simplify the Start Menu

(It's ironic that the solution is so complex.)

This solution takes the previous solution to the next step by systematically removing most of the entries. Since this specifies many different specific addresses, it should be used on only the original release version (build 950) of Windows 95.

- Copy the file *explorer.exe* from your Windows folder to a temporary working folder. You won't be able to edit the original file, as it will be in use by Windows.

- Using a hex editor (like UltraEdit-32; see "Software and the Internet" in the Preface), open the *copy* of *explorer.exe*.

- At the hex address 002C2C4, replace 50 00 72 00 6F 00 67 00 72 00 61 00 6D 00 73 with 53 00 74 00 61 00 72 00 74 00 75 00 70 00 20. (This changes the word "Programs" to "Startup," and is optional.)

- At the hex address 002C300, replace 00 00 00 00 00 00 00 00 00 00 00 00 00 00 00 00 with 20 00 20 00 20 00 20 00 20 00 20 00 20 00 20 00.

- At the hex address 002C310, replace all the characters until the address 002C41B with alternating 20 and 00.

- At the hex address 002C420, replace 80 00 00 00 00 00 00 00 with 20 00 20 00 20 00 20 00.

- At the hex address 002C428, replace 00 00 00 00 F7 01 00 00 with 20 00 20 00 F7 01 20 00.

- At the hex address 002C430, replace 00 with 20.

- At the hex address 002C434, replace all the characters until the address 002C447 with alternating 20 and 00.

- At the hex address 002C44A, replace 00 00 00 00 with 20 00 20 00.

- At the hex address 002C450, replace 52 00 75 00 6E 00 2E 00 2E 00 2E 00 00 00 00 00 with 20 00 20 00 20 00 20 00 20 00 20 00 20 00 20 00.

- At the hex address 002C460, replace 00 with 20.

- At the hex address 002C462, replace 00 00 00 00 00 00 with 20 00 20 00 20 00.

- Save the changes, and exit to DOS (or restart in MS-DOS mode if necessary). *Back up the original file*, and then replace it with your modified version. When you restart Windows, the change should take effect.

Notes and other issues

You can permanently disable Windows if you don't know what you're doing. Make sure to back up any files in a safe place before proceeding.

To change the look of the **Start Menu** button itself, see "Customizing the Start Menu Button" earlier in this chapter.

Clearing Unwanted Entries
from Explorer's New Menu ● ■

If you right-click on the Desktop or an open folder (or open Explorer's **File** menu) and choose **New**, you will be presented with a special list of registered file types that can created on the spot. Basically, Explorer will just create a new, empty file (sometimes with a special template) with the appropriate extension in that location. This list is maintained by certain Registry entries, and since most of us will not need to create new Ami Pro documents on the fly, there is a way to remove these unwanted entries.

- Open the Registry Editor (*regedit.exe*). (If you're not familiar with the Registry Editor, see Chapter 3.)

- Select **Find** from the **Edit** menu, type ShellNew, and press **OK**.

- Every ShellNew that is found will be a branch of a particular file type. If you don't want that file type in your **New** menu, delete the entire ShellNew branch.

- Repeat this for every unwanted tile type, and close the Registry Editor when finished. The changes will take effect immediately.

Notes and other issues

You can also use TweakUI (one of Microsoft's PowerToys. See "Software and the Internet" in the Preface for more information) to not only remove unwanted entries from the **New** menu, but create new, custom entries by choosing the **New** tab, and dragging a file of the desired type and dropping it onto TweakUI.

Getting Rid of Shortcut Residue ● ■

Shortcuts have two ways of telling you that they're shortcuts. When a shortcut is first created, its caption begins with the text "Shortcut To." The shortcut's icon also has a small curved arrow in the lower-left corner. Although you can simply rename the icon so that Shortcut To isn't there, there is no quick way to remove the little arrow for just one shortcut. To turn these features off for good on all shortcuts, follow these instructions (see Figure 4-9).

Get rid of the "Shortcut To" text

- According to Microsoft, if you remove the "Shortcut to" text by hand immediately after creating the shortcut at least *eight times*, then it will stop coming back. Unfortunately, this doesn't seem to always work.

- If you have TweakUI (one of Microsoft's PowerToys. See "Software and the Internet" in the Preface for more information), choose the **Explorer** tab, and turn off the **Prefix "Shortcut to" on new shortcuts** option in the Settings section. This should work in most cases, although the text may mysteriously reappear.

Figure 4-9: Cleaning up shortcuts; before and after

Get rid of the curved arrow on icons

- Open the Registry Editor (*regedit.exe*). (If you're not familiar with the Registry Editor, see Chapter 3.)

- Select **Find** from the **Edit** menu, type `IsShortcut`, and press **OK**.

- Remove any and all references to this text; keep searching until it's gone. Use this one with caution (try backing up your Registry first), as you can disable certain Windows functionality if you're not careful.

- Close the Registry Editor when you're finished, click on an empty area of the Desktop, and press F5 to refresh the Desktop so that this change will take effect.

- If you have TweakUI (one of Microsoft's PowerToys. See "Software and the Internet" in the Preface for more information), choose the Explorer tab, and change the **Shortcut overlay** option to your liking. You can choose any icon (which should be partially transparent so the original shows through), or none to remove it altogether.

Notes and other issues

The curved arrow icon can also be changed with the Microangelo Engineer utility. See "Software and the Internet" in the Preface for more information.

Enabling Iconic Preview of Bitmaps ● ■

In Explorer, when you view a folder containing icons (.ICO files), cursors (.CUR files), or animated cursors (.ANI files), their file icons are previews of their contents instead of generic icons. You can configure Windows 95 to show iconic previews of bitmaps (.BMP files) as well using the following procedure:

- Open the Registry Editor (*regedit.exe*). (If you're not familiar with the Registry Editor, see Chapter 3.)

- Expand the branches to `HKEY_CLASSES_ROOT\PAINT.PICTURE\ DefaultIcon`, and change the (default) value to `%1`. Note that if the .BMP file type is no longer associated with MS Paint, the correct Registry location will be somewhere other than in `PAINT.PICTURE`. Try `HKEY_CLASSES_ROOT\.BMP\DefaultIcon` for starters.

- Close the Registry Editor, and press F5 to refresh any open windows to reread the icons for bitmap files.

Notes and other issues

In case you've accidentally disabled it, this same process will also work for icons (.ICO files).

To view bitmaps with all possible colors, see "Using True-Color Icons" earlier in this chapter.

To turn off iconic preview of bitmaps, select **Options** from Explorer's **View** menu, click on the **File Types** tab, find the bitmap file type in the list, click **Edit**, and then **Change Icon**. Once you've chosen a new generic icon, press **OK** and then **OK** again.

Turning Off Zooming Windows ● ■

Although the zooming windows (the animation you see when opening, maximizing, or minimizing windows) is a good user-interface tool and is sort of cute when you first install Windows 95, it can quickly get tiresome. Additionally, on slower video cards, the title bars can flicker when zooming, which is never desired. To turn off the zooming windows, follow these steps:

- Open the Registry Editor (*regedit.exe*). (If you're not familiar with the Registry Editor, see Chapter 3.)

- Expand the branches to `HKEY_CURRENT_USER\Control panel\desktop\ WindowMetrics`.

- Select **New** from the **Edit** menu, and choose **String Value**.

- Type `MinAnimate` and press `Enter`.

- Double-click on the new entry to change its value, and type a value of 0 for "off" or 1 for "on."

- Press **OK** and close the Registry Editor when finished. You'll have to restart Windows for this change to take effect.

Notes and other issues

This setting can also be changed with TweakUI, one of Microsoft's Power-Toys. See "Software and the Internet" in the Preface for information.

If you're using Windows NT 4.0 or Windows 95 with the Microsoft Plus! Pack installed, and have the AutoHide setting turned on in the taskbar properties, turning off zooming windows will also disable the animation for disappearing taskbars.

If you're using Windows NT 4.0 or Windows 95 with Internet Explorer 3.0 or later installed, this setting also determines whether the various parts of Explorer are animated, such as when directory tree branches are expanded.

Cleaning Up and Customizing System Folders ●■

Some new applications don't allow you to choose where they are installed, but rather just install themselves into a directory called Program Files. It never occurred to the folks at Microsoft that a user might want to choose the installation location, say, if the disk containing Program Files was full. Program Files is a system directory, meaning that it is specified in the Registry as a special directory that can't be moved or deleted. Since many programs install to this location, it's helpful to be able to change its name and location. Other system folders in Windows include **Temp**, **Start Menu**, and **Fonts**.

If these weren't enough, applications such as those in the irritating Microsoft Office line create other useless folders, including My Documents and Personal. Internet Explorer insists on creating the altogether-too-precious Favorites folder. All these folders seem to have the same purpose but have different names and locations, none of them necessary. It seems once again that the people in charge of these various products at Microsoft neglected to consult each other. Since these products have misled the operating system into thinking that they're important, you can't easily delete them, even if the applications are removed.

If you've decided to clean up your hard disk and remove these useless folders, new applications may continue to cause these problems. To remove the clutter and try to eliminate future problems, follow these instructions. Note that it's a *really* good idea to back up your Registry before continuing.

Change most of the system folders

- Open the Registry Editor (*regedit.exe*). (If you're not familiar with the Registry Editor, See chapter 3.)

- Most of the system folders are stored in the Shell Folders and User Shell Folders keys in the Registry, underneath `HKEY_CURRENT_USER\ Software\Microsoft\Windows\CurrentVersion\Explorer\`.

- Supposedly, the standard Windows system folders are specified in `Shell Folders`, while additional folders from newly installed applications are stored in `User Shell Folders`. In practice, however, any changes made to either of these should be duplicated in both keys. Additionally, some settings may find their ways into `HKEY_ LOCAL_MACHINE\SOFTWARE\Microsoft\Windows\CurrentVersion\ explorer\User Shell Folders`.

- The folders that can be changed in this way include Personal, Desktop, Favorites, Fonts, Nethood (for the Network Neighborhood), Programs (inside the **Start Menu**), Recent (for the Documents menu), SendTo, **Start Menu**, Startup (also in the **Start Menu**), and Templates.

- Depending on the item you're changing, you may have to search the Registry for other occurrences. Make sure to get them all. Note that some references may include the short filename, while others may include the long one (see the next solution for more information).

- If you're changing Personal or My Documents, you may have to start *each* of your installed Microsoft Office applications, choose **Options** from the application's **View** menu, and specify a new default location.

- Make changes to any desired folders, and close the Registry Editor when finished. You'll need to restart Windows for these changes to take effect.

Change the Program Files folder

- Since nothing in the Program Files folder is necessary when Windows is installed, it can be deleted. However, some applications may install *shared* files there. The first step is to move all of the current contents to the new location—whatever destination you choose.

- Next, open the Registry Editor.

- Expand the branches to `HKEY_LOCAL_MACHINE\SOFTWARE\ Microsoft\Windows\CurrentVersion`, and look for values named `ProgramFilesDir` and `CommonFilesDir` to the right. If they're not there, create each of them by selecting **New** from the **File** menu, then **String Value**, typing the name, and pressing **OK**. Double-click on each of the values, and change their contents to any new path you choose. You can make them both the same, if you wish.

- Select **Find** from the **Edit** menu to accomplish the following. Replace every occurrence of C:\Program Files and C:\PROGRA~1 with the new folder you've chosen. You can even use your Windows folder if you wish. C:\WINDOWS\MSAPPS is a good alternative, as some older Microsoft applications use it for the same purpose. See "Searching the Registry Effectively" in Chapter 3 for hints on searching and replacing.

- Close the Registry Editor when finished. You'll need to restart Windows for these changes to take effect.

Change the Temp folder

- Your temporary files are stored in the Temp folder. Since these files can be numerous and can often get corrupted, it's a good idea to put your Temp folder on a drive different from your Windows folder, not only for the sake of performance but for reliability as well.

- The Temp folder isn't specified in the Registry like the others. Instead, it's an environment variable. Changing an environment variable depends on the version of Windows you're using.

- For Windows 95, open a text editor, such as Notepad, and open C:*autoexec.bat*. You can create the file if it's not there. Then, add (or change) the following lines:

```
SET TEMP=D:\TEMP
SET TMP=D:\TEMP
```

where D:\Temp is the new desired location of your Temp folder. Make sure both lines point to the same path. Yes, you need both lines, as some older applications still use the .TMP variable.

- For Windows NT, duplicate this setting in the system properties icon in the Control Panel.

Notes and other issues

Changing the location of Program Files can cause problems when installing some new software, which may incorrectly recreate the Program Files folder as PROGRA~1, instead of reading the proper location from the CommonFilesDir key as described above. If an application does not let you choose the installation directory, but rather insists on installing here, make sure to write the program designers a note telling them how you feel about this "feature."

For some reason, the person who designed the Registry Editor did not include a search-and-replace feature. However, you can use the Registry Search and Replace utility for this purpose.

Tips and Techniques

The most important topic here is "Customizing Context Menus," wherein you will learn about one of the best features of object-oriented interface design. While Windows 95 and Windows NT don't necessarily exhibit the best in modern user-interface design, the concept of context menus is quite useful. Read these topics to learn more and improve your working experience with Windows.

Customizing Context Menus ● ■

New in Windows 95 and Windows NT 4.0 is the nearly global functionality of context menus. A context menu is what you see when you use the right mouse button to click on a file, folder, application titlebar, or nearly any other object on the screen. Most of the time, this menu includes a list of actions appropriate to the object on which you've clicked. In other words, the options available depend on the context.

For example, the context menu for file icons depends on the type of file selected. Usually you'll see **Copy**, **Paste**, **Delete**, **Rename**, **Open**, and **Properties** (among others). You may have noticed that some programs have added customized items to these menus, extending the power of the context menu paradigm. Here's how to add your own options to these menus (see Figure 4-10).

For file icons

* Select **Options** from the **View** menu in a folder window or in Explorer, and click the **File Types** tab.

* Select the desired file type from the list, and click **Edit**.

* Here, you can specify a new name for this file type (to be listed in the type column in Explorer's **Details** view), as well as the default icon for files of this type.

* In the box entitled Actions is a list of the customizable context menu items. The bold item is the default (the action carried out when you double-click on a file of this type) and appears at the top of the context menu.

* You can add new actions, change the default actions, and remove unwanted actions here. For new items, specify the program with

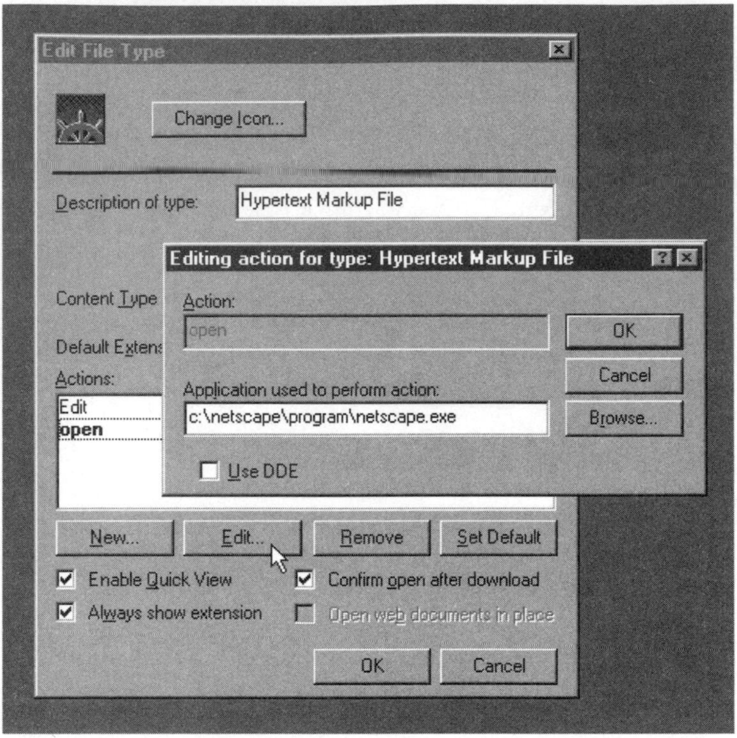

Figure 4-10: Customizing the context menu for HTML files saves time and effort

which you want the action performed. Then you can check the **Enable QuickView** option (if available) to show the **QuickView** action in the context menu.

- Press **OK** and then **OK** again when finished. The changes should take effect immediately.

For folder icons

- Open the Registry Editor (*regedit.exe*). (If you're not familiar with the Registry Editor, see Chapter 3.)

- Expand the branches to HKEY_CLASSES_ROOT\Directory\shell\.

- Select **New** from the **Edit** menu, and then select **Key**.

- Here, type the name of the new item you want added to the list, and press Enter.

- Highlight the new key, select **New** from the **Edit** menu, and then select **Key** again.

- Type command for the name of this new key, and press Enter.

- Double-click on the (default) value in the right pane, and type the full path and filename of the application you want associated with this entry.

- Close the Registry Editor when finished. The result is the same for the previous solution, but since the previous solution won't work for folders, we must do it the hard way. Your changes should take effect immediately.

For Desktop items

- Use the same method as for folder icons, described earlier.

- To find the Registry location of the various Desktop items, refer to "Changing the Icons of System Objects," previously in this chapter.

Notes and other issues

For other examples where this functionality is put to use, see "Clearing Unwanted Entries from Explorer's New Menu," "Customizing My Computer," "Printing Out a Directory Listing," "Using QuickView with Any File," and "Preventing Programs from Changing Your File Types" elsewhere in this chapter.

See "Understanding File Types" in Chapter 3 for a detailed examination of how file types are stored in the Registry.

Using QuickView with Any File ● ■

A handy tool that comes with Windows 95 is the QuickView application. By right-clicking on some files, you'll see an option called QuickView that will allow you to view the contents of a file without opening the application. The problem is that this doesn't work with just any file. To get either your favorite files or all files on your hard drive to work with the QuickViewer, follow these steps:

Solution 1: All files with extensions

- Open the Registry Editor (*regedit.exe*). (If you're not familiar with the Registry Editor, see Chapter 3.)

- Expand the branches to HKEY_CLASSES_ROOT\.

- Look for a key that reads "*" —if it isn't there, add it (select **New** and then **Key** from the **Edit** menu).

- Under this key, add a new key, and call it QuickView.

- Set the value of the (default) value to "*" (without the quotation marks) and close the Registry Editor.

- This should work for all files with extensions except those that Quick-View doesn't understand and, for some reason, .PCX files. Files without extensions won't have the QuickView option.

Solution 2: Just the files you want

- Double-click on the My Computer icon, and choose **Options** from the **View** menu.

- Click on the **File Types** tab and select a file type or extension from the list.

- Click **Edit**, turn on the **Enable QuickView** option, and press **OK**.

- Note that this option may not be available for some file types because Windows has been warned that QuickView doesn't support some file formats. You can override this by using one of the other solutions here.

- If the type of file with which you want to use QuickView is not listed, click **New Type** to add the extension of the desired file to the list, and then follow the steps listed above. You'll have to do this for every file you want to use with QuickView.

Solution 3: Use the Send To menu

- Create a shortcut to *quikview.exe* (in your \Windows\System\Viewers folder) in your \Windows\SendTo folder.

- This way, QuickViewer will be accessible from the **Send To** context menu when you right-click on any file.

Solution 4: For unknown (unregistered) files only

- Open the Registry Editor (*regedit.exe*). (If you're not familiar with the Registry Editor, see Chapter 3.)

- Expand the branches to HKEY_CLASSES_ROOT\Unknown\shell\ openas\command.

- Double-click on (default), and replace what's there with C:\windows\ system\viewers\Quikview.exe, or any other desired program.

Solution 5: Use a Desktop receptacle

- Create a shortcut on the Desktop for *quikview.exe*, allowing you to drag any files onto it to be viewed.

Notes and other issues

QuickView may not have a filter for every file you view, but sometimes viewing the raw data is better than nothing at all.

If you have Windows 95 on floppies, see "Software and the Internet" in the Preface for more information.

Getting Find to Look Where You Want ● ■

The Find feature included with Windows is quite handy for finding files on your hard disk or network. The problem is that when you access it from the **Start Menu**, it defaults to looking in the drive on which Windows is installed. If you have more than one drive, it can be quite helpful to search across all your drive letters rather than one. While you can type or point to the desired search destination, there's no way to set the default search location for the **Find** command in the **Start Menu**. There are, however, other ways to use **Find**.

Solution 1

- Open the Registry Editor (*regedit.exe*). (If you're not familiar with the Registry Editor, see Chapter 3.)

- Expand the branches to HKEY_CLASSES_ROOT\Directory\shell\find\ddeexec.

- Double-click on (default), and replace the value with:

  [FindFolder("C:\", C:\)]

  replacing C:\ with whatever folder pathname you wish.

- Close the Registry Editor when you're finished. The change should take effect immediately.

Solution 2

- Right-click on the My Computer icon on your Desktop, and select **Find** to begin your search from the top level.

Solution 3

- Open any folder in which you want to search, and press F3 or Ctrl-F to search that folder and all folders beneath it. F3 also works on the Desktop, although Ctrl-F does not.

- If you're using Explorer, you can also select **Find** from the **Tools** menu to search from the current folder.

Solution 4

- Open the **Find** window in any of the usual ways (as described above), and choose the desired find location. Choose **Save Search** from the **File** menu. This will put a file with the .FND extension on your Desktop.

- Store the .FND file in another folder, if desired, such as your Windows directory, and create a shortcut to it on the Desktop. Rename the shortcut to something simple, like **Find**.

- Double-click on the icon to redo the search. The location and any other search parameters you've specified are saved.

Printing Out a Directory Listing ● ■

Although there is no built-in way to print a directory listing (all the file-names in a folder), there is a way to add this functionality to Windows. Since DOS can list the contents of a folder in a way that can be saved to a file, you can then open the file and print it. To automate this process, follow these instructions:

- Open a text editor, such as Notepad, and type the following two lines into a new document:

```
CD %1
DIR >LPT1
```

This assumes the printer you wish to use is connected to printer port 1. Change LPT1 to LPT2 if necessary.

- Save the two-line file into your Windows\Command folder, and call it *printdir.bat*.

- Find the file in Explorer, right click on it, and select **Properties**.

- Choose the **Program** tab, turn on the **Close on Exit** option, choose **Minimized** from the **Run** listbox, and click **OK**.

- Next, open the Registry Editor (*regedit.exe*). (If you're not familiar with the Registry Editor, see Chapter 3.)

- Expand the branches to HKEY_CLASSES_ROOT\Directory\shell.

- Select **New** from the **Edit** menu, and then select **Key**.

- Type Print for the name of this new key, and press Enter.

- Highlight the new Print key, select **New** from the **Edit** menu, and then select **Key** again.

- Type command for the name of this new key, and press Enter.

- Double-click on the (default) value in the right pane, and type the following:

```
C:\Windows\Command\PRINTDIR.BAT
```

  assuming that C:\Windows\ is your Windows folder.

- From now on, when you right-click on a folder icon, you can click the **Print** option to print its contents.

Notes and other issues

The *dir* command is used to display the contents of the current directory in the command prompt. To specify the desired sort order, change the line above to the following:

```
DIR /O:xxx  >LPT1
```

where xxx can be any or all of the following letters, in order by preference: N to sort by name, E for extension, S for size, D for date, G to group directories first, A by last access date (earliest first). Precede any letter with a minus sign to reverse the order. Some examples include /O:EN to sort by extension and then name, /O:-D to sort by reverse date, and /O:SAG to sort by size and last access date, grouping directories first. Also, try the /B switch to display "bare" filenames (without all the extra information), and the /W switch to condense the filenames into multiple columns. Type DIR /? to see all the possible options. See Appendix A for information on setting the default sort order for the *dir* command.

Choosing Your Short Filenames • ■

When you try to open a file with a long filename in an older 16-bit Windows or DOS application, the filename is truncated to the old 8.3 DOS standard format. That is, a file named *A Big Blob.txt* will appear as *ABIGBL~1.TXT*. You can configure Windows 95 to drop the ~1 suffix from short filenames, making them more accurate than their long counterparts. In addition, choosing long filenames wisely will make the short versions easier to understand.

Solution 1 (more permanent, and more dangerous)

- Open the Registry Editor (*regedit.exe*). (If you're not familiar with the Registry Editor, see Chapter 3.)

- Expand the branches to HKEY_LOCAN_MACHINE\System\CurrenControlSet\control\FileSystem.

- Select **New** from the **Edit** menu, and then select **Binary Value**.

- Type `NameNumericTail` for the name of the new value, and press `Enter`.

- Double click on the value, enter 0 (zero), and click **OK**.

- Close the Registry Editor when you're finished. From now on, short file-names will not use the ~1 suffix, although successive long filenames with the same short name will have a numeric suffix.

Solution 2 (less permanent)

- Using a 16-bit application (or a non-long filename-aware 32-bit appli-cation), create a document with a short filename, such as *ABIG-BLOB.TXT*.

- Then, in Explorer, rename the file to *A big blob that ate Manhat-tan.TXT*, or something like that.

- Go back to the 16-bit application, and instead of *ABIGBL~1.TXT*, you'll see the same, original 8.3 filename. This is due to the fact that the long and the short versions are so similar and that the short ver-sion was created first. If the long filename is too different, this won't work.

Notes and other issues

Several users have reported unpleasant side effects with Solution 1, so use it with extreme caution (try backing up your system first).

In a related discussion, you might notice that there's no way to have a file-name with fewer than eight letters be all uppercase because Windows 95 thinks it's a short filename. To get around this, try inserting a space some-where into the filename.

Use Solution 2 with caution, as some older 16-bit applications might not work with long filenames truncated to their short versions.

System Administration

This final section closes things up with what I'm defining as system administration. This rather vague term encompasses such topics as secu-rity, the DOS prompt, tips for multiple users, and designating drive letters. The first topic should set the tone for the section, although the topics here are a little diverse.

Changing the Registered User Information ● ■

During the installation of Windows, you were asked your name and company to be used throughout the operating system. In addition, you were required to enter a CD key, a form of copy protection. All this information is stored in the Registry and can be easily edited once installation is complete.

- Open the Registry Editor (*regedit.exe*). (If you're not familiar with the Registry Editor, see Chapter 3.)

- Expand the branches to HKEY_LOCAL_MACHINE\SOFTWARE\ Microsoft\Windows\CurrentVersion.

- To the right, among a myriad of settings, are the three settings in which we're interested. You can change the RegisteredOwner (your name), RegisteredOrganization (your company), or ProductId (the CD key) to anything you want simply by double-clicking on them and typing.

Notes and other issues

This setting can also be changed with WinReg 95. See "Software and the Internet" in the Preface for information.

This will change the registered user information only for Windows, not for the applications already installed on your system. However, many newer applications will use the current user name and organization as defaults during their installation procedures.

If you change the CD key (ProductId) to something other than the original CD key, and try to run Windows setup on the same system (installing over your current installation), you'll need to enter the new CD key before continuing. However, the old CD key will still be used when the product is installed elsewhere.

Booting Directly into DOS ●

In previous versions of Windows, you were required to load DOS before running Windows. In Windows 95, DOS is still there, but the command prompt is skipped when loading Windows 95. To go to the command prompt before loading Windows, follow these instructions.

- Open the file *C:\msdos.sys* with any text editor, such as Notepad. You'll probably have to unhide the file before you can edit it. See Appendix A for more information.

- Find the line that reads BootGUI=1, and change it to BootGUI=0.

- Save the file and reboot your computer. You'll be placed directly into DOS, where you can type win to start Windows 95.

Notes and other issues

For more information, see Appendix D, *Contents of MSDOS.SYS File*.

See "Creating a Startup Menu" in Chapter 6, *Troubleshooting*, for an important application of this solution.

This setting can also be changed with TweakUI, one of Microsoft's Power-Toys. See "Software and the Internet" in the Preface for more information.

How to Exit to DOS •

Users of Windows 3.x have become accustomed to the ability to shut down Windows 95 completely into DOS, without having to restart the computer. You may have discovered that choosing **Restart the computer in MSDOS mode** from the **Shutdown** menu doesn't unload Windows 95 completely from memory. Unfortunately, Microsoft, in an effort to hide DOS from users of Windows 95, has made this difficult. Here's how you do it:

Solution 1

- If you delete the shutdown logos (*logos.sys* and *logow.sys*) from your Windows directory, you will be returned to the DOS prompt whenever you choose "shut down your computer." See "Replacing the Startup and Shutdown Screens" in Chapter 2 for more information.

Solution 2

- Follow the instructions in "Booting Directly into DOS" earlier in this chapter.

- When the shutdown screen informs you that "it is now safe to turn off your system," type MODE CO80 and press Enter to be returned to the command prompt. You won't see the letters as you type until you press Enter.

- If you're launching Windows 95 from *AUTOEXEC.BAT* (with the *win* command), you can also include this command at the end of the file to display the command prompt automatically.

Notes and other issues

You can configure certain drivers to be loaded when you exit Windows, but you must use a special shortcut to do so. See "Do I Still Need *CONFIG.SYS* and *AUTOEXEC.BAT*?" in Chapter 6 for more information.

Sharing System Folders Between Users ■

You'll notice after installing Windows NT 4.0 that there is a separate **Start Menu** folder, Send To folder, and Desktop folder for each user. By default, there are three users: Administrator, All Users, and Default User. It shouldn't take you long to realize that precious hard drive space is being wasted by all of these folders. If you know you don't need a separate Send To folder for each user (especially if you're the only one), try using a solution that takes advantage of two features of Windows. First, when you rename or move a system folder with drag-drop, Windows keeps track of the change and records it. The other nice feature is that when you drag-drop a folder from one place to another and there is another folder in the destination with the same name, it combines the contents of the two folders (see Figure 4-11):

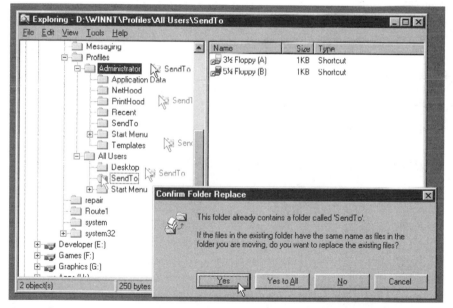

Figure 4-11: Drag-drop a folder from one user to another to share it

These two features come into play when you drag a system folder from one user's directory to another (refer to Figure 4-4). Windows will then point to the same folder for both functions, and you'll reduce some of the clutter.

Notes and other issues

Another example of this use of these features is if you've installed Windows 95 and Windows NT 4.0 on the same system. You can have both installations share the same **Start Menu**, Desktop, Program Files, or Send To folder. You can either drag-drop some folders (as already described), or use Microsoft's TweakUI utility (see "Software and the Internet" in the Preface) to reassign some system folders from one installation to the other.

This won't work for the Fonts folder. To share fonts between two installations or versions of Windows without taking up twice as much disk space, you must use a different procedure. First, start the version of Windows without all the extra fonts. Then open a Find window, and search for *.TTF; *.FON (all your font files, each type separated by a semicolon) in the Fonts folder of the other installation of Windows. Select all the files and drag them into the Fonts folder of the running version with the right mouse button. Select **Create Shortcut(s) Here**, and Windows will allow you to share the fonts across both versions.

If you are installing two versions of the operating system on the same machine, you may not need to install all your applications for each version repeatedly. Start by making sure each operating system can see the system folder of the other. Add the system directory to the path (with *AUTOEXEC.BAT* in Windows 95 or Control Panel in Windows NT). Then, using the Registry Editor (see Chapter 3 for more information), create Registry patches for all your software by exporting selected portions of HKEY_LOCAL_MACINE\Software and HKEY_CURRENT_User\Software. Just apply the patches in the other operating system to migrate the settings.

How to Implement Security in Windows 95 •

Windows NT 4.0 comes with more security features than the average home user requires; Windows 95 doesn't seem to come with enough. Whether you're trying to protect your computer from prying children or protect valuable data from prying coworkers, there are ways to implement various forms of security. Although there's no way to secure a system entirely, here are a few hints that should help:

Solution 1: Use the Policy Editor

- Open the System Policy Editor (*poledit.exe*) on your Windows 95 CD-ROM (in the Admin\Apptools\Poledit folder). If you have the floppy disk version of Windows 95, see "Software and the Internet" in the Preface.

- If you are asked to "open a template file," choose *admin.adm* in the same folder, and click **OK**.

- Select **Open Registry** from the **File** menu.

- Search through the branches for the various options to find the ones that will help implement the security measures you want. You can eliminate certain features from the Desktop, the **Start Menu**, and Explorer by turning on or off any of the options here.

Solution 2: Use third-party software designed for heightened security

- Windows interface replacement, Route 1 Pro, comes with several security features, such as password protection for specific features and software, and protection for shutting down and restarting the system. Used in conjunction with some of the settings in the Policy Editor (see Solution 1), this software can help you create a fairly secure environment. Route 1 Pro is available for download on the Internet at *http://www.creativelement.com/software/route1.html* .

Solution 3: Configure multiple users

- By setting up multiple users on your system, each with a different password, you can restrict access to certain features and software (also using the Policy Editor described already) to some users, while providing full access to others. Enabling passwords for the various users helps ensure that nobody has unauthorized access. See "Preventing New Users from Logging In" in Chapter 2 to plug an potential hole in security.

Notes and other issues

If you find yourself using the Policy Editor quite a bit, you may want to copy it to your hard disk rather than accessing it from the CD every time. Copy all the files from the Poledit folder on the CD to your Windows folder. The next time you're asked to locate *admin.adm*, choose the one you just placed in your Windows folder, and you'll never be asked again.

Connecting SCSI Devices Without Restarting Windows ● ■

One of the great things about SCSI technology, besides the fact that it's Plug & Play that actually works, is the ability to plug in or turn on an SCSI device and use it without having to restart your computer. However, since Windows doesn't systematically scan your SCSI card for newly attached or disconnected devices, you have to do it manually when connecting devices. After you've properly connected and turned on the device, follow these instructions:

- Right-click on the My Computer icon, and select **Properties**.

- Choose the **Device Manager** tab, and select **Computer** from the top of the list.

- At this point, you may need to click the **View devices by connection** option at the top of the window.

- Click **Refresh**. This will take several seconds, but the new device(s) should appear in the list.

- If you can't find your new device, choose the **View devices by connection** option, find your SCSI card in the list, and expand it out to see all the devices attached to it.

- If you're using Windows NT 4.0, you can accomplish this with the SCSI icon in the Control Panel as well.

Notes and other issues

There are some non-SCSI devices for which this process will also work, but most other devices require that you power down your computer before connecting or disconnecting them. There are also some SCSI devices for which this will not work; you may still have to restart your system to force Windows to recognize newly attached devices.

The Plug & Play system may require that you insert the appropriate drivers when Windows detects a new device, including the above method.

If you change the SCSI ID of a device connected to your system, Windows may not recognize the change and will still report the device as having the original ID. In this case, you will need to restart your computer. A design flaw in Windows' Plug & Play technology will not recognize the old device with the new ID, thereby treating the device as a newly attached device and requiring that you supply the appropriate drivers. If this happens, try specifying your Windows/System folder (among others) so that Windows will simply use the driver files already on your system.

Transferring Windows 95 onto Another Hard Disk •

With the release of an operating system as large as Windows 95, it's quite reasonable that many users may need to upgrade their hard disks. While one can simply reinstall Windows 95 on the new drive, it isn't always the most attractive solution. However, it's not that easy to transfer Windows 95 either. Now you'll have to first follow the instructions included with the new drive for connecting it to your computer.

The following assumes that each drive has only a single partition, as installing two drives with multiple partitions causes additional problems. If you've got a tape drive or some other backup device, your best bet is to back up your system and restore it onto the new hard drive. Otherwise, follow these instructions:

- Connect both hard disks to your computer at once, configuring the new one as the slave and the old one as master. If these are SCSI drives, make the SCSI ID of the old drive lower than that of the new drive.

- At the DOS prompt, type FORMAT d: /U /S, where d: is the drive letter of your new disk.

- Copy all the files and folders from the root directory of the old drive to the root directory of the new drive from within Windows 95. You can do this by selecting all the contents of the root directory of the old drive and dragging them into the root directory of the new drive.

- Make sure you include all hidden files (see Appendix A for more information), especially C:\ *msdos.sys*. You'll need to replace the one on the new drive with the existing file. However, don't try to copy your Swap File (*win386.swp*). Not only won't it work, but it is a waste of time.

Notes and other issues

If you need to copy the files in DOS, use the XCOPY32 utility, which will preserve your long filenames (the standard XCOPY won't). Use the undocumented /h parameter to copy hidden files, although system files will still be ignored.

Designating Drive Letters ● ■

Each disk drive on a PC, whether it's a CD-ROM, a floppy, a removable, or a hard disk, has its own drive letter. Some drives are separated into several sections, called partitions. Each partition has its own drive letter. There are two ways that drives are assigned drive letters. The first kind are the ones controlled by your BIOS that don't require any software to be recognized. These usually include the floppy and most hard drives, for which drive letters are created when your system is first turned on. The second kind of drives are controlled by software or, more specifically, drivers (usually included in Windows). These types of drives include CD-ROM drives, removable cartridge drives, network drives, and sometimes SCSI hard disks.

Generally drive letters are assigned to these drives depending on the order in which they are loaded. Your first floppy drive is always assigned to A:, and the second floppy, if you have one, is assigned to B:. The hard disk letters always start at C:, and go from there. What follows are any software-controlled drives, such as CD-ROMs and network drives. For example, assume a computer with three hard disks, two floppies, and a CD-ROM drive. Two of the hard disks are IDE drives (drives 1 and 2) and are controlled by the computer's BIOS. The third is an SCSI drive and is controlled by SCSI drivers built into Windows. For the sake of argument, each hard disk has two or more partitions. In Windows 95, drive letters will be assigned to the drives in the following manner:

Device Name	Default Drive Letter	Notes
Floppy Drive 1	A:	
Floppy Drive 2	B:	
Hard Disk 1, First Partition	C:	
Hard Disk 2, First Partition	D:	
Hard Disk 1, Second Partition	E:	
Hard Disk 1, Third Partition	F:	
Hard Disk 2, Second Partition	G:	
Hard Disk 3, First Partition	H:	*
Hard Disk 3, Second Partition	I:	*
CD-ROM	J:	*

Note that the first partitions of the two BIOS-controlled drives are listed first. Then, starting back with the first drive, the rest of the partitions are listed. Once all of the partitions of the BIOS drives are listed, Windows 95 adds Hard Disk 3 and the CD-ROM drive. In Windows 95, those drive letters marked with an asterisk can be changed. BIOS-controlled devices can't be reassigned in Windows 95. In Windows NT, the drive letters are assigned similarly, except that all hard disks are treated equally, regardless of whether they're controlled by the BIOS or by software:

Device Name	Default Drive Letter	Notes
Floppy Drive 1	A:	
Floppy Drive 2	B:	
Hard Disk 1, First Partition	C:	*
Hard Disk 2, First Partition	D:	*
Hard Disk 3, First Partition	E:	*
Hard Disk 1, Second Partition	F:	*
Hard Disk 1, Third Partition	G:	*
Hard Disk 2, Second Partition	H:	*

Device Name	Default Drive Letter	Notes
Hard Disk 3, Second Partition	I:	*
CD-ROM	J:	*

Here, the first partitions of all drives are listed first, followed by the rest of the partitions of each drive, and then the CD-ROM. In Windows NT 4.0, the drive letters marked with an asterisk can be changed. Virtually all drives except for the floppies can be changed. Most users will have only a single drive with a single partition, probably a CD-ROM drive, and one or two floppy drives.

Here's how to designate drive letters for drives that support it:

Solution 1: For Windows 95

- Double-click on the System icon in the Control Panel, and click on the **Device Manager** tab.

- Find the device (CD-ROM drive or otherwise) that you wish to config-ure from the list, and select it.

- Click **Properties**, and choose the **Settings** tab.

- If the **Removable** option is not turned on and the **Reserved drive let-ters** listboxes below are disabled, turn it on now. If initially turned off, make sure to turn it off it again when you're done with this proce-dure.

- In the section entitled **Reserved drive letters**, choose the same letter for both the **Start drive letter** and **End drive letter**. If the letter you choose conflicts with any other drive and the other drive is controlled by Windows 95, it will reassign the other drive to make room for the one you're configuring.

- You'll have to restart your computer for this change to take effect.

Solution 2: For Windows 95*

- Open the Registry Editor (*regedit.exe*). (If you're not familiar with the Registry Editor, see Chapter 3.) It's a very good idea to back up your Registry at this point.

- Open one of the following branches, depending on the type of device you wish to configure (your system may vary).

- For all SCSI devices, and most non-SCSI CD-ROM drives, expand the branches to HKEY_LOCAL_MACHINE\Enum\SCSI.

---

*Use with caution, and only if Solution 1 doesn't work.

- For IDE hard disks, expand the branches to HKEY_LOCAL_ MACHINE\Enum\ESDI.

- For standard floppy drives, expand the branches to HKEY_LOCAL_ MACHINE\Enum\FLOP.

- Expand the subbranch of the particular device you wish to configure, and click on the numbered key under that device (if you have two of the same device, there will be two keys here).

- Double-click on the string value called UserDriveLetterAssign- ment (create it if it's not there by selecting **New** and then **String Value** from the **Edit** menu).

- In the box that appears, type the desired drive letter *twice*, in all capi- tal letters (for example, type NN to configure this drive to use **N**:).

- Next, double-click on the string value called CurrentDriveLet- terAssignment.

- In the box that appears, type the desired drive letter *once*, in all capi- tal letters. If this device is partitioned into more than one logical drive, include all drive letters (for example, type J to configure this drive to use J:. If this drive has three partitions, you might type DFG to configure this drive to use D:, F:, and G:).

- Close the Registry Editor when you're finished, and restart your com- puter immediately for this change to take effect.

Solution 3: For Windows NT 4.0

- Run the Disk Administrator (*windsk.exe*, located in the System32 folder). This utility allows you to change any drive letter (with the exception of floppy drives), regardless of how the drive is controlled.

- Right-click on the drive or partition you wish to change, and select **Assign Drive Letter**. Choose a desired drive letter from the list that appears and follow the on-screen instructions. You'll be able to choose from any available drive letters.

- Windows NT may be able to change the drive letter on the spot, with- out rebooting. Reassigning drive letters for hard drives controlled by the BIOS will require the system to be restarted.

Notes and other issues

To change the letters of network drives connected through a Microsoft Windows network, see "Setting Up a Workgroup" in Chapter 7.

In Windows 95, neither Solution 1 nor Solution 2 will work if the drive in question is controlled by software loaded in your *CONFIG.SYS* or

AUTOEXEC.BAT, since Windows 95 doesn't have control over these devices. If the devices are supported in Windows 95, you should remove the old drivers from these files. See "Do I Still need *CONFIG.SYS* and *AUTOEXEC.BAT?*" in Chapter 6 for more information.

Some SCSI controllers have a built-in BIOS and therefore are treated like BIOS-controlled IDE drives by DOS and Windows 95. Windows NT should have no problem with this type of drive either. Contact the manufacturer of your drive if you encounter problems.

Adjusting Your Printer Timeout ●■

If you've ever printed in Windows 95, your work has undoubtedly been interrupted with the little "Windows will automatically retry in 5 seconds" window that appears if your printer is not turned on, out of paper, or is just warming up. The time that Windows 95 waits before notifying you that the printer isn't ready is called the *timeout*. In Windows 3.x, the timeout was easily changed to suit the user's printer and work habits, but this adjustment can be difficult to find in Windows 95. It can be irritating to have to look at this retry window every 5 seconds (see Figure 4-12). Here's how to do make it more tolerable.

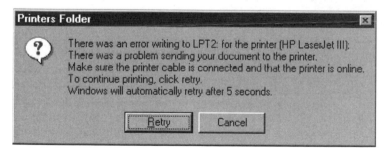

Figure 4-12: The printer timeout window is just plain irritating

- Double-click on the Printer icon in Control Panel, and choose the **Details** tab.

- For an unknown reason, the timeout for "not ready" is called Not Selected here. Set this value *and the value below it* to something more useful, like 120 seconds.

Notes and other issues

This solution won't work for some systems, as the little box will still appear, regardless of this setting. Other than obtaining specialized printer drivers from the manufacturer of your printer, or an update from Microsoft if it becomes available, there's no other way to change this setting.

You may have noticed that if your printer is not plugged in to your computer, this box does not appear at all. In fact, Windows may never notify you that it can't print in this situation.

Using the Third Mouse Button ● ■

Although most PC mice come with two buttons, some makers (such as Logitech) include three buttons on their mice. The third (middle) mouse button, while not really used by Windows, can be programmed to take the function of another operation such as double-clicking, copying to the clipboard, or deleting text. Since the Mouse icon in Control Panel doesn't have any settings for the third mouse button, you'll need special drivers for your mouse (obtained from the manufacturer). However, if you have a Logitech three-button mouse, you can set the middle mouse button to double-click with the following instructions.

- Open the Registry Editor (*regedit.exe*). (If you're not familiar with the Registry Editor, see Chapter 3.)

- Expand the branches to `HKEY_LOCAL_MACHINE\SOFTWARE\ Logitech\ Mouseware\CurrentVersion\SerialV\`.

- Select **Find** from the **Edit** menu, and search for `DoubleClick`.

- When you find a value (*not* a key) named `DoubleClick`, double-click on it, and change the `000` to `001`.

- You'll have to restart Windows for this change to take effect.

Notes and other issues

If you're left-handed and have switched the left and right mouse buttons, this solution will still use the physical left button, meaning that you are actually double-right-clicking. So far, there is no way to overcome this limitation.

It's far more effective to use the drivers specific to your version of Windows, if the manufacturer of your mouse has made them available.

Turning Off the PC Speaker ● ■

Most of us who are annoyed by the various beeps and sputters of our sound cards and the good old PC speaker have turned off most of the sound "events" using the Sounds icon in Control Panel. However, on some computers, turning off all of the sound events means that the PC Speaker is used instead for the default beep. Since there's no way to remove the PC speaker driver permanently from the Device Manager, and there's usually no other way of turning the thing off, it can get quite frustrating. Furthermore, the volume control included with Windows doesn't have any effect on the PC speaker.

Solution 1

- Yank the PC speaker out of your computer. It's usually connected by a two-conductor wire to the motherboard, which can be easily removed. You'll find it remarkably liberating.

Solution 2

- Using the sound recorder, create a small .WAV file of simple silence, and specify it for the Asterisk, Default Sound, and Exclamation events in Control Panel. Instead of an annoying .WAV file or the PC speaker, this silent file will be played, allowing you to work in peace.

Solution 3

- Obtain and install TweakUI, one of Microsoft's PowerToys. See "Software and the Internet" in the Preface for information. Under the General tab, in the Effects section, turn off the **Beep on Errors** option.

5

In this chapter:
- *Fine-Tuning Your System*
- *Upgrading Your Computer*
- *Improving Work Habits*

Maximizing Performance

The two strategies used when upgrading your computer involve making the most of what you've got and buying new equipment. Naturally, if money were no object, you could simply upgrade a system entirely to improve performance. On the other hand, there's only so much you can do with your old hardware. Luckily, you can combine the two and improve your system while spending the least amount of money doing so.

The first portion of this chapter deals with the configuration of your system and how you can squeeze more out of your existing components. The main focus is removing bottlenecks. There are usually one or two specific characteristics of your system, hardware or software, that generally cause the most slowdowns. Anyone who upgraded from Windows 3.x knows how much of a bottleneck software can be. Windows 95 runs your computer so much more efficiently than the old Windows, one wonders how much this version is *still* hindering the speed demon that lay beneath.

There is a very important factor to keep in mind throughout this chapter. Spending time fine-tuning your hardware and software and spending money replacing certain components *can* make a difference, but there is a certain point past which your computer is going to turn into a money pit. It's easy to calculate the point of diminishing returns; just compare the estimated cost of an upgrade (include *your* time here as well) with the cost of a new system (minus what you'd get for selling or donating your old system). I stress this, as I've seen it happen all too often; people end up spending too much and getting too little in return. A simple hardware upgrade ends up taking days of troubleshooting and configuring, and then one finds out that something else needs to be replaced. Taking into account that the final result will need to be upgraded soon, it can be more cost-effective to replace the entire system and either sell or donate the old parts. That said, it can also be quite cost-effective to replace components one by one, as long as it's done right. While this book does focus on customizing the Windows operating system and not upgrading your hardware, we will rationalize it by referring to the upgrade as *customizing* your Windows hardware.

The one aspect of performance that is usually overlooked is *your* work habits. You can save a lot more time by learning a few keystrokes, mouse clicks, and shortcuts than you would by buying faster hardware. These tips include keyboard shortcuts used in Windows as well as other applications, some advanced time-saving features of Windows 95 and Windows NT, and some additional software that may make your life easier.

Fine-Tuning Your System

You'll be amazed at how a few adjustments can improve a computer's performance significantly. Hopefully, you won't have the chance to be amazed at how easily you can mess up a computer, however. Make sure to write down any settings before you change them. For example, if you're changing jumpers on some card, be sure to make a note of where they were, just in case you need to undo your changes. For the same reason, you should back up any configuration files before making changes that could adversely affect your system.

Hardware

We'll start with fine-tuning your hardware and move on to Windows afterward. What follows is a collection of tips, hints, and tweaks that can really make a difference in the hardware you've already got. See "Upgrading Your Computer" later in this chapter for detailed information on replacing these components. Whenever drivers are mentioned here, refer to Chapter 6, *Troubleshooting*, for more information.

Monitors

Good use of your monitor is important, especially if you use your computer for long periods of time. You shouldn't be looking up or down at a monitor; it shouldn't be tilted at all, but rather placed directly at eye level. If you're too high or low for this, raise the monitor or use a higher chair. Using a monitor at eye level is not only more comfortable but decreases the risk of back and neck injury. If you keep the glass clean, your images will be sharper as well. Spray some window cleaner on a paper towel (not on the monitor directly) to clean it. If you wear glasses, consult your optometrist for eyewear made especially for computer screens. Reading or driving glasses don't have the proper focal length for this purpose. The contrast and brightness should be set so that black appears dark black and not washed-out gray (try adjusting these with a full-screen DOS session) and text is bright and high-contrast. Try turning the contrast control all the way up and the brightness a little above all the way down.

Video cards (also known as display adapters)

While there's not much you can do to a video card to make it perform better short of replacing it, you can significantly improve its performance by making sure you have the newest drivers (obtained from the manufacturer). Drivers optimized for your video card can increase speed, offer higher resolutions with more colors, and offer better stability than the plain-vanilla drivers that come with Windows.

BIOS

The settings available in a computer's BIOS setup vary significantly from one system to another, but some settings are common throughout them all. The BIOS setup is usually accessed by pressing a key immediately after powering on your system, such as `Delete` or `ESC`. You're then presented with a menu or a screen full of settings. Refer to your manual for details. Make sure all of your settings are correct. The configuration of your hard disk, floppy drives, keyboard, and ports should all match your system. Make sure your BIOS correctly reports the amount of memory in your system; it's possible that it isn't using all that's installed.

If your motherboard has I/O ports (serial and parallel) built in, you can usually configure them in the BIOS setup as well. If your mouse or printer is plugged into a separate card, this is not the case. You should disable any ports that aren't being used, and make sure there aren't any conflicts here with other devices in your system. Some computers can configure their ports automatically. You should turn this feature off, as it doesn't always work correctly. If your BIOS has built-in antivirus support, disable it immediately. This feature causes compatibility problems with Windows and can slow down your system. Additionally, antivirus software does a much better job of this, because it can be updated to support the newest viruses. Many systems have advanced BIOS settings that can improve performance as well; a little investigation can yield some good results. Just make sure to write down all settings before you change them.

Floppy diskette drives

The only thing you can really do with a floppy drive is to keep it clean. Dust can slow down the drive and even make the disk unreadable. For faster and more reliable floppy formats, see Chapter 6.

Hard disks

As far as the physical hard disk goes, the best thing you can do is to make sure your drive is securely fastened to your computer case. It shouldn't wobble or rattle at all. Air should flow past the drive easily, as it should throughout the entire case. On the software side, you should run Scandisk every other day to check the drive for errors and Disk Defragmenter once a week to defragment the drive. See Chapter 6 for more information.

In addition to regular maintenance, you can adjust a few Windows settings to optimize your hard disk performance to your needs. Double-click on the System icon in Control Panel, and choose the **Performance** tab. Click **File System** and choose the **Hard Disk** tab to display the hard disk performance settings for your machine. The disk cache is configured by selecting one of three options for the "Typical role of this machine." Experiment with each of these to achieve the best results, although most users will benefit most by choosing **Desktop computer** here. If you choose **Network Server**, Windows will devote more memory to the disk cache, which, while resulting in better disk performance, will reduce the memory available for applications. Adjust the **Read-ahead optimization** all the way to the right, unless you know you want to lower it for some reason. Click **OK** when you're finished.

Hard disk controllers

Most hard disk controllers don't have any settings (see the following item for SCSI controllers). However, some of the more expensive caching controllers have memory on them. These types of controllers generally require special drivers, some of which aren't available for Windows. Even if the controller is supported, it may not be offering much of a performance increase. If either of these is the case, the memory on your disk controller can be put to much better use by placing it on your motherboard (if it fits). Combining this memory with your system RAM will provide more memory for applications, reducing the need for excessive disk access and yielding better overall performance than if you left the memory on the controller card.

SCSI controllers

Each SCSI device attached to your SCSI controller may have different requirements. If your controller supports it, make sure settings like data rate and synch negotiation are properly matched to each of your SCSI devices. Check to see if your SCSI bus is properly terminated as well. Active terminators, while more expensive than their passive counterparts, usually do a better job. You should be using native 32-bit drivers made especially for your adapter. Any lines in CONFIG.SYS or AUTOEXEC.BAT are just slowing things down. See "Do I Still Need CONFIG.SYS and AUTOEXEC.BAT?" in Chapter 6 for more information.

CD-ROM drives

Make sure the driver for your CD-ROM drive is a native 32-bit driver made especially for your version of Windows. Any lines in CONFIG.SYS or AUTOEXEC.BAT are just slowing things down. See "Do I Still Need CONFIG.SYS and AUTOEXEC.BAT?" in Chapter 6 for more information. If the drivers are all correct, double-click on the System icon in Control Panel, and choose the **Performance** tab. Click **File System** and choose the **CD-ROM** tab to display the CD-ROM performance settings for your machine. Adjust the **Supplemental cache size** to your liking; the resulting memory required is displayed below. The more memory you use here, the better. If you have the RAM to spare, move the slider all the way to the right. If you don't use your CD-ROM much, move this slider more to the left to leave more memory available for other applications. Finally, match the setting of **Optimize access pattern for** to the speed of your drive. Click **OK** when you're finished.

Modems

The most common cause for slow connection speeds is noisy phone lines. Try connecting a handset to the phone line if it isn't already there. When placing a call, if your connection isn't crystal clear, you may be able to reduce the amount of noise. Try replacing the wall jack and the phone cord connecting the modem to the wall with new ones. Note that the phone cord shouldn't be any longer than is necessary. Make sure there isn't anything else on the line between the computer and the wall; any answering machines, fax machines, and telephones should be plugged into the back of the computer, and the computer should be plugged *directly* into the wall.

On the software side, make sure you have a driver made especially for your modem. While a generic modem driver may work with your modem, a new driver supplied by the manufacturer of your modem might enable higher connect speeds (such as 33,600 bps for 28,800 bps modems), as well as better error correction and compression.

Printers

Old printer cables commonly cause problems, such as lost data and slow printing. Your printer cable should be new and securely fastened at both ends. Although long printer cables can be convenient, shorter ones are more reliable and may provide faster printing. Don't use a longer cable than is necessary. Additionally, some computers have more than one printer port. If yours has two or more, try them all, as one or more may be bidirectional, which should yield faster printing. Remove any switching boxes or printer sharing devices unless they are absolutely necessary. As far as the software goes, most of the drivers included with Windows should work fine. In fact, many new printers come with special software that allows you to control the printer on-screen but usually requires lots of memory and disk space. If Windows supports your printer without this special software, use the Windows driver instead for the fastest printing.

If your printer is shared by two or more computers over a workgroup, the printer should be connected to the computer that uses the printer the most. See "Network cards," the next section, for more tips.

Network cards

You should be using the most recent drivers for all of your network adapters for the best performance. Since longer cables can contribute to lost data, you shouldn't use cabling longer than is necessary. Some network adapters come with special software, while others are installed with third-party network operating systems. Windows will always perform best over a network if it's using its own native 32-bit drivers, and not older drivers loaded in AUTOEXEC.BAT or CONFIG.SYS. See "Do I Still Need CONFIG.SYS and AUTOEXEC.BAT?" in Chapter 6 for more information. Furthermore, Windows has a tendency to install more drivers than are truly necessary for the type of connection you're using. See Chapter 7, *Networking*, for more information on the drivers required for your connection, and try removing all unnecessary ones. Extra drivers not only waste memory but slow network communications as well.

Sound cards

Many sound cards come with DOS drivers and other DOS configuration software. These drivers may be necessary for DOS games, but they are almost never needed in Windows. These drivers take up valuable memory, slow system startup, and may cause slowdowns when you try to use sound in Windows. See "Do I Still Need CONFIG.SYS and AUTOEXEC.BAT?" in Chapter 6 for more information on removing these drivers. Make sure you have the most recent drivers for your sound card (obtained from the manufacturer). Newer drivers may add new features, such as full duplex (used for Internet communication programs) and advanced mixer and sound recording utilities.

Mice

If you have any software that came with your mouse, it's probably unnecessary and just taking up memory and disk space. Unless you need it for some advanced features, such as using the third mouse button, you should remove the software, as Windows supports most mice out of the box. This doesn't include any special mouse drivers that may be needed, but rather the "utilities" package (such as "Intelli-point" for Microsoft mice or "Mouseware" for Logitech mice) that may have come with your mouse. Other than that, keep the ball clean, and use a clean mouse pad for best performance.

Double-click on the Mouse icon in Control Panel to adjust the sensitivity of your mouse. You can also adjust the double-click speed and turn on "pointer tails" to increase visibility on laptop displays. Since the mouse is a primary method of input, fine-tuning these settings can go a long way to improving your relationship with your mouse.

Keyboards

Double-click on the Keyboard icon in Control Panel to adjust the various settings of your keyboard. Moving the Repeat Rate slider all the way to the left will make your computer seem faster, especially when scrolling through a long document or moving the cursor through a lot of text. The Repeat Delay is different, though. Just adjust this to your liking, and test the setting below.

Sticky keys can slow things down as well. You can pull your keys off one by one and remove whatever is caught underneath. Some people have been successful cleaning the entire keyboard by immersing it in plain water (unplugged, of course), and then waiting for it to dry. Keyboards are cheap; you might as well replace it if it's not in top condition.

Everything else

Keep it clean, keep it cool, and make sure you have the latest drivers.

Software

Apart from using the latest versions of all the software in your computer, the one major piece of software that can gain the most from configuration and tweaking is Windows itself. Keep in mind, however, that one can accomplish only so much by fine-tuning Windows. Fine-tuning your hardware and upgrading still remain the best ways to maximize performance.

Stopping Windows 95 from Wildly Accessing Your Hard Disk •

Many users who have installed Windows 95 without taking the time to customize the way it uses the hard disk are disappointed to find that it frequently seizes up for up to a minute because of random, pointless disk activity. This is due to the way that Windows 95 is set to handle disk caching and virtual memory. Windows 95 loads drivers and applications into memory until it's full, and then starts to use part of your hard disk to "swap" out information, freeing up more memory for high-priority tasks. This type of "virtual memory" can slow performance significantly if it's not configured correctly. Although Windows 95 instructs you to "let Windows handle disk cache settings" for best results, this obviously does not yield the best results. Here's how to eliminate the random disk activity and improve system performance:

Part 1: Virtual Memory

- Right-click on the My Computer icon, select **Properties**, and choose the **Performance** tab.

- Click **Virtual Memory**, and then select **Let me specify my own virtual memory settings**.

- The location and size of your swapfile are now displayed in front of you. If you want to choose a different drive for your swapfile, run Disk Defragmenter on that drive first, and then select it here.

- Specify the same value for the **Minimum size** and the **Maximum size**, so Windows 95 won't spend so much time resizing the file. A good size is roughly **two and a half** times the amount of installed RAM (i.e., create a **40** megabyte swapfile if you have **16** megabytes of RAM).

- Press **OK**, and then **OK** again, and confirm that you want to restart your computer.

Part 2: Defragmenting the swapfile

- One of the reasons that the default settings yield such poor performance is that since the swapfile grows and shrinks with use, it quickly becomes very fragmented (broken up). Once you've set the swapfile size to be constant (see Part 1), you won't have to worry that it will become fragmented again. However, you'll need to defragment it at least once for it to remain that way in the future.

- If you have Norton Utilities 95 (with Speedisk), you'll be able to optimize the swapfile without moving it.

- If you don't have such a utility and have the time to do it right, you can defragment it manually. If you have more than one partition or hard disk in your system, you can defragment the swapfile by moving it from partition to partition. First, defragment a partition other than the one containing the swapfile. Then move the swapfile to that partition (keeping its size constant). Then defragment the original drive, and move the swapfile back.

- Although it's also possible to disable the swapfile entirely while you defragment the drive (and then reenable it so it will be recreated whole), it isn't advisable because Windows 95 may not be able to start without a swapfile.

Part 3: Virtual cache*

- Open the file *system.ini* for editing using a plain text editor, such as Notepad.

- Add the following two lines to the [vcache] section (add the section if it's not there):

```
MinFileCache=4096
MaxFileCache=4096
```

- These values, in kilobytes, regulate the size of the VCache, so you can stop it from filling up all available RAM and paging all loaded apps to disk. If you have more than 16 mb of RAM, then set the above values (both of them) to about 25 percent of the amount of installed RAM.

- See Chapter 3 for more information on INI files.

Part 4: RAM

- You may have thought we overlooked the obvious: add more RAM! The more memory you have, the less frequently Windows 95 will use your hard disk, and the better your system performance will be.

---

* Only if you have 16 megabytes of RAM or more.

- Since Windows 95 isn't very efficient or compact (by any stretch of the imagination), you'll need to feed it as much memory as you can afford. Eight megabytes is the absolute minimum, but 16 is much better. If you have the money, 32 megabytes will make Windows 95 fly.

- When Windows 95 was first released, 32 megabytes of RAM cost around a thousand dollars. That same memory at the time of this writing can be purchased for around $130. See "Upgrading Your Computer" later in this chapter for more information.

What to Throw Away

When you first install Windows, your hard disk is littered with files you don't need. Whether you need a particular file can be subjective, so it is assumed that if you feel you don't need WordPad, you can go ahead and delete it. Note that deleting files from your system can cause Windows to stop functioning, so it's better to move, rename, or back up files before deleting them for good. Here are some files that can be deleted.

In the root directory of your boot drive (usually C:\)

- Any files with the extensions *.TXT, *.PRV, *.LOG, *.OLD, *.- - -, and *.DOS (unless you use the dual-boot feature).

- If you don't plan on uninstalling Windows 95, you can delete *win95undo.dat* (if it's there).

In your Windows directory

- Anything with the extensions *.LOG, *.OLD, *.- - -, *.BAK, and *.000, *.001, *.002 (and so on).

- Almost any files with the following dates can also be deleted, as they belong to old versions of Windows:

  03/10/92—Windows 3.1
  09/30/92—Windows for Workgroups 3.1
  11/01/93—Windows for Workgroups 3.11
  12/31/93—Windows 3.11

- If you've upgraded your Windows 95 system to Windows NT 4.0, you should also be able to delete any files dated 7/11/95.

- Do a search (select **Find**, **Files** or **Folders** from the **Start Menu**) and search for any *.BMP and *.TXT files in the Windows directory. Use QuickView to view them, and delete them if desired.

In your Windows\System directory

The entire WIN32S directory under your System directory is used only in Windows 3.x to allow certain 32-bit applications to run, but some older applications install it in Windows 95, or may be around if you upgraded from an earlier version of Windows. If you remove this directory, make sure to remove any references to it in your *SYSTEM.INI* file, and restart Windows.

In your Temp directory (usually Windows\Temp)

Ideally, all files in this directory are placed here temporarily by open applications and automatically deleted when not in use. Therefore, you should never delete any files that may be in use. However, many applications don't behave and forget to delete these files. If you find files in your Temp directory that have a date or time *earlier* than the last time you started your computer, you can delete them. Additionally, if you exit Windows, you can safely delete any files in that directory, as none of them will be in use when Windows isn't running.

Anywhere else on your system

- Other files that can be deleted include *mscreate.dir*, an absolutely useless, empty, hidden file created by Microsoft's newer installation programs. There may be hundreds of these empty files on your hard disk (see Slack Space in the Glossary).

- *~msssetup.t* is a temporary directory created during the installation of a program and can be freely deleted if it still exists after an installation is complete.

- If you're trying to create more disk space, you may want to delete help files (**.HLP*) for applications that don't need them (see "Notes and other issues" below). Also, many applications include bitmaps (**.BMP*), which take up enormous amounts of disk space for virtually no reason.

- Some programs (including the tutorial that comes with Windows) insist on installing video clips (**.AVI, *.MOV,* and **.MPG*) to your hard drive. These files can be quite large, each eating up to several megabytes of disk space. To see what the video contains before deleting it, double-click on it to open the appropriate video player.

Files not to delete

- Any files from your SYSBCKUP directory. These files are used to store backups of important system files that may become corrupted or overwritten by older applications.

- Your Registry (*system.dat, system.da0, user.dat, user.da0*), as well as *system.1st* (in the root directory of your boot drive), which you can use if the Registry in use becomes corrupted.

- Any files in your root directory, as well as the Windows and Windows/System folders not already mentioned.

- Files and folders in your Program Files or Windows\MSAPPS directory that have names like Microsoft Shared and Common Files. These files can be used by several applications simultaneously, which is why they haven't been placed in the folders of the applications that put them there.

If in doubt

- If you're not sure if something should be deleted but want to try anyway, try moving it to another directory first to see if everything works without it for a day or so.

- Check the file's date. If it's recent, most likely it's still being used. For information on removing a particular application, contact the manufacturer of that application, or refer to the application's documentation.

- See "Clean up and Customize System Folders" earlier in this chapter for more information on all the extra empty folders that Windows won't let you delete.

Notes and other issues

See "Getting Rid of WinHelp's Contents Screen" in Chapter 2 for more information on the several files that may be created on the fly for use with help files and which ones may be deleted.

Upgrading Your Computer

When asked which component is the most important in a system, the answer is both easy and impossible. On one hand, all of the components work together to form a complete system and therefore are equally important to a well-tuned computer. On the other hand, the quality and speed of certain components can affect the overall system performance and efficiency more than others. Additionally, certain parts that are important to some users may be insignificant or even unnecessary to others. One thing that is for sure is that a single component can be a significant bottleneck, hindering the performance of the rest of the system.

Computers are designed to be completely modular; nearly all the parts in one computer are upgradable and interchangeable with those found in other computers. Upgrading single components rather than replacing the entire system is usually much less expensive and allows you to spread out the cost of a new computer over a long period of time. If many components in your system need upgrading, however, you may be better off buying an entirely new system. That way, you'll have two working computers rather than one machine and a pile of obsolete parts. If you're upgrading several computers, you may be lucky enough to combine the leftover parts into an entirely new system.

When purchasing a new system, you should be aware that the quality of the components is usually below what you'd get if you bought the components separately. Computer system vendors make more money by including substandard, generic parts in their systems rather than name-brand, top-of-the-line components. If you know how to build a computer from scratch and have the time, you're usually better off doing so for this reason. Most companies allow you to customize your system with various components so make sure you demand the best. Some companies, especially the larger mail-order firms, tend to include a long list of top-of-the-line components for one low price, so shop around. When buying a new system, look at more than just the CPU speed and the sticker price.

Name-brand components are important in that you know they'll be supported in the years to come. Many users were disappointed to find out, for example, that they were unable to get appropriate drivers for their no-name video cards when Windows 95 was released and were forced to use generic drivers or replace the cards altogether. A good test for a hardware manufacturer is to see if it still supports products it stopped making years ago. Check the technical support area of a company's Internet Web site to see if it has drivers and troubleshooting information for old products. If it supports yesterday's products today, it's likely to support today's products tomorrow. If a company doesn't have some kind of support on the Internet, it's time to choose a different company. Do your research before you spend a dime.

Since a computer is just the sum of its parts, you can improve an existing system or know what to look for in a new system by being able to choose the components effectively. There are some general considerations to keep in mind in choosing new components. For example, if you buy something you know is going to be obsolete in a half-year, such as the CPU, don't buy the top of the line, as the extra money will be getting you close to nothing in the long run. However, spending a lot on a good monitor that will last for years and years is smart and will pay off in the long run.

Monitors

The monitor is arguably the most important single component in a computer system, and next to the printer, usually the most expensive. My advice to those looking for a new computer is that it's best to take some money out of the budget for the computer and spend it on the monitor. *Don't skimp here.* Your monitor is what you spend the most time looking at, and your eyes will thank you for choosing wisely, especially if you wear corrective lenses or are prone to headaches. The monitor is the component least likely to become obsolete. A good monitor will probably outlast every other component in your system, so it's the best place to put your money.

A large, clear monitor makes your computer more pleasing to use. Don't settle for anything less than a 15-inch display. If you can afford it, invest in a 17-inch monitor and postpone that CPU upgrade for a while. Look for a flat, square screen surface. Bulging, round screens are old and ugly, and distort images. You'll want lots of controls to adjust not only brightness and contrast, but image size and position, color temperature, rotation, and the "pincushion" effect. Insist on digital controls (push buttons). Analog controls (dials) don't have memories, so you'll need to adjust the controls every time you change the video mode (which happens more frequently than you may think). Don't waste your money on built-in speakers unless you have limited desk space or can afford the novelty. Separate speakers provide better sound and save you some money.

Go to one of those big computer stores and carefully compare all of the available monitors in your budget. It's important to get one you like and don't be afraid to ask who makes the picture tube inside. This is an important factor when considering a laptop as well. There aren't any laptop screens currently available that are as good as the cheapest Desktop monitors, so if your eyes are bad and you don't need the portability, go for a Desktop system.

Video cards (also known as display adapters)

The video card is what puts the image on your monitor, so a faster video card will mean a faster display. The video card is responsible for the resolution, color depth, and refresh rate. The resolution (the number of pixels on the screen) and the color depth (the maximum number of colors that can be displayed simultaneously) are both dependent on the amount of memory on the card. The more memory on a video card, the better. Higher resolutions and more colors mean better picture quality. The refresh rate is not the speed at which your video card can draw things on the screen but rather how many times per second the image on the screen is redrawn. If your screen flickers, the refresh rate isn't high enough. Make sure your video card supports a resolution of 1024 × 768, a color depth of 65,536 colors, and a refresh rate of at least 72 Hz.

Most video cards on the market today are accelerated, meaning that they can do certain calculations so that your CPU doesn't have to. Faster video cards produce smoother animation, better-quality video, faster-scrolling text in your word processor, and windows that snap into place rather than crawl. Newer cards even accelerate certain types of 3D graphics. These types of cards often rely on special controller chips on the card itself. If your video card has a common controller chip rather than a proprietary one, your card is more likely to be supported by the software you wish to run.

If your computer has VLB (vesa local bus) or PCI (peripheral computer interconnect) slots (see "Motherboards," the following section), get a video card of the same type. These cards run faster than normal cards but don't cost much more. If you're also considering upgrading your CPU and motherboard, your money is best spent on a new PCI card rather than a VLB card, meaning that this would be a good time to upgrade that old 486 to a Pentium. It's important to have a brand-name video card; no-name or clone video cards aren't widely supported and can be difficult to get to work in later versions of Windows. Make sure the manufacturer has drivers made especially for your version of Windows before you buy.

Motherboards

The motherboard holds the CPU chip, the memory, and all of the expansion cards. Different motherboards have different features, but you should choose a motherboard that matches the type of CPU you wish to use. For example, you'll need a Pentium-class motherboard to use a Pentium chip. Most motherboards support a wide range of CPU speeds, so it's best to choose a motherboard that can accommodate a faster chip later.

Since the motherboard also connects all of your expansion cards, you'll need one that has lots of slots, all of the right kind. The basic type, ISA (industry standard architecture), has been around for 15 years and is what most cards plug into. EISA is an enhancement of this architecture but isn't worth the additional money. For 486-class systems, look for boards with VLB slots, which allow VLB cards to run faster than normal ISA cards. For Pentium systems, you'll want PCI slots for your cards. Devices that commonly use these types of slots include video cards, hard disk controllers, SCSI controllers, and some network cards. New motherboards never come with more than eight slots, but the stingier manufacturers include only five or six slots on their boards. Insist on as many as you can get.

A good motherboard has built-in serial and parallel ports, as well as a built-in hard disk controller, lots of slots for additional memory (four is the norm, but six or eight is better), and a large secondary cache (256 K or larger). A motherboard with lots of jumpers and switches can be difficult to configure, so look for boards with only a few, well-labeled jumpers. In fact, make sure *all* of the connectors are clearly labeled in English, and not simply numbered. The last tip is to look for a motherboard made in the U.S.A. They're getting rare, but are definitely worth it.

CPU

The processor docs all the work—and what becomes obsolete the fastest. Don't settle for anything less than a Pentium chip, but you don't necessarily need to get the fastest one. The faster the processor speed (measured in megahertz), the faster your computer will be. Do some math before deciding, however. Divide the processor speed by the price to get the megahertz-per-dollar of each chip. You'll find that the fastest chips are rarely the best deal. True, a faster chip will last longer before it needs to be upgraded, but the extra money to get the top of the line today won't matter so much when it's time to upgrade later. You're best bet is one or two steps below the top of the line, if you can afford it. If money is tight, go for a slower processor. You can always upgrade later if you have a motherboard that supports faster chips.

Your motherboard must support the chip you put into it, so unless you buy a new motherboard, you might only be able to get a faster 486 than what you already have. That said, compare the price of a new chip with that of a new motherboard and chip. For example, upgrading your 486-33 processor with a 486-100 processor won't require a new motherboard but also won't yield the performance increase of a new Pentium motherboard and chip. Additionally, if you plan on getting a new video card, your money is better spent on a PCI card than a VLB card, meaning that this would be a good time to upgrade that old 486 to a Pentium.

Remember to get a fan to mount on that chip as well. A well-cooled processor will last longer and perform better.

Memory

The more memory, the better. When Windows 95 was released, the price of memory was nearly the same as it had been for the previous three years. By the time Windows NT 4.0 had been released, the price of memory had dropped 85 percent, making a memory upgrade an inexpensive way to improve performance.

Most memory comes in SIMMs (single inline memory modules), small circuit boards holding a varying number of memory chips. You must choose the type of SIMM that your computer requires, including the number of pins (usually 30 or 72) and the speed (usually 60 or 70 nanoseconds). Since 60 ns SIMMs are faster and don't usually cost any more than 70 ns, they're a better investment.

Adding more memory to a computer will almost always result in better performance. Windows loads drivers, applications, and documents into memory until it's full. Once there's no more memory available, Windows starts storing chunks of memory on the hard disk (in the form of your swap file) to make room in memory for more information. Since your hard disk is quite a bit slower than memory, this swapping noticeably slows your system. The more memory you have, the less often Windows will use your hard disk in this way, and the faster your system will be.

While Windows 95 requires a minimum of 8 megabytes of RAM, and Windows NT requires at least 16 megabytes, you're most certainly better off with 16 and 32, respectively. If you use a lot of graphics programs, such as Photoshop, you'll benefit from even more memory.

Computer case

The computer case doesn't directly affect performance, but there are differences in designs that warrant attention. Look for a case with several fans for better cooling, plenty of drive bays for future expansion, and easy access. A well-designed case won't have sharp edges inside and won't require you to dismantle the entire computer to accomplish something as simple as adding more memory. Some newer cases can be opened without even a screwdriver, making that task just a little easier.

Hard disks

A hard disk should be fast, capacious, and reliable. Look for a solid brand rather than a close-out deal. Get the largest capacity you can afford because you'll use it. Probably the most important feature, however, is the speed. The speed of a hard disk is measured in two quantities: access time and transfer rate. The access time, measured in milliseconds, is the average length of time required to find information, and the transfer rate, measured in megabytes per second, is the speed that the drive can transfer data to your system. While the access time is almost always quoted with the capacity of a drive (look for 11 ms or smaller), the transfer rate isn't always publicized. However, if you're looking for maximum performance, it's a good thing to look for. Lower access times and higher transfer rates are better.

Hard disks today come in two primary flavors: SCSI and IDE. IDE drives plug into an IDE controller, which often is built into the motherboard. SCSI drives require an expensive adapter (see "SCSI Controllers" later in this chapter), but if you already have one, it's not an issue. IDE drives are generally cheaper and nearly as fast as SCSI drives. Installation is relatively easy as well. SCSI drives, while more expensive, offer benefits such as larger available capacities, faster transfer rates and access times, and easier installation. SCSI hard disks, like other SCSI devices, can also be external, a handy feature if you don't have any free space or just want to share the drive between multiple computers. If you're seriously considering either of these, refer to the discussions of the respective controllers, which follow.

Hard disk controllers

The hard disk controller is what your hard disk and floppy drives plug into. With the exception of SCSI controllers (see the following section), the discussion of hard disk controllers focuses on IDE controllers. IDE is a very inexpensive solution; the controller is either built into the motherboard or is available as an expansion card, costing no more than around $15. If your controller is built into your motherboard (a good thing to look for in a new motherboard), you don't need one. Otherwise, look for the cheapest one you can find; they're all the same. Most include parallel and serial ports for printers and mice, respectively. Look for a card where the jumpers or switches are labeled in English *on the card*. There are more expensive IDE controllers available, but unless you really need the advanced options they offer, don't bother.

An IDE controller can support up to two drives. Some cards come with two IDE controllers, bringing the total up to four. You can plug IDE hard disks and IDE CD-ROM drives into an IDE controller, but once you've hit the limit, that's it. See "SCSI Controllers," the following section, for a comparison.

SCSI controllers

SCSI adapters can be used with any SCSI devices, including hard disks, CD-ROM drives, scanners, tape drives, removable cartridge . drives, optical drives, and CD recorders. There are several varieties of SCSI, including SCSI-1, SCSI-2, Fast SCSI-2, SCSI-3, Ultra-SCSI, Wide-SCSI, and UltraWide-SCSI. For most users, SCSI-2 is sufficient, but check the requirements of all of the devices you intend to use with it to see what you'll need.

A good SCSI controller will have its own BIOS, so you can boot off your SCSI hard disk. Look for a Plug & Play SCSI adapter in either a PCI or VLB variety (see "Motherboards" previously in this chapter) for best performance. Controllers with bus mastering offer better performance than those without, as well as being less of a burden on the rest of the system while in use. It's very important to get a solid brand-name SCSI controller to ensure compatibility with any SCSI devices you intend to use, as well as to make obtaining the latest drivers for any version of Windows easy.

The two most common devices used with an SCSI controller are hard disks and CD-ROM drives. Since these two drives are also available in IDE (see "Hard Disk Controllers," covered earlier), there's usually a choice to be made between SCSI and IDE. Since you can mix and match devices (you can have an IDE CD-ROM drive and a SCSI hard disk, or vice versa), you'll never be entirely committed to your decision. The primary advantage to IDE is that IDE controllers are cheap, and IDE devices are usually less expensive than their SCSI counterparts. SCSI devices offer better performance than IDE devices, and the higher end SCSI controllers don't burden the system as IDE controllers do. While most IDE controllers support only two hard disks, SCSI adapters support up to seven. SCSI is more flexible, supporting many different kinds of devices, while IDE controllers support only hard disks and CD-ROM drives. An SCSI device can be internal (mounted inside your computer), or external (in its own case, connected with a cable to your computer). IDE devices can only be internal. If you don't plan on using other SCSI devices, such as a scanner or CD recorder, you probably don't need to spend the extra money for an SCSI controller. Refer to "Hard Disks," already covered, and "CD-ROM Drives," the next section, for more details.

CD-ROM drives

A CD-ROM drive should do two things well—it should be fast, and it should recognize all of the different types of CDs you want to use: CD-ROMs, multisession CDs, recordable CDs, audio-CDs, PhotoCD, and enhanced-CDs (sometimes called CD-Plus). The speed of a CD-ROM drive is measured by how much faster it is than a normal audio-CD player; a quad-speed drive is obviously four times faster. The two numbers to look for in your CD drive are access time and transfer rate. The access time, measured in milliseconds, is the average length of time required to find information, and the transfer rate, measured in kilobytes per second, is the speed that the drive can transfer data to your system. CD-ROM drives are much slower than hard disks, so access times will be in the range of 120 ms to 300 ms, as opposed to 8 ms to 14 ms for hard disks. Look for an access time of 200 ms or smaller. The transfer rate is about 150 kilobytes per second times the speed of the drive. A quad-speed drive should have a transfer rate of about 600 kilobytes per second. Lower access times and higher transfer rates are better.

The brand of CD drive you purchase isn't that important. Windows should support nearly anything you throw at it. In fact, CD drives are getting to be as common as floppy drives; so as long as it's fast and supports all of the different types of CDs, it should be all right. The more expensive drives aren't necessarily any better than the cheap ones. The only choices worth mentioning are the loading mechanism and whether the drive is IDE or SCSI. There are two types of loading mechanisms: motorized tray and caddy. The caddy is a cartridge that holds the CD and helps keep dust out of the drive and away from the CD. Motorized trays are less expensive, more common, and don't require caddies. Just place the CD on a tray that extends out of the drive, and close it. The problem with motorized trays is that nearly all of them are very flimsy and easily breakable. Look for a sturdy drive, if nothing else.

The other choice is between IDE and SCSI. IDE drives plug into an IDE controller, which often is built into the motherboard. SCSI drives require an expensive adapter, but if you already have one, it's not an issue. IDE drives are generally cheaper and are nearly as fast as SCSI drives. Installation is relatively easy as well. SCSI drives, while more expensive, offer benefits such as faster transfer rates and easier installation, and they don't burden the system as much as IDE drives when they're in use. SCSI CD drives, like other SCSI devices, can also be external, a handy feature if you don't have any free space in your case or just want to share the drive between multiple computers. If you're seriously considering either of these, refer to the discussions of the respective controllers in previous sections.

Modems

A modem allows your computer to communicate with other computers over standard telephone lines. Modems need to support dozens of different protocols (languages), but nearly all modems today support all of the protocols you'll need. The primary considerations are speed and price. Faster modems are more expensive, but since many online services (including the phone company) charge you for connect time, you shouldn't skimp here. Don't settle for less than 28,800 bps. Some modems go up to 33,600 bps. Look for a brand name; you want to be sure not only that your software supports the modem but that it is going to be supported in the future.

ISDN adapters technically aren't modems, but basically they perform the same task. If you are able to get an ISDN phone line into your home or office (contact the phone company) and can afford the extra expense of the adapter and service, this will offer much better performance than any modem.

Sound cards

A good sound card is Soundblaster-compatible. Look for lots of features, such as 16-bit sound, wavetable, a CD-ROM connector (so you don't need another controller), 32 voices, Plug & Play support, and a MIDI connector. Some sound cards support 3D sound, although it isn't worth it unless you have the software to take advantage of it. Get yourself a fairly good set of speakers, but don't spend too much. Your computer isn't able to produce sound quality high enough to take advantage of them.

Network cards

The most important feature of a network card is compatibility. Make sure it is able to communicate with the rest of your network and comes with drivers for your version of Windows. Buying a name brand will help ensure that you'll always be able to find drivers. Look for a Plug & Play network card, but don't waste your money on a VLB or PCI card unless you really need the extra performance. See Chapter 7 for more information on setting up a local network.

Printers

There's such a wide range of printers available that it's impossible to cover all of the choices. The decision is usually based on your budget and your needs. Get a solid brand-name printer; a good printer should be a workhorse, lasting for years. The choice is usually between inkjet and laser printers. Laser printers are more expensive, faster, and have better print quality than inkjet printers. Inkjet printers are less expensive, take up less space, and often print color.

A laser printer should have a resolution of at least 600 dpi (dots per inch; higher numbers are better) and should print at least six pages per minute. Some printers go up to 16 pages per minute. Check the price of a new toner cartridge for each printer you're considering, as this can be an expensive maintenance consideration.

Inkjet printers are also available in 600 dpi, and commonly print 3 to 5 pages per minute. Look for support for color, even if you don't think you'll need it. If you do get a color printer, make sure it has at least two cartridges: one for black printing and one for color. Some older color printers require you to swap cartridges whether you're printing black text or color. You can't do both at the same time.

Mice

Cheap mice don't last long. Try lots of different kinds, and choose one that's sturdy, comfortable, and not too ugly. Make sure the ball is placed under your fingers instead of under your palm for greater control. It should have a long cord and a plug with thumb screws so you don't need a screwdriver.

Some mice have two buttons, and some have three. Windows uses only two, but a third button can be programmed to take over other operations, such as double-clicking or pasting text. Three buttons aren't necessarily better than two, however—just different. (Unless the mouse won't work without it, don't bother installing the software that comes with your mouse.)

Personally, I hate mice. I use a pressure-sensitive, cordless, battery-less stylus on a tablet. A stylus is just a pen, and the tablet is just what the pen draws on. The pen is more comfortable, more precise, more natural, more fun, and more flexible than any mouse. My advice: Try a tablet before you invest in another rodent.

Keyboards

Get yourself a solid keyboard. The brand doesn't matter. Just make sure it has a long cord and isn't too hideous. Too many keyboards are flimsy and cheap. Shop around to find one with a solid feel and good-quality keys. Some people like soft-touch (mushy) keyboards, while others like tactile (clicky) keyboards. Get one that suits your taste and won't hinder your work. Additionally, ergonomic keyboards are now getting affordable. Some of the more radical designs have split, adjustable keyboards, curved to fit the motion and shape of your hands. Try these before buying, as they aren't for everyone. If you're worried about hand injury, see a doctor, or at least get yourself one of those soft, gel-filled wrist-wrests. Some keyboards have a few extra keys made especially for Windows 95, providing quick access to the **Start Menu** and other things. Don't spend any extra money for this type of keyboard, but some people like them.

Tape drives, removable cartridge drives, and CD recorders

These types of drives allow you to store a lot of data on special media. Research the cost of the cartridges before investing, however. A drive that seems like a good deal in the store may turn out to be a money pit when you take into account the expensive media. Try comparing your cost to store, say, a thousand megabytes (one gigabyte) using a certain drive, including the cost of both the drive and the media. Other things to consider are speed, reliability, and availability of the media. Don't forget portability. How likely are others able to read these cartridges?

Improving Work Habits

What follows is a collection of tips and tricks, keyboard shortcuts, and additional software that can make the time spent in front of your computer more efficient.

Tips and Tricks

Search the Registry

You can learn a lot from using the Search command in the Registry Editor. Even if you don't edit any information (it's good to play it safe), just looking at your Registry can provide valuable insight to nagging problems. See Chapter 3 for more information on the Registry and the Registry Editor.

Clean up your hard disk

By erasing unneeded files and folders on your hard disk, you'll not only get more space but will make your drive faster and more responsive. Additionally, removing drivers and applications that are no longer used will clear more memory for your other applications, which can substantially improve overall system performance. Be careful, however. Removing files that are still needed can cause some applications, or even Windows 95 itself, to stop functioning. It's always good practice to move any files in question to a different directory or drive (or just simply rename them) before deleting them entirely. Again, backing up your entire hard disk is very important. See "What to Throw Away" earlier in this chapter and "Do I Still Need CONFIG.SYS and AUTOEXEC.BAT?" in Chapter 6 for details.

Use file extensions

Start by opening the My Computer window, selecting **Options** from the **View** menu, and choosing the **View** tab. Turn off the **Hide MS-DOS file extensions for file types that are registered** option, and click **OK**. This will display the three-letter filename extensions that are normally hidden by Windows. These extensions not only tell Windows what to do with a file, but can tell *you* what to with it as well. For example, files with the .TXT extension and .INI extension both open Notepad when you double-click on them, but they are intrinsically different types of files. Another consequence of this design flaw in Windows is that some documents have the same icon as the applications that use them. For example, if your word processor has the same icon as the documents it creates and your file extensions are hidden, you won't be able to tell the difference between the program itself (with the .EXE extension) and your documents.

Speed up the Start Menu

In the Registry Editor (see Chapter 3 for details), go to HKEY_CURRENT_USER\Control Panel\desktop, and add a string value named MenuShowDelay, with a value specifying the delay (in milliseconds) between the time you click on a menu and the time it actually opens. A value of 400 is default, and smaller numbers are faster. Try 0 (zero) for the fastest response. See "Stopping Menus from Following the Mouse" in Chapter 4, *Advanced Customization Techniques*, for more information.

Change a file association on the fly

You know that when you double-click on certain files, the associated application is opened with the file. If you select **Options** from Explorer's **View** menu and choose the **File Types** tab, you'll see a list of all of these associations. While you can change any of them with the **Edit** button, there's a faster way. Hold the Shift key while right-clicking on a file, and select **Open With...** to choose a new program to use with that file type. See "Customizing Context Menus" in Chapter 4 for more information on file types.

Edit the Send To menu

When you right-click on any file icon, one of your choices is to send the file to a list of other places, such as floppy drives and other applications. You can configure this list by removing or adding desired shortcuts to the Send To folder (usually C:\Windows\SendTo). Just drag-drop any folders, programs, or drive icons into this folder to add their shortcuts to the **Send To** menu. A good trick is to drag a shortcut for the Send To folder into the Send To folder itself. It makes it easy to add new objects later.

Index all the files on your system

Select **Find** and then **Files or Folders** from the **Start Menu**, select a drive (or use My Computer for all drives), and click **Find Now** without specifying anything in the **Named** field. This may take a few seconds but will list all of the files on the selected drive. You can then sort the results by clicking on the appropriate column heading, especially useful for finding the largest or most recent file on your system. You can then double-click any file shown to open it, or drag-drop it somewhere else, as though you were looking at the folder containing the file.

Better floppy formats

Although you can right-click on a floppy drive in Explorer or My Computer and select **Format** to format a floppy or other drive, there's a better way (albeit slightly more laborious). Type Format a: /u at the MS-DOS prompt (substitute A: for whatever drive letter you wish). Using DOS instead of Windows to format floppies will yield better multitasking; you'll be able to do other things while formatting floppies (strange how Windows multitasks DOS programs better than Windows applications in this case). Furthermore, using the /u parameter specifies an unconditional format, meaning that it won't save unformat information, yielding a faster format and more free diskette space. This format isn't available in Windows. To erase a floppy, type Format a: /u/q. This is much quicker than a full format, but will not ensure an error-free disk (see Chapter 6 for more information). If Format reports any bad sectors, throw away that floppy immediately.

Load Doskey in a DOS box automatically

Right-click on *DOSPRMPT.PIF* (in your **Start Menu** folder), and select **Properties**. This file is used by default to load the command prompt. Choose the **Program** tab, and enter DOSKEY in the field labeled **Batch File**. Doskey is a little toy that comes with Windows as well as with previous versions of DOS which keeps a memory of all the commands you enter in DOS. Use the up and down cursor keys to cycle through commands you've typed before.

Limit access to others

Load up the System Policy Editor (poledit.exe), located on your Windows 95 CD-ROM in the Admin\Apptools\Poledit folder. If you have the floppy disk version of Windows 95, see "Software and the Internet" in the Preface. If you are asked to "open a template file," choose *admin.adm* in the same folder, and click **OK**. Select **Open**

Registry from the **File** menu, and then double-click on the Local User icon. `Open Local_User\ Shell\` Restrictions for the most useful of these settings. Set the desired options here, and select **Save** from the **File** menu when you're finished.

Useful Windows 3.x programs that didn't make it to the new version

There are a few programs that came with earlier versions of Windows that aren't included in Windows 95 or Windows NT. While they are older, 16-bit programs, they do provide some functionality that otherwise isn't supported. Cardfile (*cardfile.exe*) is a simple electronic address book. The Macro Recorder (*recorder.exe*) allows you to record and play back series of mouse movements and keystrokes, although it may not work with some newer applications. Although Windows 95 and Windows NT have replaced Write (*write.exe*) with Wordpad, you won't be able to save .WRI files. If you still need to write to Write files, you can still use the old Write utility. Before you delete that old DOS directory, make sure that there's a new counterpart in the Windows\Command directory. If not, you should be able to use it with your version of Windows.

Use the DOS prompt

The DOS prompt can still do some things that Windows can't. For example, you can rename multiple files with wildcards (type `ren *.TXT *.DOC` to rename all *.TXT* files to *.DOC* files). Print out directory listings by using the *dir* command (try it with the /b switch). See "Printing Out a Directory Listing" in Chapter 4 for more information. You can quickly print any text file by typing `copy filename.txt lpt1:`, where `filename.txt` is the filename of the file you wish to print, and `lpt1` signifies printer port #1 (use `lpt2` for port 2). Finally, the DOS *Attrib* command allows you to view the attributes (read-only, system, hidden, and archive) of all the files in a directory simultaneously (Windows NT can do this, too), and it will allow you to turn on or off the system attribute of a file—something that right-clicking on a file and selecting Properties won't allow you to do. See Appendix B for more information.

Use the task list

Taskman is really a holdover from earlier versions of Windows. You can use it to activate certain applications that don't seem to respond when you click their buttons on the taskbar. You can also use it to end any running program—useful when the program won't respond and safer than pressing `Ctrl-Alt-Del`.

Speed up system bootup

There are several factors that can affect the amount of time it takes for your computer to load Windows:

- You don't have enough free RAM—you should have a minimum of 8 megabytes, but 16 is better.

- Your hard disk is too slow—try optimizing it using the Disk Defragmenter. If you have some money burning a hole in your pocket, you might want to invest in a new, fast, huge hard disk.

- You don't have enough free disk space for a sizable swapfile. You should have 20 to 40 megabytes of free disk space (including the size of the swapfile, *Win386.swp*).

- You have 850 fonts installed—if you can survive without all those fonts, try removing 600 to 700 of them to see if that makes a difference.

- Your network drivers (LAN, Dial-Up Networking) take too long to load. Try disabling them to see if it makes a difference.

- If you're using Windows 95, there's a timed delay when you first turn on your computer that you can eliminate. Using a plain text editor, such as Notepad, edit your *MSDOS.SYS* file in the root directory of your boot drive (usually C:\). It's hidden, so you'll have to unhide it before editing it. Add BootDelay=0 to the [Options] section of the file, and save. For more information, see Appendix D, *Contents of MSDOS.SYS FILE*.

Remove DriveSpace from memory (Windows 95 only)

If you're not using DrivSpace (or the older DoubleSpace), the disk compression utility that comes with Windows, the drivers may still be taking up valuable memory and slowing system startup. Simply delete *Drvspace.bin* and *Dblspace.bin* from the root directory of your boot drive (usually C:\) and from your Windows\Command folder. Don't do this if you are currently using DriveSpace or DoubleSpace to compress your hard disk!

Keyboard Shortcuts

- Press F1 at almost any time to get help. If you're lucky, and not using a Microsoft application, you may get a useful help screen at this point.

- Switch between running applications. Press Tab repeatedly while holding Alt. Hold the Shift key to go in reverse.

- To switch between open documents in an application, press Ctrl-Tab. If an application decides to interpret this keystroke differently, as do most word processors, you can also use Ctrl-F6 for this purpose.

- Press Alt-F4 to close the current application window, or Ctrl-F4 to close the active document without closing the entire application.

- Switch easily between a full-screen and windowed command prompt by pressing Alt-Enter at any time.

- Open the **Start Menu** by pressing Ctrl-Esc.

- Move to the next field when entering data. Press Tab. Hold the Shift key to go in reverse.

- In a tabbed dialog (such as Display Properties in Control Panel), move to the next tab by pressing Ctrl-Tab. Hold the Shift key to go in reverse.

- Send the active window to the bottom of the pile by pressing Alt-Esc.

- Go to an application's menu without opening any specific menu by pressing the Alt key by itself. Use the cursor keys to navigate, and press Enter to make a selection.

- Keyboard equivalents of **Undo**, **Cut**, **Copy**, and **Paste**. Hold Ctrl while pressing Z, X, C, and V, respectively. In many applications, the following will also work: Alt-Backspace, Shift-Del, Ctrl-Ins, and Shift-Ins, respectively.

- In Explorer or the Registry Editor, use the left and right cursor keys to expand or contract any branches you wish. Press * (the asterisk key) to expand all of the branches (don't do it in the Registry Editor). If the Desktop in Explorer is selected, all directories in all drives will be expanded.

- In Explorer, use the Backspace key to go to the parent folder (go up one level). This works in file dialog boxes, folder windows, the Registry Editor, and most other hierarchical structures.

- Switch to the taskbar with the keyboard by first pressing Ctrl-Esc to bring up the **Start Menu**. Press Esc to close the menu while keeping the taskbar active, and then press Tab to switch to the row(s) of running applications on the Taskbar. Press Tab again to switch control to the Desktop. You can use the cursor keys at any time to navigate the active section.

- To display an object's context menu with the keyboard (normally accessible by right-clicking on the object) press Shift-F10.

- To display the control menu for the active window, press Alt-Space.

- When you're in a file dialog (such as when opening or saving a file), press the F4 key to shift the focus to and open the drive and directory drop-down listbox at the top of the window.

6

Troubleshooting

Due to the sheer number of components that make up a modern computer system, it can be quite difficult to isolate the cause of a given problem. Hardware conflicts, buggy drivers, and poorly written software can all contribute to any number of different problems. You may be experiencing frequent lockups (your system stops responding, requiring you to restart), error messages (an application can't complete a certain task), malfunctioning hardware (a device doesn't work), or data loss (your files aren't where you left them). These problems can be distilled into two basic forms: hardware or software malfunction, and data loss due to this malfunction.

To cope with malfunctioning hardware or software, you need to isolate the problem and then take steps to solve whatever trouble you've uncovered. Most problems like this are caused by incompatibilities or conflicts, where two or more components (software or hardware) don't work together. Drivers provide the link between your hardware and operating system, and are vital to the proper functioning of your system. You'll find a few tips concerning the different types of drivers and how to make sure you have the latest and greatest drivers on your system.

Dealing with data loss entails two strategies: preventative maintenance and data recovery. Assuming you've isolated and solved the source of the data loss, there are several methods you can employ to make sure your work is safe, and recover it when it isn't safe.

What follows in the "Configuration" section are several more specific topics, some of which employ the hints outlined in the earlier sections.

General Troubleshooting Techniques

Just a few words of advice before we begin: if it ain't broke, don't fix it. Many problems are actually caused by people looking for problems to solve—for example, installing a new device driver just for the sake of having the newest drivers on your system may introduce new incompatibilities. While the material presented here is to aid troubleshooting and data recovery, some of the solutions can cause other problems, so in general back up your entire hard disk before continuing.

Drivers

Drivers are small programs that allow your computer to communicate with the various devices attached to it. For example, your printer has a driver that contains all the capabilities of your printer, such as paper sizes and print resolution. The beauty of this design is that an application like your word processor can simply send your document to whatever printer driver is installed, and the driver can then interpret the document appropriately so that it prints on your specific printer correctly.

The problem arises when a driver is defective or outdated. Outdated drivers designed either for Windows 95 or a previous version of Windows or a previous version of the device can create problems, as can bugs in the drivers. It's usually a good idea to make sure you have the latest drivers installed in your system when troubleshooting a problem. Newer drivers usually offer improved performance, added features and settings, better stability and reliability, and better compatibility with other drivers in your system.

The other thing to be aware of is that some drivers may not be the correct ones for your system. For example, when installing Windows 95, it may have incorrectly detected your video card and hence installed the wrong driver. Make sure that **Device Manager** (double-click on the System icon in the Control Panel, and click the **Device Manager** tab) lists the actual devices you have installed on your system. Devices to investigate for the correct drivers include your video card, sound card, CD-ROM drive, modem, printer, network adapter, scanner, monitor, SCSI controller, tape drive, and any other drives or cards you may have. If you're not sure of the exact manufacturer or model number of a device, take the cover off your computer and look, or refer to the invoice or documentation that came with your system. Note that hard disks, floppy drives, keyboards, power supplies, and CPU chips don't usually need special drivers.

To obtain the latest drivers for your system, start by looking through Windows to see if support is built in. To find out if Windows 95 includes support for a specific device, double-click on the Add New Hardware icon in the Control Panel. Click **Next**, choose **No** when asked if you want Windows to search for your new hardware, and then click **Next** again. Choose a type of hardware from the list shown, and then click **Next** to display a list of manufacturers and their products (see Figure 6-1). If you have a disk containing drivers for your device, you may be able to use it at this point by clicking **Have Disk**, although you should always read the device's documentation before attempting to install a driver in this way.

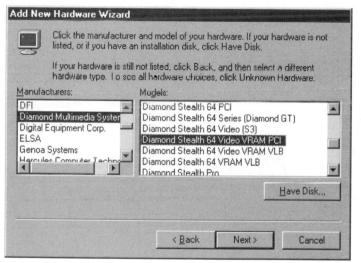

Figure 6-1: List the devices supported by Windows 95 by using the Add New Hardware Wizard

The method used to determine which drivers are installed varies by type of hardware, but you can usually tell by looking at the devices listed in Device Manager. Installing new drivers also varies with the hardware. Try choosing a device, clicking **Properties**, and then choosing the **Driver** tab (if it's there). If the tab is there and you've chosen it, click **Change Driver** to view all the devices supported by Windows. Only video cards will be shown if you're viewing the properties for your video card, and so on.

Even if your device is listed, your manufacturer may still have a newer driver. If you have access to the Internet, you can start at the company's Web site (see "Software and the Internet" in the Preface). Most companies today make all their drivers freely available for download. Don't let them charge you for something that other companies offer their customers for free. Refer to the instructions that come with the new drivers for the particular installation procedure. An indicator of a good computer product manufacturer is if it has drivers available for discontinued products. If it is supporting yesterday's products today, it will likely be supporting your product tomorrow.

It's important that any drivers you use with Windows 95 or Windows NT 4.0 be designed *especially* for your platform. Using drivers made for older versions of Windows or DOS may cause problems ranging from poor performance, to crashes, to the device's not working at all. Newer 32-bit drivers offer much better performance and stability, as well as extra features like support for Plug & Play, and the additional setting required for compatibility with other devices in your system. If a new driver isn't yet available, you should be able to use an older Windows driver, although this isn't recommended. If you are loading DOS drivers in your CONFIG.SYS or AUTOEXEC.BAT files, you may be preventing Windows from detecting your devices and installing drivers of its own. See "Do I Still Need CONFIG.SYS and AUTOEXEC.BAT?" later in this chapter for more information.

Some users may be disappointed to discover that a manufacturer of a discontinued product has either stopped supporting the product, or the company has just gone out of business. If this happens, you may be out of luck and forced to replace the device if it isn't supported in your version of Windows (see Chapter 5, *Maximizing Performance*, for information on upgrading your system). There is a way out, however. Many products, such as video cards, modems, and SCSI controllers, use similar components that are widely supported by the industry. For example, many varieties of S3's video card chips are used commonly in video cards today. By looking at your video card, you should be able to determine which variety of chipset it uses (look for the brand and model number). Even if the manufacturer of your video card has gone out of business, there may be other video cards that use the same chipset and therefore may use the same driver.

Don't install more than one new driver at once. By upgrading one driver at a time, you can easily isolate any potential new problems, as well as recognize when an existing problem has been solved. If you install several new drivers at once, you'll have a difficulty trying to find where you went wrong.

My last piece of advice is to put a copy of the latest drivers for all of your devices on floppy disks for easy access the next time you need them.

You'll be glad you did when you realize that you can't download the driver for your modem if your modem isn't working.

Error Messages

Error messages rarely describe a problem accurately. Usually the computer will report that a program has crashed or isn't able to load, but the problem may be something completely unrelated to what the message is reporting. There are many different kinds of error messages, but only the more "popular" ones displayed by Windows 95 and Windows NT 4.0 are discussed here. If you're looking for a list of all possible error messages (or error codes), you're out of luck. This doesn't exist.

If only a specific application displays an error message, your best bet is to contact the manufacturer of the application for technical support with its products. Many companies now have troubleshooting, updates and patches, and FAQs (frequently asked questions) on their web sites (see "Software and the Internet" in the Preface for more information).

Common error messages usually tell you that a file is missing or corrupted, an error has occurred, or a specific device isn't working or turned on. Error messages that tell you that *you've* done something wrong don't really apply here, for obvious reasons.

Errors during startup

You may have seen a strange message when Windows 95 is loading, either during the display of the Windows 95 logo screen, or after the taskbar appears. This can be caused by many different things, but there are a few common culprits.

A driver won't load

When Windows is starting up, it loads all of the installed drivers into memory. A driver may refuse to load if the device it's designed for isn't functioning or turned on, or if the driver itself isn't installed properly. If you remove a device, make sure to take out the driver as well. Even if it isn't generating an error message, it could be taking up memory. Driver errors may also be caused by hardware problems. Refer to the section on hardware later in this chapter for more information.

A program can't be found

After Windows loads itself and all of the drivers, it loads any such-configured programs. These include screensavers, scheduling utilities, all those icons that appear in your tray, and any other programs you may have placed in your Startup folder. If you removed the application, for example, and Windows still tries to load it, you'll have to remove the reference manually.

A corrupt Registry

See Chapter 3, *The Registry*, for any errors regarding your Registry.

A corrupt or missing file

If one of Windows's own files won't load and you're sure it isn't a third-party driver or application, you may have to reinstall Windows to alleviate the problem. I'll take this opportunity to remind you to back up frequently.

An error message of this sort will usually include a filename. To help isolate the problem, you can search your hard disk for the file and look in several places on your computer for the reference to the file. If you don't know what the error means exactly, you should do both. A lot can be learned by finding how and where Windows is trying to load a program. However, if you know that the file or files are no longer on your system, you can proceed to remove the reference. Conversely, if you know the file *is* still on your system. and you want to get it working again, you'll probably need to reinstall whatever component or application it came with to alleviate the problem.

The following are places that files or drivers can be specified to load when Windows 95 starts. Often simply removing the reference to the file solves the problem. At the very least, locating the driver will help determine the culprit.

- Look in your Startup folder (usually found in your **Start Menu** folder) for outdated or unwanted shortcuts. When you've installed an application, it may have placed a shortcut here for some reason. If you've moved or deleted the application, the shortcut may still be there, irritating you every time you turn on the system. Right-click on any shortcut and select **Properties** to learn more about it.

- Older programs might still install themselves in your *win.ini* file (anywhere on the line that starts with LOAD= or RUN=). Use a text editor such as Notepad to edit this file. You may want to back it up before proceeding.

- Some older drivers are specified throughout your *system.ini* file. Use a text editor such as Notepad to edit this file. You definitely want to back it up before proceeding. Neither *win.ini* nor *system.ini* is used by Windows 95 or Windows NT 4.0, but they are kept around for compatibility with older applications and may still contain references that cause problems.

- Search your Registry for the filename in the message. If you don't know the name of the file, try looking in HKEY_LOCAL_MACHINE\ SOFTWARE\Microsoft\Windows\CurrentVersion\Run and HKEY_ LOCAL_MACHINE\SOFTWARE\Microsoft\Windows\CurrentVersion\ RunOnce for other programs and drivers loaded at Windows startup.

- Search your hard disk for the file. If you find a .DLL or .EXE file, but you're still not sure what it is or how it got there, right-click on it and select **Properties**. Click on the **Version** tab to view the various information presented. Software developers often place the name of the application or manufacturer associated with the file here. If the version tab isn't there, neither is the information. You can also Quick-View the file (if you have QuickView installed) to see other information that may be of help.

- Programs notorious for putting things in these places include backup utilities that automatically load their useless scheduler programs and the software that comes with older versions of Microsoft mice and keyboards. If in doubt, throw it out.

Page-fault, illegal operation, and fatal exception

These errors are usually caused by a bug in software, where an application or driver tries to use part of your memory that's currently being used by another program. You should expect this to happen occasionally, due to the nature of software, but if it happens more frequently than once a day, it could be the sign of a more serious problem. When software crashes, it can cause one of these error messages to be displayed or cause your system to hang or even restart.

Often these error messages are accompanied by lists of numbers (accessible by clicking **Details**). Since this information will generally be of no use to you, there's no point in it unless you're asked to do so by someone, say, in the technical support department of the manufacturer of the application causing the problem.

The first step is to see if you can reliably reproduce the problem. If it seems to be application or device specific—the same action in a program or the repeated use of a certain device causes the crash—then you've found the culprit. This is the most common cause of crashes, especially today with companies shortening application testing periods to get their products to market faster. In the same way, buggy drivers can often be the cause of crashing. For example, if your system crashes every time you try to use your scanner, first check the scanner driver. It's then only a

matter of fixing the problem. Hardware and software issues are discussed
later in this chapter.

If the occurrences instead appear to be random and not associated with
any piece of hardware or software, there are some remaining possibilities.
Errors in your system's memory and on your hard disk can cause these
problems as well. To diagnose and repair any problems on your hard
disk, use the Scandisk utility included with Windows, or one of the more
powerful third-party utilities available. While there are programs that can
test system memory, a quicker and more reliable method is to replace
your computer's memory, one SIMM at a time, until the problem is
solved. See "Bad RAM" later in this chapter for more information.

Crash and burn

If an application crashes and *doesn't* display an error message, it usually
has just frozen. Depending on the severity of the crash, the application
may simply be not responding to the mouse or keyboard or has turned
the screen black. In most situations, you can press the Ctrl, Alt, and
Del keys to display the Close Program box (see Figure 6-2).

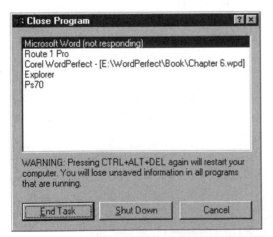

Figure 6-2: Pressing the Ctrl, Alt, and Del keys displays the Close Program box,
allowing you to close a hung application

You now are fortunate to have the option of closing a misbehaving
program or shutting down Windows completely. You can close any
running program here by selecting it from the list and clicking **End Task**,
whether it has crashed or not. In fact, it's a good way to close programs
that don't have windows, such as screensavers and other background
programs (note that 16-bit applications closed in this way may behave
unpredictably). If an application has stopped responding, you'll notice

the text ("not responding") appears next to the application's name. A program doesn't have to be misbehaving in order for you to have access to this window, however. Note that applications that aren't responding don't always allow themselves to be shut down. Conversely, it's possible for an application reported as not responding to be doing so only temporarily. Some programs, such as those that access certain devices, may appear to hang during normal operation. For this reason, it's best to have patience and give all hung applications a few minutes to correct themselves. Additionally, once you've used End Task on a hung application, it may take a little while for Windows to be able to close it.

Another thing to be aware of is that many applications are made up of several components. It's possible for one of those components to crash and leave the rest of the program in operation. This can cause problems, although it certainly varies with the program. Try pressing `Ctrl`, `Alt`, and `Del` again to see if the program is still running.

Since any crashed program can cause system-wide instability in Windows 95, it's good practice to restart Windows every time a crash occurs. The Windows NT system is more robust, and this isn't usually necessary. Note that while Windows NT also allows you to close a nonresponding application by pressing `Ctrl`, `Alt`, and `Del`, as described above, the screen does look different from the Windows 95 version shown in Figure 6-2.

The following programs are part of Windows and commonly appear in the Close Program window. Closing them with the above method can solve some problems temporarily, but may not stop many other problems from reoccurring.

MSGSRV32 (not responding)

MSGSRV32.EXE is a program that's actually part of Windows 95 and runs invisibly in the background. It performs several necessary functions, including the following (from Microsoft's knowledge base):

- Mediate Plug & Play messages among various parts of the operating system.

- Coordinate automatic responses to Setup programs. This includes checking whether a Setup program has improperly overwritten Windows 95 files, and optionally restoring the Windows 95 versions of those files. See "Your Sysbckup Folder" later in this chapter.

- Display the initial logon dialog box if networking is enabled.

- Play the system startup and shutdown sounds.

- Load installable Windows drivers at startup and unload them at shutdown.

- Run the shell program (usually *explorer.exe*), and rerun the shell if it fails to respond.

Because of the varied nature of this program, almost anything can cause it to crash. If it does, it's best to restart Windows 95 immediately.

RUNDLL32.DLL

This program is used by some applications to run parts of other applications and therefore doesn't necessarily correspond with any particular error. However, the following two circumstances relate to this file:

- If you get the message "Rundll32—This program has caused an illegal operation and will be shut down," it could be caused by a missing entry in your *system.ini* file. Using a text editor, such as Notepad, to edit the file, look for the line that starts with `drivers=` in the `[boot]` section. If *mmsystem.dll* isn't specified on the right side of the equals sign, add it. If you continue getting this error, try removing all other drivers from the line until *mmsystem.dll* is alone.

- If the Close Program window reports "Rundll32.dll (not responding)," end the task, and try whatever it was you were doing again. This has been known to happen when a modem fails while trying to connect to another computer using Dial-Up Networking (see Chapter 7, *Networking*, for more information).

Hardware Issues

The most common type of hardware problem is a conflict: two devices try to use the same resource, such as an IRQ or memory address. The telltale signs of a conflict include the one or more devices not working, one or more devices not showing up in Device Manager, or your system crashing every time one or more devices are used. The first step in diagnosing a problem like this is to check the drivers (see "Drivers" earlier in this chapter).

Devices use different resources of your computer, including memory, interrupts (IRQs), I/O addresses, DMA addresses, SCSI IDs, and serial and parallel ports. If two or more devices try to use the same resource, it causes problems ranging from slow performance to system crashes. On many devices, you tell the hardware which resources to use by setting appropriate jumpers or switches on the devices themselves. Newer devices allow their settings to be changed with software. The newest Plug & Play products work with your Plug & Play BIOS (part of your computer) to configure themselves automatically to work with other Plug & Play devices and other legacy (older) devices, theoretically avoiding all conflicts.

Some devices, such as printers, which connect to your computer's parallel port, don't use any resources of their own. However, the port to which they're connected does use resources. You can usually change the resources used by a particular device (parallel ports included). The trick is to configure all of your devices to use different resources so that no conflicts occur. All devices are different. Refer to the documentation included with the device, or contact the manufacturer for specific configuration instructions.

To determine which resources are available in your system, open the Device Manager by double-clicking on the System icon in Control Panel and choosing the **Device Manager** tab. Select **Computer** from the top of the list, and click **Properties** (see figure 6-3). Device Manager is available in Windows 95 only. In Windows NT, the devices are spread around several different icons in Control Panel. Although the screens are different from Windows 95, the technique is the same.

By choosing any of the four types of resources (IRQ, I/O, DMA, or Memory), you'll be presented with a list of the resources used by the various devices in your system. Any gaps in the numbers represent available system resources, and you should be able to assign them to new devices. Most resource conflicts are shown here as well, but be aware that some devices *can* share resources. For example, your communication ports share IRQs (Com2 and Com4 both use IRQ 3, and Com1 and Com3 both use IRQ 4).

If you find a conflict, start by removing or reconfiguring one of the devices involved. You may be required to reconfigure several devices, literally shuffling resources around until all the conflicts are resolved. Again, the method used to change the resources used by a particular device depends on the device itself. You should be able to see all the resources used by a given device by selecting it in Device Manager, clicking **Properties**, and choosing the **Resources** tab.

The information presented in Device Manager may not reflect the current state of your system. Especially if your computer is older and doesn't support Plug & Play entirely (or at all), you may have devices installed that don't show up here, as well as devices displayed that aren't actually

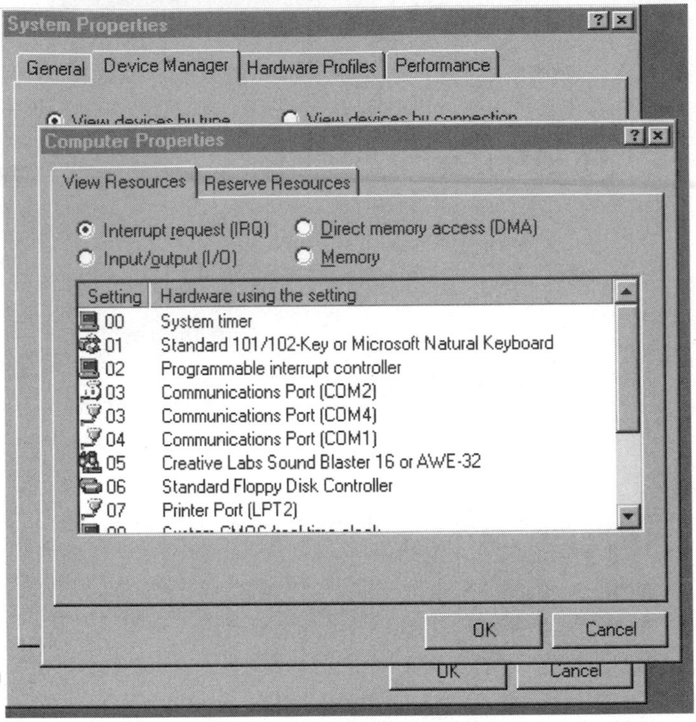

Figure 6-3: You can determine which resources are being used by looking at the Computer Properties in Windows 95's Device Manager

installed. The **Refresh** button is used to reread the devices in your system but won't detect anything more than is normally seen when Windows starts. Refresh is used primarily to detect devices attached to or disconnected from your system without restarting. To have Windows redetect the hardware attached to your computer, use the Add New Hardware icon in Control Panel, and confirm that you want it to search for new hardware when asked.

If you're installing a new product and need to set its resources manually, do so after checking with Device Manager to avoid any conflicts. If you're installing more than one device, do so one at a time. It's much easier to isolate problems when you know which device has caused them. Furthermore, when installing Plug & Play devices, you should expect the device to be quick, automatic, and painless—theoretically. However, many devices, while able to configure themselves automatically, may not be able to adapt entirely to your system. Be prepared to reconfigure or even remove some of your existing devices to make room for new ones.

If you're trying to get an existing device to work, try removing one of the conflicting pieces of hardware to see if the conflict is resolved. If removing a device solves a problem, you've found the conflict. If not, try removing all devices from the system, and then reconnect them one by one until the problem reappears. Although it may sound like a pain in the neck to remove all the devices from your system, it is the easiest and most sure-fire way to find the cause of a problem like this. Since there are so many different combinations of resource settings, it can be a laborious task to resolve conflicts. Some devices come with special software designed for this task. The software can advise you of proper settings or even make the changes for you. Make sure to review the documentation for any mention of such a utility.

A feature found in many new devices is user-upgradable firmware. Firmware is actually software stored in the device ROM used to control the device. To find out what firmware version a certain device uses, select the device in Device Manager, click **Properties**, choose the **Settings** tab, and look at the **Firmware Revision** setting. If you're experiencing problems with a certain device, see if there's a newer firmware revision. If so, you may be able to download a software "patch" that will update the firmware to the newest version, which may not only fix many problems but may improve performance as well. Devices that commonly have user-upgradable firmware include more expensive modems; CD-ROM drives; removable, optical, and tape drives; motherboards (in the form of an upgradable BIOS); SCSI controllers; and some video cards. Some older devices allow you to change the firmware by upgrading a chip. It's not as convenient as software-upgradable firmware, but it's better than nothing. When shopping for new hardware, look for user-upgradable firmware; it can mean not only a lower maintenance cost but a cheaper upgrade path. Imagine upgrading that video card without even opening your computer!

Bad RAM

Bad memory can manifest itself in anything from frequent error messages to your system not starting. Errors in your RAM aren't always steady or reliable either. They can be intermittent, occurring at completely random intervals. Nearly all newer computers (those capable of running Windows anyway) use SIMMs, which are easy to install and remove, but these rules should apply to any type of RAM. The first thing you should do is pull out each SIMM and make sure there isn't any dust or other obstruction between the pins and your motherboard (don't use a wet rag to clean this, however). Look for broken or bent pins, broken SIMM holders, metal filings or other obstructions, and burn marks. Make sure all your

SIMMs are seated properly; they should snap into place and should be level and firm (be careful not to break them testing their firmness, however).

If all that is in order, there are two ways to determine if your RAM is actually faulty. The first way is to use a software testing program (CheckIt, a commercial package, is the only one I know of that does this) to run a continual test of your RAM (have it repeat the test many times, perhaps overnight). However, testing your RAM with software is not 100 percent reliable, and once you've found a problem, you need to follow the next method anyway to find and replace the faulty SIMM.

The second method of finding and replacing bad RAM is to go to your local computer store and buy more RAM. It's necessary only to buy one SIMM, as most likely only one SIMM in your system is faulty. Replace each SIMM in your computer with the new one, and try it out. If the problem seems to be resolved, you've found the culprit. Throw it out immediately. If the system still crashes, try replacing the next SIMM with the new one, and repeat the process. If you replace all the memory in your system and the problem persists, it may be a bad CPU or motherboard. To eliminate the possibility of the problem's being caused by another device rather than the RAM, remove all unnecessary devices from your system before testing your RAM in this way. Many computer stores have more advanced ways of testing RAM, but they may charge you more to test your RAM than it would cost to replace it.

Software Issues

Most of this book is devoted to troubleshooting software, namely Windows 95, so there isn't much point in elaborating here. Hardware conflicts occur when two devices try to use the same resource in your computer; software conflicts can occur when two applications try to use the same resource. For example, if you've ever tried to open a document in one application when it's currently open (or being viewed) in another, you'll get an error such as, "You don't have permission to open this file" or "Sharing violation." What's more serious (and just as common) is when a program tries to use a file that's corrupted, missing, or the wrong version, and that's what we'll discuss here. (Note that any problems with specific applications should be addressed by the manufacturers of the applications.)

Disk or file corruption

Occasionally a file becomes corrupted (the causes are too numerous to mention here). The first step in recovery is to run Scandisk, the program included with Windows 95 to diagnose and fix many file corruption problems. Since there's a DOS version as well, you can run it if Windows 95 doesn't start, although you should use the Windows version when possible. See "Preventative Maintenance and Data Recovery" later in this chapter for more information.

Missing files

Files can simply vanish from your hard disk, by user error, or file corruption (see the previous section), or because another program has removed or renamed the file (see the next section). There's not much you can do about this, other than to keep backups of files that tend to disappear, making it easy to replace them when necessary. If you've discovered that a file that came with Windows or another application is missing, you usually will need to reinstall the application to restore the file. If a file is missing, it's likely that other files are missing as well, and reinstalling ensures that all necessary files are present. If you know that a single file is missing, you can usually retrieve it from the distribution disks.

To save distribution costs, companies often compress their files, thereby reducing the number of disks or CDs required to store the application. If you're trying to retrieve the file from a newer Microsoft application (including Windows itself), the files are stored in cabinets (see Appendix A). Otherwise, the company may be using the industry standard ZIP format (see "Software and the Internet" in the Preface), or Microsoft's old Compress/Expand utility. If the names of the distribution files look like *ctl3d.dl_*, you should be able to restore it to its usable state by typing expand ctl3d.dl_ ctl3d.dll in DOS.

Version control

Here's a tough one: many different programs share files with each other, called DLLs (dynamic link libraries). These files provide functionality that many applications can use (such as how you can see the same File Open box on many applications). In fact, Windows is primarily a collection of DLL files used by the various applications that run in the operating system. The problem arises when one errant application overwrites a newer version of a DLL with an older (or just different) version. This problem has been addressed with something called Version Control, where each file contains specific version information. For example, when you install a new application, the setup program will test every file it copies to your hard disk with any files it's replacing. If it detects that a newer file is on your hard disk than what came with the application, it will skip the file.

In theory, this works quite well. However, older applications don't always follow the rules, and newer applications sometimes come with shared files that introduce new bugs. Microsoft is notorious for replacing files shared by many different programs with new, buggy versions that either cause problems or change some basic interface components to suit their own products. While this practice of Microsoft's is frowned on, its monopolistic position in the industry pretty much ensures that it can do what it wants, and let the other manufacturers clean up the mess.

There are two ways to determine what version of a file you're using. The old way is to look at the file's date; the problem with this is that many programs change the dates of the files they install, so this isn't very reliable. With most .EXE and .DLL files, version information is available to you in the file properties sheet. Right-click on any .DLL on your hard disk, and click **Properties**. You should see a **Version** tab (if not, the file you've chosen doesn't contain any version information). This tab displays the version of the file, some copyright information, usually the name of the manufacturer, and a short description of the file. Shuffle through the items in the **Item name** list to see the various clues.

Usually, newer versions of .DLL files are just that: the same contents as the original version, but with more functionality added. In some situations, a certain .DLL file can be replaced with a completely different file, with which all it has in common is the filename. This is rare, with the possible exception of *WINSOCK.DLL* discussed shortly.

There are more .DLL files than can be listed in any one place, let alone this book. Many come with Windows, but many more are installed on your system by any of the thousands of applications and drivers currently available. There are a few troublemakers, however, which are common enough both to cause a problem on your machine and be easy to fix.

WINSOCK.DLL

This file and its 32-bit counterpart, *WSOCK32.DLL*, are used by most, if not all, Internet applications, and the version on your hard disk depends on which Internet dialer you're using. If you're using Dial-Up Networking (see Chapter 7), the file should be dated 7-11-95 for Windows 95 and 8-02-96 for Windows NT 4.0. Files with later dates may have been placed there by updates from Microsoft. The problem occurs when another dialer (such as Trumpet Winsock and Netscape Navigator) replaces the file on your hard disk with its own version. Since the various creators of this file have included entirely different functionality in each version, it is not advantageous to have the latest version on your system. If your Internet applications stop working, check this file. You may need to replace it with the one appropriate to your dialer. See the discussion of the Path, which follows, for an important consideration.

CTL3D.DLL

This file and its cousins, *CTL3DV2.DLL* and *CTL3D32.DLL*, seem to cause lots of problems. It's used by older applications to display certain 3D effects, where the controls in some windows look carved out. Software designed especially for Windows 95 or Windows NT already contains this functionality, but older applications rely on this file for basic operation. Although the newer versions usually are preferred, some applications will display an error if you use anything but the specific version that came with the product. You guessed it: bad programming. As of this writing, for *CTL3D.DLL*, you should have version 2.05; for *CTL3DV2.DLL*, you should have version 2.29; and for *CTL3D32.DLL*, you should have version 2.29. If you don't have these versions, don't panic; it's just a guideline if you are having trouble with any of these files. Make a habit of backing up these files so that you can easily restore them if they become overwritten.

THREED.VBX

This is a custom control used by some applications written in the Visual Basic programming language. Custom controls—.VBX files (16-bit) and .OCX files (16 and 32-bit)—are .DLL files that add modular functionality to programs. *THREED.VBX* is just one of these, and is mentioned because of its popularity. The problem actually exists with all .VBX and .OCX files, just as it does with .DLL files. Be aware that these files have version information as well, and that newer versions of these files can be overwritten with older ones just as easily.

Operating system settings and diagnostics

Often by investigating settings in the operating system and using the built-in diagnostic tools, you can eliminate a pesky problem or performance issue. In Windows 95, start with the System Performance box. Double-click on the System icon in Control Panel, and choose the **Performance** tab. Click **Advanced** and then choose the **Troubleshooting** tab for some additional settings you can try. If you're having trouble with sound or motion video, try snooping around the Multimedia Properties box in Control Panel.

In Windows NT 4.0, the Windows NT Diagnostics utility (*winmsd.exe*, located in the WinNT\System32 folder) allows you to investigate system settings, especially handy since NT doesn't come with a Device Manager.

In the Control Panel, the Services and Devices icons list many functions and drivers controlled by Windows and whether they are functioning.

The path less traveled

The path isn't emphasized as much as it used to be, but it is still an important setting in both Windows 95 and Windows NT and can cause problems. If a directory is included in your path, you'll be able to run a program in that directory from DOS *without* making it the current directory. For example, say you had the program *notepad.exe* in the directory C:\windows, which just happens to be in the path. In DOS, if you're in a different directory, say C:\myfolder, you can *still* type notepad to run the application, even though you're not in the same directory.

You may not think it applies to you, but it may. The same rules that apply to programs also apply to files in Windows, such as .DLL files. If you have multiple versions of a file floating around in different directories on your hard disk and some of those directories are in your path, Windows may be using the other versions rather than the latest one. For example, say you have the appropriate version of the file *WINSOCK.DLL* in your Windows/System directory, but you have another, older copy of *WINSOCK.DLL* in your C:\Winsock directory. It's possible that some programs might try to use the older version because it found it in a directory in the path.

How do you escape this trap? First remove any unnecessary directories from your path. The path is specified in *AUTOEXEC.BAT* for users of Windows 95, and in the System icon of Control Panel in Windows NT. Next, search your hard disk for any filename you suspect to be causing problems. Start with any of those mentioned in the previous section. Then find the most recent version (if applicable—be careful here), and place it in your Windows\System directory. Remove all other copies of the file from your hard disk. Not only will you be reducing the risk of software conflict, but you'll be retrieving some free disk space as well. Make sure to back up those files before deleting them, at least until you know everything is working properly.

Your Sysbckup folder

In Windows 95, you'll find a hidden folder called Sysbckup under your Windows directory. This folder contains copies of some of the important files used in Windows, kept around in case the originals get overwritten or corrupted. If an application replaces a file in your Windows\System directory that's also in your Sysbckup folder, Windows 95 will automatically fix the problem and replace the file with the known good copy.

You can use this to your advantage by placing copies of any files you wish to protect in this way into the Sysbckup folder. Be careful when doing this, however, not to replace any vital files with improper versions, and make sure not to delete any files in this directory. For more information, see the reference to MSGSRV32 (not responding) in the section "Crash and burn" earlier in this chapter.

Preventive Maintenance and Data Recovery

There's no substitute for backing up, and there's no better method of disaster recovery than having a good copy of all your data. Any stolen or damaged hardware is easily replaced, but the data stored on your hard disk are not. Unfortunately, hindsight is 20/20, and if you didn't back up, there's not much you can do about it after the fact. We'll begin our discussion with some preventive maintenance before covering any disaster recovery techniques.

Back up your entire system

There are more ways to back up your data than to store it. The sole purpose of a backup is to have a duplicate of the data on your hard disk that can be easily retrieved in the event of data loss. Imagine if your computer were stolen, and you had to restore a backup to a brand-new computer. Could you do it? If the answer is no, you're not backed up. You need to be able to complete a backup easily and often, and store the backup in a safe place, away from the computer.

The minimum back up should entail one or more floppy disks, containing your recent, most important documents and data. Floppies are cheap, and all computers have floppy drives. The downside is that floppies are slow, too small to back up large amounts of data, and very unreliable. Although it's most important to back up your recent documents, it's best to have all your documents, as well as Windows and all your applications backed up as well. This will save you time and aggravation when you need to restore your system to its full working order.

Ideally, you should be able to back up your entire hard disk on a single piece of media. Since floppies aren't suitable for this task, you should invest in a backup solution if your data are at all important. The hardware you use should be fully supported by your version of Windows. You can't use 16-bit software to back up long filenames, so make sure you have 32-bit backup software. The back up media (the tapes, cartridges, or disks) should be cheap and reliable, and you should be able to use them over and over again.

Whichever backup solution is appropriate for you depends on your work habits. Tape drives, optical drives, removable cartridges, and writable CD-ROMs are selling like hotcakes these days, and for good reason. While removable cartridge drives (Syquest, IOmega Zip and Jaz, and Magneto Optical drives) are great for quickly archiving data (storing important projects for long-term, frequent use), they still aren't as appropriate for backing up as tape drives.

Tape drives are still the most cost-effective, reliable, and appropriate method for recovering your system after a disaster. Removable drives and CDs offer random access; you can simply open Explorer and read or write to any file immediately. Tape drives require special backup software and tend to be slower than comparably priced removables, especially when restoring single files. However, remember what's important here: you need to store the contents of your entire system on one cartridge and be able to back it up and restore it in one step, without user intervention.

Basically, you need to find the method that works best for you and fits in your budget. Do some research before investing in any one technology, and make sure your version of Windows supports it fully. Try this: add the cost of the drive you're considering using with the media required to store the entire contents of your hard drive, and compare it with other solutions. Say you want to compare the backup cost of a $500 recordable CD drive with a $500 tape drive. To back up that 2-gigabyte (2000-megabyte) hard disk with the record-able CD, you'll need to spend $500 for the drive and $15 for each CD. Since CDs hold 650 megabytes, you'll need three, bringing the total to $545 for the first backup. Now, since CDs can be written to only once, you'll need to spend an additional $45 for each successive backup. The tape drive uses $10 cartridges that hold 2 gigabytes each, which means you need only one cartridge per backup, and since the cartridge is reusable, you don't need to spend more money every time you want to back up. While both drives back up data at approximately the same speed, you'll need to be there to switch CDs, while the tape drive continues unattended. Performing an unattended backup overnight is ideal. While the numbers discussed here may change substantially with time, the methodology doesn't. Do your research, and it will save you time and money in the long run, not to mention that extra peace of mind.

Get the latest drivers

It's always a good idea to keep up with the latest drivers, but remember to back up your Registry before installing any of them. It takes only a few seconds and can save you hours of work if your system decides not to boot up with the new drivers. Refer to the discussion of drivers earlier in this chapter, and see Chapter 3 for more information on the Registry.

Format floppies

Diskettes are still the standard, despite the fact that they're unreliable, slow, and small. However, everyone has a floppy drive, the disks are cheap, and it's a great way to transport small amounts of data. To avoid a headache, always format every floppy diskette before you use it. It'll take an extra couple of minutes, but it may save you hours in the long run. Floppies are very unreliable. They are highly susceptible to dust, damage, and heat and can turn on you in an instant. Use DOS to format your floppies. It's faster and more reliable than using Windows' format feature and will give you more free space, as well as yield better multitasking. Just type Format a: /u at the MS-DOS prompt (substituting a: with whatever drive letter you wish). The /u parameter specifies an unconditional format, meaning that it won't use up part of the floppy with the unnecessary unformat information that the Windows format includes. This yields an even faster format, more free diskette space, and a much more reliable format. If there are any errors (bad sectors, or sectors not found) reported on the diskette, throw it out *immediately*. Disks cost around 30 cents apiece. If in doubt, throw it out.

Never use floppies to store any information for more than a few hours. That's what your hard disk is for. Floppies should be used only to install software and transport data from one computer to another. See "Back Up Your Entire System" (previously in this section) for more information.

Make a startup disk

You'll never need a boot disk until your system doesn't start, and then you'll wonder why you never took five minutes to make one. A boot disk is a floppy with a few special files on it, enabling you to start your system if something goes wrong with your hard disk. It's easy, quick, and *very* useful.

Windows 95 even has a built-in method for doing this. Double-click on **Add/Remove Programs** in Control Panel, choose the **Startup Disk** tab, and then click **Create Disk**. If you're a do-it-yourselfer, you can just as easily do this through DOS. Just type Format a: /u/s at the

MS-DOS prompt (see "Format floppies," previously in this section, for more information). The /s parameter tells your computer to install the special system files on the disk (no, you can't just copy these files manually). For added security, you may want to store a copy of your Registry on this or another disk. See Chapter 3, *The Registry*, for more information. No matter which of these methods you use, you still need to complete one' more step that Microsoft doesn't tell you about. Copy the hidden file *MSDOS.SYS* from the root directory of your boot drive (usually C:\, unless you're using DriveSpace) onto the floppy, replacing the one that's there. This will enable you to run Windows when you boot from the floppy, a task that otherwise isn't possible.

If you're using the CD version of Windows 95 (this doesn't apply to Windows NT or the floppy-based version of Windows 95), put the DOS drivers for your CD-ROM drive on the startup disk. Since you can't access your CD-ROM drive without having Windows 95 running or the DOS CD-ROM drivers installed, you won't be able to reinstall Windows 95 if it becomes necessary. Having the drivers already set up on your startup disk will make this problem trivial. Refer to the instructions that came with your CD-ROM drive for details, as the procedure varies across different types of drives. Just make sure you can boot from the floppy and be able to access your CD-ROM drive right away and without any additional steps. See "Restoring Windows After a Crash" later in this chapter for more information.

In Windows NT 4.0, you can create an emergency repair disk. Use the Repair Disk Utility to create the repair disk, or update an existing disk with the most recent configuration. The advantage of NT's design is that several configuration files are also stored on the disk, as well as an emergency recovery program, which automates the recovery procedure.

For either platform, label the disk with the date, write-protect it, and put it in a safe place. While the Windows NT repair disk can be used to repair your system, the Windows 95 disk just allows you to boot into DOS when the hard disk won't. See "Booting Directly into DOS" in Chapter 4, *Advanced Customization Techniques*, for an alternative for Windows 95 users.

The Registry

Back up your Registry often. It's just a few files, and takes only minutes. See "Backing Up the Registry" in Chapter 3 for more information.

Hardware

Most of these topics deal with software issues: protecting your data, creating boot disks, and so forth. However, there are a few things you can do to reduce the likelihood of problems with your hardware. Don't block any vents on computer or your monitor, and routinely vacuum all around to remove dust (too much dust can cause your components to overheat). Make sure you have a fan in your power supply and one mounted directly on top of your CPU. An extra fan won't hurt. Just make sure that air can flow freely inside from the front of the computer to the back. Overheated components can cause system crashes, slow performance, and data loss. If every device is connected to a surge protector, the possibility of damage by an electrical surge is virtually eliminated.

Make sure all your cables are tied neatly behind the computer so pins and plugs don't get broken and plugs don't become loose. Tighten all those cable thumbscrews! Clean the ball of your mouse; and use a mouse pad. Don't spray glass cleaner on your monitor; spray it on a the paper towel instead. Don't place those floppies next to your monitor!

Data Recovery

All that said, there are certain measures you can take to restore your system after a disaster. This section covers only data recovery; recovering hardware (for example, if it were destroyed in an earthquake) requires ample insurance or a fat checkbook.

If you've backed up your system, you can make repairs without worrying about losing any more data. For example, to bring a hard disk back to working order, you may be required to format it. If you don't have data to recover, you can format without worry. However, if you haven't backed up, you'll need to try to recover as much data as possible before repairing the damage. The following paragraphs describe several different extremes of damage, each with its own symptoms and solutions.

File corruption

If you can't access a certain document or start a certain application (including Windows itself), but everything else seems to work, the problem is most likely due to one or more corrupted files. This can almost always be fixed with Scandisk. Usually Scandisk will be able to fix the problem by repairing the damaged file or marking a small portion of your hard disk as unusable, depending on the severity of the damage. If the problem was fixed but one or more files are no longer operational, you'll need to replace the files or reinstall the application to which the files belong. See "Software Issues" earlier in this chapter for more information on Scandisk and replacing missing files.

Registry error

This is the same thing as the previous item, but it applies only to the files that make up your Registry. See Chapter 3 for more information on backing up and recovering a damaged Registry.

Disk error

A disk error is a physical defect on your hard disk, often called a bad sector. This manifests itself by reporting some type of read error whenever you try to access a particular file. Nastier problems will cause the computer to stop responding for up to a few minutes whenever a certain file is accessed. The Scandisk utility is able to find most bad sectors and mark them as unusable. Any files located on the bad sector will be moved to a good sector, although this often means the file has been irreparably damaged and should be deleted. You shouldn't be worried if your hard disk develops one or a few bad sectors over the course of its lifetime, but if the number of bad sectors continually increases, usually the drive needs to be replaced. To find out, format the drive completely. If the problem doesn't go away, replace the drive immediately. Otherwise, you've apparently fixed the problem.

Sector not found, invalid directory entries, or other errors where you see gibberish instead of filenames

This usually means that your hard disk needs to be reformatted but probably not replaced. Try to back up as many files as you can as quickly as possible. This type of problem tends to grow quickly. Once you've recovered as much as you can (if necessary), reformat the drive, and start filling it. If you have access to one of the commercially available utilities packages, such as Norton Utilities for Windows 95, you may be able to repair the directory structure without reformatting. Note that Scandisk is usually not up to the task of fixing this type of problem, although it may be worth a try.

Disk crash

If your hard disk has crashed, you most likely can't get it to turn on. Old hard drives can simply die—another good reason to back up often. There's not much you can do at this point, but a professional computer consultant or the manufacturer of the hard drive may be able to recover some or all of your data. Be careful here; it's possible to make your data nonrecoverable by trying to recover material yourself.

Once you've solved whatever caused the problem in the first place, you can restore your data onto your hopefully-functioning hard drive.

Restoring Windows After a Crash

The purpose of backing up is to give you the opportunity to restore your system to its original state if something unforeseen should happen to your hard disk—whether theft, malfunction, or user error. You'd be surprised at how many people back up their system without having any idea how to restore it later if the problem should arise. The backup doesn't do you any good if you can't get at your files later, so make sure you can restore your system from scratch.

If you back up your hard disk using backup software made for your version of Windows (either the included Backup utility or a third-party solution), and your hard disk crashes, you'll have to reinstall Windows as well as your backup software from scratch before you can restore anything else. That doesn't mean you've lost your Windows settings. When you restore your own copy of Windows on top of the freshly installed version, all your settings will be restored as well. This does have a few implications, however. For example, if your copy of Windows is on a CD, you can't use your CD-ROM drive without either having Windows running or special DOS CD drivers installed. This means that you should have a startup disk containing all the necessary DOS CD-ROM drivers installed and ready to go. See "Making a Startup Disk" earlier in this chapter for more information. Make sure that you have a floppy disk version of any drivers or special software necessary for your backup device handy. Make sure that tape backup software is kept on a floppy and not on a tape, for example.

The other thing to be aware of is that you won't be able to restore some of the files to your Windows directory because they're system files and will be in use while Windows is running. It is a good idea to be aware of all these issues before your computer crashes, as there are ways of getting around them. Following are a few different techniques you can use to back up and restore your system after a crash. It's best to review the technique *before* a crash so you can make sure you can reproduce the steps when you need to.

Using Windows software

- Back up your entire hard disk with native Windows software, including the Windows directory itself.

- After the crash, install a bare-bones version of Windows 95 into a directory different from your original Windows directory, such as C:\Barewin. For Windows NT, it's best to install it to the original location and hope for the best. If you're using a third-party backup program (other than the one that came with Windows), you'll need to re-install it at this point as well.

- Restore *all* the files on your system to their original locations, including your Windows directory. For Windows 95, the bare-bones version will have a different directory name; you won't have to worry that some files will be skipped because they're in use by Windows. For Windows NT, keep track of any files skipped by your backup program for this reason, and restore them into a temporary directory to be copied back into Windows later manually.

- Windows 95 keeps track of where it's installed with the file *MSDOS.SYS* in the root directory of your boot drive. If you make sure to restore this file as well, overwriting the one put there by the bare-bones version, you'll be automatically "switching" to your "good" version at this point. When you're done, just restart your computer, and your restored version of Windows 95 should be used. You can then delete the temporary bare-bones installation in its entirety.

Using DOS software (for Windows 95 only)

- If you can obtain a DOS version of your backup software (some Windows software packages come with an emergency DOS restore just for this purpose), you can still back up your system with the Windows counterpart. Otherwise, you'll have to back up and restore with your DOS software.

- The major drawback to DOS software is that it won't back up your long filenames. This may seem trivial, but since many programs rely on these filenames, including Windows 95 itself, it's imperative that you take it into consideration.

- If your DOS software doesn't do it for you, you'll have to back up your long filenames manually. To accomplish this, Microsoft has included a command-line utility on the CD version of Windows 95, called Lfnbk, located in the \Mig_kit\Admin95\Apptools\Lfnback folder. It is called "Temporary Compatibility," as it is only for use with programs that don't yet support long filenames—a situation assumed to change soon. Read the included documentation file for more information on its use and limitations.

- After a crash, you'll only have to reinstall your backup program before you can restore your computer. You should be able to restore all the files on your system without incident. When restoring the long filenames, make sure you have a copy of Lfnbk on a floppy, as you most likely won't be able to access your CD-ROM without Windows 95.

Notes and other issues

It is a good idea to back up your Registry frequently. See Chapter 3 for more information.

If you're having trouble getting your tape drive to work with Windows, see "Getting Things to Work," the next section.

Getting Things to Work

While the number one rule for getting your various devices to work remains obtaining a driver from the manufacturer, this isn't always as easily done as one would like. For many users, obtaining the correct driver may be impossible, either because the company has stopped supporting the device or the driver hasn't yet been released. There are, however, some techniques for getting certain kinds of devices to work. Where upgrading your hardware is discussed, refer to Chapter 5 for more information.

Getting most hardware to work in Windows requires obtaining the correct drivers and eliminating any hardware conflicts. To resolve a possible conflict, see "Hardware Issues" earlier in this chapter.

Video cards (also known as display adapters)

Most likely, without the correct video driver installed, you still should be able to use Windows at a resolution of 640 × 480 with 256 colors—a standard mode supported by nearly all VGA cards. If you don't have a VGA-compatible card, buy one. A high-performance video card can be purchased for less than $75 and is worth the investment, especially if your current card isn't supported by Windows.

Most modern video cards are based on a certain chipset, usually identifiable by the large, square chip in the center of the card itself. If the chip is covered with a sticker, remove the sticker to see what's printed on the chip surface. Windows may be able to detect the type of chip, even if it can't determine the make and model of the card. Common chipset manufacturers are S3, Cirrus Logic, ATI, Tseng, and Western Digital. Each chipset comes in several varieties as well. If you can determine the type of chipset on your video card uses, you should be able to use a generic video driver made for that chipset or a driver for another card that uses the same chipset.

If you know you are using the correct video driver but can't use all of the resolutions it supports, try changing the driver for your monitor.

Monitors

If Windows knows what type of monitor you're using, it can determine which resolutions and color depths you can use. Note that some older monitors may not be able to display the high refresh rates or resolutions generated by newer video cards. A video card and a monitor don't have to be matched to work, but it's worth investigating whether your monitor can support all of your video card's modes. Note that newer Plug & Play monitors automatically provide Windows with the necessary information and don't need a driver.

The manufacturer of your monitor isn't likely to have any drivers for you, although it might be able to tell you which supported monitor is compatible with yours. Try a few different models by the same manufacturer, if available. Since many monitors use the same tubes, you should be able to find one that works. Additionally, you may be able to use a higher resolution or color depth with your monitor by lowering your video card's refresh rate. In Windows 95, you'll need a special video driver, but Windows NT comes with the necessary adjustment in the Display Properties window.

Hard disks and floppy diskette drives

These drives almost never need special drivers, unless they use some proprietary interface (such as your parallel port). To get Windows to recognize your hard disk, you need to find a driver for your hard disk controller. Most hard disks (with the large exception of SCSI) require that you specify their parameters in your computer's BIOS setup, usually accessible by pressing some key just after you first turn on your system.

Hard disk controllers

Most hard drives available today are the IDE type. Since IDE controllers can be purchased for around $10, throw out your existing IDE controller if it needs a driver. Most other types of controllers don't need drivers either (with the large exception of SCSI; see the following topic). If Windows doesn't support your controller and you can't get a driver from the manufacturer, you're out of luck.

SCSI controllers

Most SCSI controllers are supported by Windows or have drivers available. If your SCSI card doesn't have either, you may still be able to use it if it uses the same SCSI controller chip (sometimes called a miniport) as another supported card. Common miniport manufacturers are Adaptec, BusLogic, Future Domain, NCR, and Trantor. You may have a sound card that has a built-in SCSI controller for your CD-ROM drive. If you can find out the make and model of the miniport, you should be able to use a driver for another SCSI card that uses the same miniport.

CD-ROM drives

Most CD drives don't need special drivers. In fact, if you plug in a CD drive and then start up Windows, it should detect it and display an icon for it in My Computer automatically. If your drive isn't detected, first check the controller. Most CD-ROMs connect to your IDE or SCSI controller (see the previous topic). For those that connect to proprietary devices, such as sound cards, or other special controller cards you'll need a driver made especially for your controller-drive combination.

Tape drives

Obtaining a driver for your backup device usually isn't enough to use it. Tape drives require special backup software to operate them. If the manufacturer of your tape drive doesn't supply any software made especially for Windows 95 or Windows NT, you'll probably need to purchase third-party commercial backup software. Note that 16-bit backup software designed for earlier versions of Windows won't support long filenames, and pretty much defeats the purpose of backing up. When purchasing backup software, make sure it specifically supports your tape drive. Otherwise, it probably won't work at all. It's also a good idea to compare the price of new backup software with the price of a whole new tape drive that includes its own 32-bit backup software.

If you must use old backup software with Windows 95 (this doesn't apply to Windows NT), either because of monetary limitations or to maintain compatibility with other computers running older versions of Windows or DOS, you can still back up your long filenames with a separate utility. Microsoft has included a DOS utility on the CD version of Windows 95 called LFNBK, located in the \Mig_kit\ Admin95\Apptools\Lfnback folder (if you don't have the CD version, see "Software and the Internet" in the Preface). Microsoft calls it "Temporary Compatibility," as it is only for use with programs that don't yet support long filenames. Read the included text file for more information.

Removable, optical, and recordable CD drives

Due to the proprietary nature of these devices, you're usually out of luck if you can't find a driver made especially for your version of Windows. However, since most of these types of devices connect to SCSI controllers, you may be able to find support from the manufacturer of your SCSI card. Newer SCSI drivers may either add support for your drive or fix a bug that prevented it from working before.

Recordable CD drives require special recording software in addition to an appropriate driver.

Modems

If your modem is slower than 9600 baud, it's not worth the time to get it to work. You can get a 14,400 or 28,800 baud modem for less money than it would cost in long-distance support calls to find drivers for the old one. While choosing the appropriate driver is important, you can usually get by with one of the standard modem drivers included with Windows. In fact, Windows might call your modem a "standard modem" if it can't auto-detect the make and model, even though a driver for your modem may be included with Windows. If after checking the list of supported modems and contacting the manufacturer of your modem for a driver, you can't find the correct driver, you should still be able to use the standard modem driver.

Essentially, the only piece of configuration information Windows really needs to use your modem is an initialization string—a long string of nonsensical characters, beginning with **AT**, used to send commands to your modem to prepare it for dialing. If your modem still doesn't work, try entering your modem's initialization string into Windows. Double-click on the Modems icon in Control Panel, select your modem from the list, click **Properties**, and choose the **Connection** tab. Click **Advanced**, and type your initialization string into the field labeled **Extra settings**. To obtain your modem's initialization string, either contact the manufacturer of your modem or refer to the documentation. If you have older software that works with your modem (that came with it or was available separately), a good trick is to snoop around the configuration section of the software to find the configuration string it's using. If that doesn't work or you can't find the initialization string, try using HyperTerminal and entering ATZ, a simple reset command. You should receive an "OK" after the successful completion of this reset.

Since modems are constantly receiving commands from your computer, it's possible for the modem to become confused if it is sent a garbled or incomplete command. The easiest way to correct a confused modem is to turn it off and then on again. If the modem is an internal model, you'll need to power down your computer and then turn it on again. Pressing the **Reset** button may not be sufficient.

If you know the software is installed and configured correctly, there are external factors that can prevent modems from working or that can slow performance. Start by removing all other devices from the phone line, including answering machines, fax machines, autodialers, and handsets. Some of these can interfere with the modem, preventing it from detecting the dial tone or causing it to hang up prematurely. Other factors include bad phone cables and wall sockets. Try replacing the old cable with a new one, as short as will reach the jack.

Since ISDN adapters aren't really modems, these techniques won't apply. You'll need to obtain the latest drivers for the manufacturer to use an ISDN adapter with Windows. If you have an internal ISDN adapter and wish to use it with Dial-Up Networking, you may need Microsoft's *ISDN Accelerator Kit*, but make sure to check with the manufacturer first. External ISDN adapters still need the appropriate drivers, but don't need this special software to be used with Dial-Up Networking. See Chapter 7 for more information.

Printers

Windows can print plain text on nearly all printers without knowing what kind of printer you have. Even if you don't have a driver made especially for your printer, you still may be able to use it with Windows by installing the Generic/Text Only driver included with Windows. To use fonts or print graphics on your printer (only for printers that are capable of printing graphics), you may be able to find another driver that works with your printer. Try installing a driver for another printer by the same manufacturer with a similar model number. Often different models use the same driver. Since many printers are compatible with Hewlett-Packard's PCL (printer control language), you may be able to use the driver for the Hewlett-Packard Laserjet Series II (for laser printers) or the Hewlett-Packard Deskjet (for inkjet printers). If you have a postscript laser printer, you should be able to use the driver for one of the Apple Laserwriter varieties.

Scanners

Scanners not only require the appropriate drivers to function in Windows, but special scanning software as well. Most scanner manufacturers have drivers for Windows 95 that come with scanning software, but a manufacturer that supports Windows NT 4.0 will be harder to find. If you have an application that supports Twain, such as a photo-retouching or optical character recognition package, you'll need Twain drivers made especially for your scanner to use it with Twain. While 16-bit Twain drivers and 16-bit scanning software should work in Windows 95, it's best to obtain the newest 32-bit equivalents from the manufacturer of your scanner. If you're searching for third-party scanning software, make sure it specifically supports your scanner. If the manufacturer of your scanner won't provide 32-bit drivers and software for use with your scanner, you're probably out of luck. Many companies have their scanners made by other manufacturers, however. If this applies to your scanner, you may be able to obtain a driver from the original manufacturer or another company that sells its version of the same scanner.

Sound cards

Any sound card worth its weight is compatible with the Soundblaster sound card by Creative Labs. If you can't find a driver for your sound card, try this one. If your sound card is older and doesn't support digi-tized sound (prerecorded sound effects and speech), it may still support MIDI synthesis (cheesy synthesizer music) compatible with the Ad Lib card. Windows should be able to detect your sound card, as well as the resources it uses. If your system crashes while trying to play sound on your sound card, and you know you have the correct driver installed, try changing the resources used by the card. See "Hardware Issues" earlier in this chapter. If you can't get it to work, and can't contact the manufacturer for the latest 32-bit drivers, you're probably going to have to replace it.

Network cards

Windows should be able to detect your network adapter and install the correct drivers for it automatically. However, there are so many different types and manufacturers of network cards, and so many of those are completely proprietary, that you may be out of luck if you can't obtain drivers made specifically for your version of Windows. Due to the nature of Windows, you will have several drivers installed for any given network adapter, including the dial-up adapter (which isn't a network card at all. See Chapter 7 for more information). Since there are no generic or standard network drivers, if you can't find a driver for your network adapter, your only hope (other than replacing the card) is to use a driver for another card.

Configuration

Following are specific topics dealing with troubleshooting hardware, soft-ware, and Windows itself. By default, Windows is configured to work reliably on a variety of different systems, but rarely will you receive the best performance without some tweaking.

Stopping Windows from Randomly
Searching the Floppy Drive ● ■

A bizarre and annoying quirk has appeared in Windows 95, where the floppy drive is searched every time an application is launched or even every few seconds, for no apparent reason. The most common cause might seem that the user launched a program from the floppy drive at some point, and Windows has now made this the *current* drive. However, this problem manifests itself even when the system is restarted, meaning that there's more going on than just the "current drive" problem. There are many things that can cause this problem, such as references to the floppy drive in certain places, as well as some third-party software. Try the following:

Windows 95 only

- Clear your **Documents** menu. See "Turning Off the Documents Menu" in Chapter 4.

- Clear out the history of the **Start Menu**'s *Run* command, discussed later in this chapter.

- Check for any viruses on your system (some users have reported the Neuville virus). You'll need an antivirus utility for this.

- Search your hard disk for all DOS and Windows shortcuts that point to programs on a floppy drive. Select **Find**, and then **Files** or **Folders** from the **Start Menu**. Type *.lnk, *.pif in the field labeled **Named**, then choose the **Advanced** tab, type a: in the **Containing text** field, and click **Find Now**. Delete any files that are found, unless you know specifically that you want to keep them.

- Search your hard disk for all files with the extension *.INI* (configuration file) that contain the text a: (using the procedure in the previous item). If one or more is found, use a text editor such as Notepad, to edit the file and remove the reference. See "Using INI Files" in Chapter 3 for more information if you're not familiar with editing these files.

- Take out the line that reads LocalLoadHigh=1 from your *MSDOS.SYS* file. This line will be there only if you intentionally placed it there in the first place.

- Search your entire Registry for a:, looking for any references to files or programs on your floppy drive. More specifically, the path HKEY_CLASSES_ROOT/CLSID may contain references to .OCX or .DLL files located on your floppy drive.

Third-party applications that are known to cause this problem (can also affect Windows NT)

Norton Navigator '95

Clear Norton Navigator's Run history (or disable the Run history altogether). If you're noticing this behavior with only a particular application, clear the document and folder History List for that application. A bug fix is available from Symantec. See "Software and the Internet" in the Preface for more information.

McAfee Antivirus '95

Try removing this program entirely or just disabling the access and shutdown options in the **Scan Disks On** area in the **Detection** tab of the VShield Configuration Manager.

FirstAid '95

Try removing this program or disabling certain features.

Long filenames for Windows 95

Obtain a patch from View Software that supposedly fixes this problem. See "Software and the Internet" in the Preface for more information.

HiJaak for Windows 95

Turning off "Enable HiJaak shell extensions" in the HiJaak Control Panel should solve the problem.

Konica Picture Show

Try removing this program entirely.

Do I Still Need CONFIG.SYS and AUTOEXEC.BAT? ●

Before Windows 95 and Plug & Play, some devices in your system required device drivers to be specified in two files on your hard disk, called *CONFIG.SYS* and *AUTOEXEC.BAT*. While this was necessary back then, nearly all the functionality of these two files has now been replaced by Windows 95. Even if your computer shipped with Windows 95, these files may still be there, loading drivers you don't need.

The problem with these old files is that the drivers they load aren't as efficient or as stable as their 32-bit Windows 95 counterparts. They take up more memory and slow down boot time as well. Additionally, a device driver specified in one of these files might actually prevent Windows 95 from detecting and using a certain device. Ideally, you should remove these files altogether, but you first need to make sure all of the functions they provide for you can be reproduced in Windows 95.

Drivers specified in *CONFIG.SYS* usually have the extension .SYS and are often called real mode drivers. Generally this file loads drivers for your disk cache, memory manager, CD-ROM, sound card, any removable or optical drives, your scanner, and a myriad of parameters like Files=50, Buffers=20. Windows 95 eliminates the need for any of these.

AUTOEXEC.BAT is similar, although it is simply a DOS batch file run automatically when your computer is first turned on. Other CD-ROM drivers are loaded here, as well as antivirus programs, Smartdrive (a disk cache), some DOS "resident" utilities, and any other programs loaded when you turn on your computer.

These two files are text files that list drivers to be loaded every time your computer starts, and can be edited with a plain text editor, such as Notepad. Windows 95 comes with a DOS text editor as well. Just type `edit c:\config.sys` (for example) to edit the file in DOS. If you make duplicates of these files before you start tinkering with them, you'll eliminate the possibility of disabling your system. If anything goes wrong, simply replace the files you've altered with your backups, and your system will be restored to its original state. Note that some older devices may not work without drivers specified here. If this is the case, you are *strongly* encouraged to seek 32-bit windows replacements. See "Drivers" at the beginning of this chapter.

- Start by putting the word `rem` in front of *every* line in *CONFIG.SYS*, and restart your computer. The *rem* command turns each entry into a remark, which is ignored by DOS. This is better than removing the lines completely, because you may have to go back and restore one or more of the entries.

- When Windows 95 restarts, it automatically scans your computer for any new devices it finds. If you've disabled any old drivers with the previous step, Windows 95 will attempt to install a new, "native" driver at this point. Refer to the documentation that came with any specific devices if you encounter problems, and see "Drivers" earlier in this chapter for details.

- The one common problem is that Windows may need to retrieve the new drivers from your CD. If your CD-ROM drive is one of the devices that was supported by *CONFIG.SYS*, Windows 95 may not have access to the CD at all! If this happens, skip all drivers until Windows loads. If the CD-ROM is enabled at this point, you can restart Windows and load the rest of the drivers. Otherwise, you'll have to go back and enable the CD-ROM drivers in *CONFIG.SYS* and *AUTOEXEC.BAT* so that all the other drivers can be installed first. Your other option is to add support for your CD-ROM drive manually. See the next item.

- Once Windows 95 appears to have loaded all the drivers it intends to, try out all your devices. You may have to run the Add New Hardware wizard in Control Panel to search for any newly added hardware if your system doesn't support Plug & Play entirely. If a device works, you can remove its driver from *CONFIG.SYS* for good. Otherwise, remove the *rem* command you placed in front of the driver to reenable it.

• If everything appears to be working properly now that all the statements in the *CONFIG.SYS* file have been disabled, you can delete the file entirely and continue with *AUTOEXEC.BAT*.

• The same process applies to *AUTOEXEC.BAT*, with the exception of the Path statement (Windows 95 only). It never occurred to the folks at Microsoft to include Windows support for this functionality. See "Software Issues" earlier in this chapter for more information.

Notes and other issues

If you think that keeping these old drivers loaded all the time is a good idea in case you need to reinstall Windows 95, you are mistaken. You will have better performance and stability if you use the native Windows 95 drivers only. However, I strongly recommend copying all your old drivers to a bootable floppy, so they are available in the event of an emergency, such as a disk crash. Windows does not do this automatically. See "Making a Startup Disk" earlier in this chapter for details.

If you still need these DOS drivers when you run a certain DOS application, you can configure Windows 95 to load them automatically when needed, rather than keeping them in memory all the time. First, you can move any *AUTOEXEC.BAT* statements into a file called *DOSSTART.BAT*, placed also in your root directory. This file will be run whenever you restart in MS-DOS mode. You can also move any statements from your *CONFIG.SYS* file to the properties of a DOS shortcut, to be loaded when the shortcut is run. Right-click on the MS-DOS Prompt shortcut located in your Windows directory (or the shortcut for any other DOS application you need to configure), and click **Properties**. Choose the **Program** tab, click **Advanced**, turn on MS-DOS mode, and select **Specify a new MS-DOS configuration**. You can now enter any desired drivers here as though they were loaded in *CONFIG.SYS* or *AUTOEXEC.BAT*. Click **OK** and then **OK** again when finished.

See "Creating a Startup Menu" later in this chapter for a reason to keep *AUTOEXEC.BAT* and *CONFIG.SYS* around.

Stopping Windows 95 from Detecting Devices •

Although there is no way to prevent Windows 95's Plug & Play feature from detecting and installing drivers for some devices, you can disable certain devices that may be causing conflicts. The lack of a feature to remove an item from the list of detected devices (when you use Add/ Remove Hardware) is quite irritating and confusing, but problems can usually be averted by following these steps:

- Right-click on the My Computer icon, and select **Properties**.

- Choose the **Device Manager** tab, and select the device you wish to disable.

- Click **Properties**, uncheck **Original Configuration** below, and click **OK**.

You'll have to restart Windows for this change to take effect.

Notes and other issues

Some devices can't be disabled in this way, and some devices can be disabled with other methods. Refer to the documentation that came with the device for details.

Getting DOS Games to Work ● ■

There is almost nothing more frustrating or difficult than to get certain DOS games to work on a Windows system. It seems as though each game needs its own drivers and memory settings installed just to start. Additional problems, such as getting sound to work and using the CD-ROM drive when Windows isn't running, are even more difficult to resolve.

In the old days of conventional memory and expanded memory managers, one often spent hours tuning and reconfiguring so that a game would have enough memory to run. Now that Windows contains all the necessary memory managers and device drivers, you don't need to have them running just to use a DOS game. While the situation is infinitely better than it was just a few years ago, there are still problems. Some poorly designed games won't run from within Windows, but require some of the services Windows provides to work at all. Avoid products like this at all costs.

There are four ways of getting into DOS from Windows, each with its own advantages and disadvantages:

Open a DOS command prompt

Whether you use the command prompt icon in the **Start Menu**, run the DOS game directly from Explorer, or use a windows shortcut to launch the DOS game (usually), you'll be using the command prompt. The command prompt, also known as a DOS window, enables you to run most DOS programs from within Windows.

Advantages

- Most games will run in a DOS window with little or no special settings. Since Windows controls the CD-ROM and sound card, the game can access these devices without any special drivers. Since CD-ROM and sound drivers can take up a considerable amount of memory, it's often best to run DOS games in Windows.

- You don't have to restart your computer or close any of your applications to run a DOS game in this way. Note that DOS games can be unstable, so it's best not to leave work unsaved if you do this.

- You can create shortcuts in the **Start Menu** for each of your DOS games, virtually eliminating the typing normally involved.

- To specify special memory settings, or any *CONFIG.SYS* drivers or *AUTOEXEC.BAT* commands to load with the game, such as sound card drivers or a DOS mouse driver, first create a Windows shortcut to the game. Right-click on the shortcut and select **Properties**. Choose the **Memory** tab to specify the amount of memory to reserve for the game. Refer to the game's documentation for the game's memory requirements. If you choose the **Program** tab, click **Advanced**, and turn on the **MS-DOS mode** option, it's the same as restarting the computer in MS-DOS mode (see next topic).

Disadvantages

- Many games require a great deal of memory or access your hardware directly, meaning that they won't run while Windows is running.

- Since Windows is running in the background, some games may run more slowly than if Windows weren't running.

- If a DOS game only runs from within Windows, you'll have to wait for Windows to load before running the game—a bit ironic.

Restart in MS-DOS mode (Windows 95 only)

If a game won't run from within Windows, you can select **Shut Down** from the **Start Menu**, and choose **Restart the computer in MS-DOS Mode**. This unloads Windows 95, which may allow you to run nearly all DOS games that don't run in a DOS window (see previous item). Furthermore, you can create a Windows shortcut to the game to automate the process. Right-click on the shortcut, click **Properties**, choose the **Program** tab, click **Advanced**, and turn on the **MS-DOS mode** option. This will automatically restart in MS-DOS mode and run the game with a single shortcut.

Advantages

- In the Advanced Program Settings window, you can specify a special *CONFIG.SYS* or *AUTOEXEC.BAT* file to be used exclusively with the game. Since you're unloading Windows, you may need to load a DOS CD-ROM driver, a mouse driver, and sound card drivers. The requirements here depend on the game—the beauty of this design.

- You can create shortcuts in the **Start Menu** for each DOS game, virtually eliminating typing. Additionally, since Windows isn't running in the background, the game can run at its full speed.

- Configuring games to run this way doesn't mean that they can't also run with one of the other MS-DOS settings explained here.

Disadvantages

- This method, while sometimes necessary, can take more time and effort to configure. Once you've done it, however, it's a snap to use.

- You have to wait for Windows to load to run any game configured in this way, and you have to wait for Windows to reload after the game concludes, unless you shut the computer off.

- Windows doesn't unload itself entirely from memory with this method, which means that some games may still not run. See "Boot directly to MS-DOS" and "Exit to DOS," which follow.

Boot directly into DOS (Windows 95 only)

See "Booting Directly into DOS" in Chapter 4 for instructions. Booting directly allows you to start your computer and go directly to DOS without having to wait for Windows to load. While this requires that you reconfigure your startup procedure somewhat, the advantages can be worth it, especially if you play a lot of DOS games.

Advantages

- You can configure a DOS startup menu (as described later in this chapter) to allow you to choose between Windows and any number of DOS games. In fact, if you create a menu item for each game, you can specify separate *CONFIG.SYS* and *AUTOEXEC.BAT* statements for each game.

- You won't have to wait for Windows to load before running a DOS game. Furthermore, you can start Windows after the game concludes by typing `win` at the command prompt.

Disadvantages

- The DOS game you're trying to get working may not be worth the time and effort required to implement this method.

- If a game requires sound card or CD-ROM drivers, you'll have to load them when the computer starts, which requires some work. Make sure these drivers are loaded only when you use the DOS game, and not when Windows 95 is running. Furthermore, these drivers, while required by the game, also take up conventional memory, which may not leave enough left over for the game to run. It's a catch-22.

Exit to DOS (Windows 95 only)

This has all of the same advantages and disadvantages of "Boot directly into DOS" with the following exceptions. Rather than starting in DOS, this method allows you to exit Windows entirely (not the same as restart in MS-DOS mode), and run your DOS game. See "How to Exit to DOS" for instructions.

- This method has one important but not obvious advantage over "Boot directly into DOS." Many sound cards come with DOS drivers for *CONFIG.SYS* that are required to initialize the sound card settings. The drivers take up a considerable amount of memory and can even conflict with some games. The problem is that you may not get sound in some games unless these drivers are installed. In some circumstances, if you exit to DOS with this method, your sound card may be initialized sufficiently for the game to work, without having to load the pesky drivers. If you're having trouble getting sound to work in a certain game, try exiting to DOS and then running it.

Boot directly into DOS with a boot disk

This has all of the same advantages and disadvantages of "Boot directly into DOS," with the following exceptions. First, you need to create a startup diskette (as described earlier in this chapter), allowing you boot your computer without loading Windows. The advantage is that it works with Windows 95 and Windows NT 4.0 (only if your hard disk uses the FAT file system, and not NTFS). The disadvantage is that startup diskettes are a pain.

Notes and other issues

Since all DOS games are different, each game may require a different method. Try contacting the manufacturer of the game for suggestions.

See "Do I Still Need CONFIG.SYS and AUTOEXEC.BAT?" earlier in this chapter for more information on drivers and commands in each of these files.

Forcing NumLock to Behave ● ■

Ever since IBM introduced the enhanced 101-key keyboard with two sets of cursor keys back in 1984, the NumLock key on most machines is turned on by default. Since some of us seem to prefer it off while others prefer it on, there are several ways to change the default. However, many users have complained that Windows will not allow you to change this setting under some circumstances. Following are several solutions to choosing the setting you prefer:

Solution 1

- In most modern computers, you can set the default in your CMOS setup. This screen, usually accessible by pressing Del, Esc, or some other key when your computer first boots up, is where you also define your fixed and floppy drives, memory settings, the clock, and other system parameters. Refer to the manual that came with your computer or motherboard for instructions on changing this setting. It's usually something like "Numlock Default: ON / OFF."

Solution 2 (Windows 95 only)

- Include the command NUMLOCK=OFF or NUMLOCK=ON (depending on your preference) somewhere in your *CONFIG.SYS* file (on its own line). See "Do I Still Need CONFIG.SYS and AUTOEXEC.BAT?" earlier in this chapter for more information.

Solution 3 (if you have Microsoft's Intellipoint software installed)

- Open the Registry Editor (*regedit.exe*). If you're not familiar with the Registry Editor, see Chapter 3.

- Expand the branches to HKEY_CURRENT_USER\Control Panel\ Microsoft Input Devices\Keyboard. If the Keyboard key isn't there, add it.

- Select **New** from the **Edit** menu, then **String Value**, and type NumLock for the name of the new value.

- Double-click on this new value, and type either ON or OFF in the box that appears, depending on your preference.

Notes and other issues

If none of these solutions works and you do have useless Intellipoint software installed, try removing Intellipoint altogether. Microsoft is aware of the problem but seems to be more interested in selling keyboards than making sure they work.

Clearing Unwanted Entries from the Start Menu's Run Command History ● ■

Whenever you use the **Start Menu**'s *Run* command to launch a program, that program's filename is added to a history list. Since this is a possible contributor to the problem of Windows' repeatedly searching your floppy drive (discussed earlier in this chapter), a solution is provided here for clearing this list.

* Open the Registry Editor (*regedit.exe*). (If you're not familiar with the Registry Editor, see Chapter 3.)

* Expand the branches to HKEY_CURRENT_USER\Software\ Microsoft\Windows\CurrentVersion\Explorer\RunMRU\. (MRU means most recently used, and signifies many such history lists in the Registry.)

* Delete all of the values in this key—everything in the right pane, except for (Default).

* Close the Registry Editor when you're finished.

Notes and other issues

If you're using the OtherFolder utility (see "Copying or Moving to Specified Path" in Chapter 2, *regedit.exe*), you can clear its history by repeating this procedure with the following Registry path: HKEY_CURRENT_ USER\Software\Microsoft\Windows\CurrentVersion\Explorer\ OtherFolder\.

With Microsoft's TweakUI, one of Microsoft's PowerToys, these lists can be cleared automatically at startup by enabling the appropriate options under the Paranoia tab. See "Software and the Internet" in the Preface for more information.

To help solve the floppy searching problem, the process for clearing Norton Navigator's Run History is the same as the abov1e, except that the Registry path is HKEY_CURRENT_USER\Software\Symantec\Navigator\ SYMFDLG4\History_List\Run.

Creating a Startup Menu ● ■

Startup menus appear when you turn on your computer, before Windows starts. There are three varieties, each with different purposes and limitations. They are shown in order of execution. That is, if you were to use all three, they would appear in this order.

Windows NT dual-boot menu

If you've installed Windows NT 4.0 on a system with another operating system present, such as MS-DOS or Windows 95, the Windows NT installation program will automatically create this menu, allowing you to choose which operating system to load. It usually gives you a choice of Windows NT, Windows NT with the plain-vanilla VGA video driver, and a choice for each additional operating system installed. For most users, the only other operating system will be MS-DOS or Windows 95. There are two ways to edit this menu.

The first method simply allows you to select a default option, and the delay.

- For example, setting the **MS-DOS** option as the default, and choosing a delay of 10 seconds means that the menu will be displayed for 10 seconds. After that time, if no selection is made, MS-DOS will be chosen automatically.

- To change these settings, double-click on the System icon in Windows NT's Control Panel, and choose the **Startup/shutdown** tab.

- Choose the desired option from the **Startup** list, and specify the delay where it says "Show List for xx Seconds," where xx is the number of seconds you choose.

The second method requires that you edit a system file but allows you to change the text and ordering of any of the items.

- Using a plain text editor, such as Notepad, edit *boot.ini*, which resides in the root directory of your boot drive (usually C). Since this file has the System attribute set, you'll need to turn it off with the Attrib DOS command before you can edit it. Refer to Chapter 3 for more information on editing .INI files, and dealing with hidden files.

- There are two sections here, [boot loader] and [operating systems].

- The [boot loader] section contains the timeout setting (the delay discussed above) and the default setting (also discussed above).

- The [operating systems] section lists all of the items shown in the menu. Be very careful not to change any text not already enclosed in quotes. To the left of the equals sign on each line is the drive containing the startup files for the operating system. Don't change this. This is also what's used in the default setting above. To the right of the equals sign are the label (enclosed in quotes) and any settings (such as /basevideo/sos for NT's safe mode).

- You can change the labels (the text in quotes) and reorder the lines, but leave everything else alone.

- Save the file, and reboot when you're finished.

Windows 95 Startup Menu

This menu is built into Windows 95 and will appear if Windows didn't load successfully the last time the computer was used. Its purpose is primarily to provide access to the command prompt and Windows 95's safe mode to aid in troubleshooting a problem. You can display this menu manually by pressing F8 during system startup, just before the Windows 95 logo appears. This menu is not included with Windows NT. When the menu appears, you have eight choices:

1. **Normal**—Choose this to load Windows normally as though nothing has happened.

2. **Logged** (*BOOTLOG.TXT*)—This is the same as choice 1, except that all the steps of the bootup process are recorded in the *BOOTLOG.TXT* file in the root directory of your boot drive. View this file after startup to help determine if any drivers or tasks failed to load.

3. **Safe mode**—This loads Windows 95 with the default VGA display driver and no network support, so that you can change settings if you can't get into Windows 95 normally. This is useful, for example, if you've changed your video driver to a new one, which doesn't work. The F5 key has the same effect as selecting this option.

4. **Safe mode with network support**—This is the same as choice 3, except that your network drivers (if any) are loaded as well if you might need network access.

5. **Step-by-step confirmation**—This is the same as choice 1, except that Windows 95 will ask you before loading each and every driver. This is useful in isolating certain problems that may be occurring when you load Windows. If you press Shift-F8, it will either turn on or off the step-by-step confirmation, so you can use the feature in conjunction with any of the other options here.

6. **Command prompt only**—This will boot you directly into DOS after loading *CONFIG.SYS* and *AUTOEXEC.BAT*, rather than loading Windows. Press Shift-F5 either here, or when your computer first starts, to go into the Command Prompt without loading *CONFIG.SYS* or *AUTOEXEC.BAT*. See "Booting Directly into DOS" in Chapter 4 to configure your computer to use this option every time.

7. **Safe mode command prompt only**—This is the same as choice 6, except that if you start Windows 95 by typing win at the command prompt, it will load into safe mode.

8. **Previous version of MS-DOS**—If you've installed Windows 95 over an older version of MS-DOS, and have opted to have it remain on your system, you can load it with this option.

MS-DOS Startup Menu

The third type of startup menu has been around since MS-DOS 5.0 and is the most flexible of the three. While it doesn't allow you to change operating systems, you can set up any number of different configurations. You can give yourself the option of booting into DOS, loading Windows 95, loading Windows 95 in safe mode, loading another version of Windows, booting into DOS with special drivers required for your favorite DOS game, or anything else you may need. While most users won't need this menu at all, if you still use DOS applications or games, this menu will be very beneficial.

Although the Windows 95 documentation doesn't tell you how to do it (or even that it's possible), the old DOS tricks still work (it's a good idea to get your old DOS manual ready). This functionality can be useful for those who use DOS more than just occasionally and don't want to be forced to enter Windows first just to play a DOS game. Note that this procedure can be tricky and requires some basic knowledge of the *AUTOEXEC.BAT* and *CONFIG.SYS* files. See "Do I Still Need CONFIG.SYS and AUTOEXEC.BAT?" earlier in this chapter for more information.

The following example shows how to create a menu giving you a choice between DOS and Windows every time you start up. Your actual files may differ substantially, but the methodology will be the same. Remember to back up your existing files before you begin.

Step 1

- Configure your computer to boot directly into MS-DOS. See the section by this name in Chapter 4.

Step 2

- Use a text editor such as Notepad to open your *CONFIG.SYS* file, located in the root directory of your boot drive (usually C:\). If it's not there, create a new file.

- Type the following lines at the top of the file. Make sure that there aren't any commands floating around that aren't part of a particular section. Sections are denoted by [brackets]. The text will probably need some adjustments for your system.

```
[Menu]
MenuItem = MS-DOS
MenuItem = Windows 95
         ... put any other menu items you want here
MenuDefault MS-DOS,4
MenuColor 15,1
[MS-DOS]
         ... put all your MSDOS drivers here
[Windows 95]
         ... put all your Windows 95 drivers here
(should be empty for most users)
[etc.]
         ... make a section for each additional menu item,
     with each name matching a new "menuitem" command above
[Common]
         ... put all the stuff you want loaded all the time
```

Step 3

- Save *CONFIG.SYS*, and open *AUTOEXEC.BAT* in the same directory (or create it if it's not there), using the same text editor, and type the following lines at the top of the file (this may need some adjustments if you have added more menu items).

```
@echo off
Rem * If user selects "Windows 95" it must be run manually here *
IF "%CONFIG%"=="Windows 95" win
IF "%CONFIG%"=="Windows 95" goto skip

         ... put all your DOS autoexec stuff here

:skip
```

- Follow the logic in this file, as you'll probably have to change the If statements to suit your particular choices. The %CONFIG% variable is set by DOS to whatever menu item is chosen, and the If statement is used to redirect execution depending on the variable. In the example shown, if the user selects Windows 95, the win command is issued, and the rest of the file is skipped (where it says ..."put all your DOS autoexec stuff here").

• Save your changes when finished, and restart your computer to test the new menu.

Notes and other issues

The particular drivers required by your system depend on the devices you have installed. There are no standard *CONFIG.SYS* or *AUTOEXEC.BAT* files, other than the two examples given above.

7

In this chapter:
- *Setting Up a Workgroup*
- *General Networking Issues*
- *Installing Dial-Up Networking*
- *Coping with Dial-Up Networking*

Networking

A network is the connection of two or more computers to each other, allowing the sharing of files, programs, printers, and other resources. A simple network can comprise merely two computers connected with a single cable, or a single machine connected to the enormous Internet via the phone company. With the proliferation of Internet service providers (ISPs), it's becoming increasingly affordable and popular to connect to the Internet. And with hardware costs declining, and Plug & Play technology making setup easier and quicker, peer-to-peer networks are also becoming more commonplace in the home. Both of these types of networks are treated similarly by Windows, as they are in this chapter. However, since Windows 95 is the more popular platform and network support isn't quite as extensive in Windows 95, most of the screen shots and specific driver information will refer to Windows 95 instead of Windows NT 4.0.

Many annoyances and problems with Windows networking are caused by an improper setup, so this chapter starts off with walkthroughs of setting up both a workgroup (a common term for a small local-area network of two or more computer users and perhaps, a printer) and a dial-up networking connection (used to connect to the Internet and other remote services). The inclusion of these basic instructions here is very important, as the additional solutions and workarounds are closely dependent on the correct installation of the respective networking service.

The setup of either type of network requires the correct hardware to be installed, as well as the proper configuration of Windows' many drivers. The hardware is up to you, although there are a few recommendations in the sections that follow. However, pay close attention to the drivers. It's important to have them all installed and configured properly, while keeping in mind that loading extra or unnecessary drivers can decrease performance, available memory, and system reliability.

Many terms are used throughout this chapter with which you may be unfamiliar. See the *Glossary* at the end of this book.

Setting Up a Workgroup

Connecting two computers to form a basic workgroup is remarkably easy with Windows 95 and Windows NT 4.0, as long as you have the proper equipment, drivers, and a few hours. Although there are many types of local area networks, network adapters, drivers, and operating systems, we'll be dealing with a basic peer-to-peer workgroup using only the software that came with Windows and some ethernet hardware.

To set up a workgroup, you'll need the following:

- Two computers, each running some version of Windows. It's possible to network two systems running different versions of Windows, although for the sake of simplicity, we'll assume Windows 95 on both. If one or more of the systems is running Windows 3.x, it's recommended that the system be upgraded to at least Windows for Workgroups 3.11. Earlier versions don't have enough network support to make it worthwhile.

- Two network cards, preferably Plug & Play. You should be able to find such cards at your local computer store for less than $70 each. *Important*: each card should come with drivers to support your version of Windows. Each card should also have a connector appropriate to the type of connection you will be making.

- A network cable long enough to connect both your computers.

For example, a common type of inexpensive network, 10base2, requires a BNC connector on each card, a coaxial cable, two T-connectors, and two terminators. See Figure 7-1 for details. This is the cheapest type of network setup, as you can connect additional computers and printers with a minimum of additional hardware. Other technology, such as 10baseT, offers many advantages (which we won't discuss here) at some additional cost.

Once you have all of the components, follow these steps (note that network adapters vary significantly, and the particular design of your network cards may require a different procedure):

- Install a network card in each computer. Refer to the documentation included with the cards for specific hardware and software setup. Before connecting the cable, run the diagnostic or test software included with the network adapters to verify that they are functioning properly and not conflicting with any other devices. Most network installation problems are caused by hardware conflicts, and eliminating them now will save hours of work.

- When installing the drivers in Windows 95 or Windows NT 4.0, make sure you're using the most recent drivers made especially for your version of Windows. Contact the manufacturer of the network cards or go to its Internet site to acquire the latest software. If the installation program installs drivers in your *CONFIG.SYS* or *AUTOEXEC.BAT* files, you're not using the latest version of the drivers. Make sure Windows recognizes your network cards in Device Manager (or in the Devices icon of Control Panel in Windows NT) and doesn't report any conflicts.

- Determine if there are any problems before connecting the cable. This way, it's much easier to isolate problems.

- Connect the cable between the two computers. Figure 7-1 shows a photograph and installation diagram of our example 10base2 setup, but your hardware will most likely be different.

Figure 7-1: Connecting the BNC cable to your network card using the proper connectors

- Once the cables are connected, you'll probably need to restart your computer. You'll then need to configure Windows with the proper protocols and settings. Double-click on the Network icon in Control Panel to view the network settings. If your network cards have more than one type of connector, you'll also need to specify which type you're using. Refer to Figure 7-2 for a sample screen shot showing the drivers that should be installed. If you don't have the drivers shown, click **Add** and choose the appropriate items from the list. They're usually found by selecting **Microsoft** as the manufacturer.

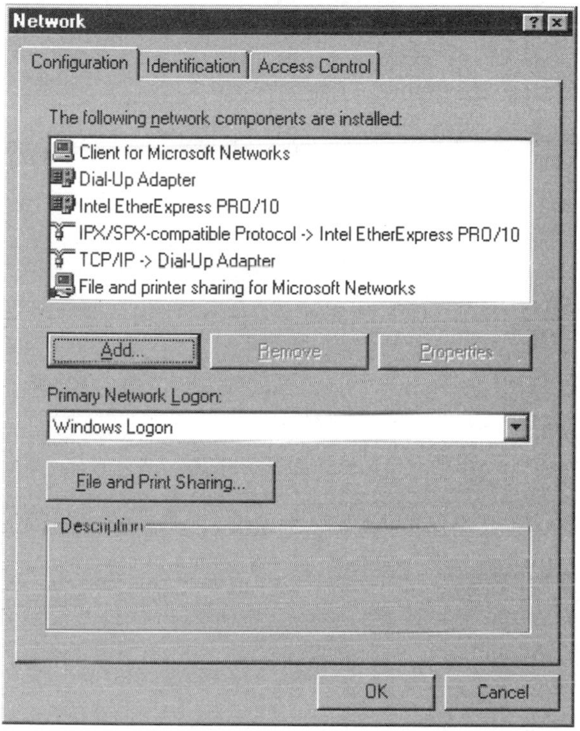

Figure 7-2: The Network icon in the Control Panel shows which network components are installed

- From the drop-down list labeled **Primary Network Logon:**, choose **Windows Logon**. Then click **File** and **Print Sharing**, and turn on both options.

- Next, click on the **Identification** tab in the Network properties window. The first field, **Computer name**, is a unique one-word name for the computer. No other computer on the network should have the same name. If you're using dial-up networking on this machine as well (see the section later in this chapter), you might want to type in your Internet logon because Windows uses it as the default when dialing.

- The **Workgroup** field should be the same for each computer on the network; otherwise you won't be able to browse that computer's shared resources.

- If you've hidden your Network Neighborhood icon as described in Chapter 2, *So You're Stuck with Windows*, you'll probably want to get it back. It provides easy access to the other computers in the work-group from your Desktop and in Explorer. You'll have to restart Windows for all of these changes to take effect.

- Determine which resources are to be shared. If a computer has a printer, drive, or folder that you want to share with the other computer(s) in the workgroup, you can do so by right-clicking on it and selecting **Sharing**. For drives and folders, use Explorer; for printers, select **Settings** and then **Printers** from the **Start Menu**. You'll see a window as shown in Figure 7-3.

```
Hard disk (C:) Properties                          [?][X]

  General | Tools | Sharing | Norton | Folder Size |

      ○ Not Shared
      ◉ Shared As:
        Share Name: [C        ]

        Comment:    [                    ]

      Access Type:
           ○ Read-Only
           ◉ Full
           ○ Depends on Password
      Passwords:
           Read-Only Password: [        ]

           Full Access Password: [        ]


              [   OK   ]   [ Cancel ]   [ Apply ]
```

Figure 7-3: Right-click on a drive, folder, or printer, and select Sharing to choose how the resource will be shared in the workgroup

- To share a device, change the option at the top of the Sharing window from **Not Shared** to **Shared As**. The **Share Name** is the name for the resource that will show up on the other computers. This is not the same as drive mapping. That comes later.

- For drives and folders, you can configure the Access Type. You'll probably want **Full**, although **Read-Only** is the default, which won't allow you to write to the resource.

- A few seconds after you press **OK**, the icon for the resource will have a small hand over it, signifying that it is being shared. You'll probably want to share any printers attached to each computer in the workgroup, as well as most of the drives, and perhaps a few selected folders, such as the Desktop folder or some shared documents folder. It's up to you and can be easily changed at any time.

- Any shared drives or folders should show up immediately on the other computers in the workgroup. Just double-click on the Network Neighborhood icon on the Desktop or select it in Explorer to view the resources available from each computer in the workgroup. The shared folders and drives should behave as though they are actually connected to the computer.

- You can also map a drive or folder on the network so that it appears as just another drive letter on your system. From Explorer's **Tools** menu, choose **Map Network Drive**. Although Windows NT 4.0 allows you to browse the network for shared devices here, Windows 95 does not, meaning you'll have to type them in manually. Note that both platforms will allow you to browse the network using Explorer or the Network Neighborhood. Assuming the other computer is called "Blue" and the drive on that computer you want to map is called "C," you'd type the following in the **Path** field:

  ```
  \\blue\c
  ```

- Then, from the list of available drives, select the new drive letter you want to use on this computer that will map to the drive you typed in. Turn on the **Reconnect at logon** option if you want Windows to map this drive every time you start. Otherwise you'll have to do it manually each time (the default is *on* here).

- For a shared printer, you'll need to install a printer driver on each computer that will be using it (Windows 95 only—NT doesn't require this). On each of the other computers in the workgroup (not the one directly connected to the printer), double-click on the Add Printer icon in the Printers window. When asked, "How is the printer attached to your computer?", select **Network Printer**, and proceed normally.

Troubleshooting

There are several things that can cause a network not to work. Try some of the following suggestions to alleviate some network problems you may be experiencing.

- If you're not able to map any network resources, make sure the Network Neighborhood icon is visible (see Chapter 1).

- If you know the network cards are functioning properly and the network cable is connected as shown in Figure 7-1, try using the diagnostic software that came with your network cards (contact the manufacturer of your adapters for more information) to test the connection. Replacing the cable or the connectors may fix the problem. If the diagnostic software reports no problems, odds are that you don't have the correct network components installed. See Figure 7-2 for an example. Note that the specific drivers required for your network adapters may be different.

- If you see other machines listed in the Network Neighborhood, it means that everything is working properly. If you don't see shared drives or folders, you need to turn on sharing for the devices you wish to share. See Figure 7-3 for more information. You may need to refresh the Network Neighborhood window (press the F5 key) to display the most recent connected resources.

- If everything shows up but the network frequently crashes or exhibits slow performance, make sure you don't have any other network software loaded that could be conflicting with the network drivers included in Windows. Contact the manufacturers of your network cards for the most recent drivers and troubleshooting tips.

- In the command prompt, type net view to see all of the machines currently logged on to your network. To see the resources offered by a particular machine, include the name of the machine in the command line. For example, assume you typed net view and got the following:

```
Servers available in workgroup MY_NETWORK.
Server name             Remark
-----------------------------------------
\\BLUE                  Blue Computer
\\RED                   Red Computer
\\GREEN                 Green Computer
The command was completed successfully.
```

You could then type net view \\red to list all of the resources shared by the machine known as Red. The advantage here is that all resources are listed, instead of just shared disks and folders in Network Neighborhood.

```
Shared resources at \\RED

Sharename   Type      Comment
-------------------------------------------
C           Disk      Red Boot Drive
D           Disk      Red CD Drive
DESKTOP     Disk      Red Desktop Folder
LASERJET    Print     Laserjet printer
The command was completed successfully.
```

General Networking Issues

Once you have your network up and running you'll undoubtedly run across some or all of the following topics.

Getting Rid of the Logon Screen ● ■

In Windows 95, if you've installed any networking drivers (including Dial-Up Networking, discussed later in this chapter), you'll get a login window asking for your username and password every time Windows starts. If you're using Windows NT, you'll get this Window regardless of the existence of network drivers. The reasoning behind the login windows in both versions is different, and therefore the solutions are different. To remove the logon box, follow the following directions:

In Windows 95, if you don't have multiple users configured

- Open Control Panel, and double-click on the Network icon.

- From the list entitled **Primary Network Logon**, choose **Windows Logon**, and press **OK**.

- You'll have to restart Windows for this change to take effect. If the logon window doesn't go away, you've configured a password for yourself. If you did, Windows 95 will always require it. Double-click on the Passwords icon in Control Panel and choose nothing (leave it blank) for your password.

In Windows 95, if you do have multiple users configured

- Open the Registry Editor (*regedit.exe*). (If you're not familiar with the Registry Editor, see Chapter 3.)

- Expand the branches to HKEY_LOCAL_MACHINE\Network\Logon.

- Double-click on the Process Logon Script value, and change the data from 0000 00 to 0000 01.

- You'll have to restart Windows for this change to take effect.

In Windows NT, regardless of the number of configured users

- Although the Ctrl-Alt-Del logon screen is virtually useless for the majority of Windows NT users, it is part of Windows NT's extensive security measures—security not found in Windows 95. For this reason, it is not possible to remove the logon screen without third-party software.

- Obtain Easy Logon for Windows NT (see "Software and the Internet" in the Preface), a utility that will automatically log on to Windows NT with a desired username and password.

Installing Dial-Up Networking

Both Windows 95 and Windows NT 4.0 come with all the software necessary to connect to the Internet, in the form of Dial-Up Networking. Dial-Up Networking uses your modem to connect to the Internet with standard phone lines. While there are other ways to connect to the Internet, such as through a commercial online service (America Online, MSN, and CompuServe), or other dial-up software (the most popular of which is Trumpet Winsock), Dial-Up Networking provides the most flexibility and the largest collection of supported software.

The most popular application of this service is to connect to the Internet. However, it has other uses, which may require different drivers and protocols. This example assumes you're setting up a standard Internet connection, and your needs may be different. Contact the system administrator to find out exactly which components you'll need before proceeding.

There are several steps involved in getting Dial-Up Networking to connect to an Internet account. Simply installing the Dial-Up Networking component of Windows 95 isn't enough. The correct drivers aren't installed, and the settings aren't configured properly. This section outlines the steps needed to install Dial-Up Networking correctly on your system and configure it for optimum performance. These are general instructions; they should work most of the time, but perhaps not in all circumstances.

To set up Dial-Up Networking, you'll need the following:

- Any Windows 95–compatible modem of at least 14,400 baud, installed and functioning. Make sure it's configured correctly by double-clicking on the Modems icon in Control Panel.

- A dial-up account with a local ISP. The account should support standard point-to-point protocol (PPP). If you don't yet have an ISP, see "Selecting an ISP" later in this chapter.

- A standard phone line. You don't need a dedicated line for an Internet connection, but it may be a good idea if you plan to spend a lot of time online.

Once you get the account, the ISP should send you the following information:

- Your username and password.

- A local phone number used to make the connection. The number should not be a toll call (ask your operator), and the modem on the other end should be as fast as your modem (ask your ISP).

- One or two Nameserver IP addresses (each with four numbers separated by periods, e.g., 204.247.136.39)

- Any special connection instructions if your ISP doesn't support standard PPP. Explain you're using Windows 95 (or Windows NT 4.0), and the ISP will tell you whether its service is compatible with Dial-Up Networking.

Both Windows 95 and Windows NT 4.0 come with an "Internet Setup Wizard" that supposedly does the job for you, but it will not be discussed here. Learning the manual installation of the required components will not only help you cover a wider variety of configurations, but aid in diagnosing and solving problems. Take the following steps to ensure you have the proper drivers installed:

Part 1 (Windows 95 only)

- Double-click on the Add/Remove Programs icon in Control Panel.

- Choose the **Windows Setup** tab, highlight **Communications** in the list of components, and click **Details**.

- Make sure you have a checkmark next to the Dial-Up Networking component. If not, check it now, and click **OK**; you'll be asked to restart your computer at this point.

- When Windows restarts, double-click on the Network icon in Control Panel.

- You should have the following network components installed:

```
Client for Microsoft Networks
Dial-up adapter
TCP/IP
File and printer sharing for Microsoft Networks
(optional)
```

- If you have another adapter installed (such as a network card), you'll probably see other protocols configured (in addition to TCP/IP). If this is the case, there will be an instance of each protocol for each adapter (see Figure 7-4). Simply remove all protocols pointing to the Dial-Up adapter that aren't TCP/IP.

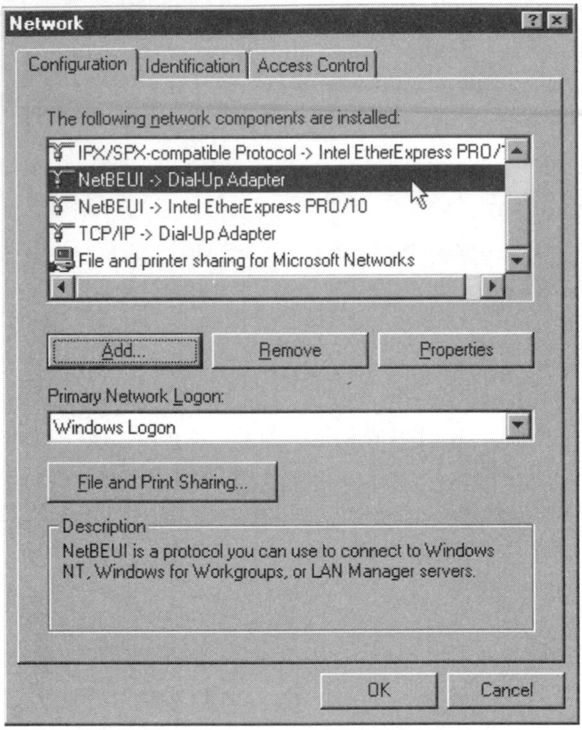

Figure 7-4: The Network properties window in Windows 95 shows the protocols installed for each available network adapter

- If one or more of the components listed here aren't installed on your system, click **Add** to add them to your list. Note that the IPX/SPX Protocol is installed by default, but isn't needed and can be removed for the dial-up adapter. When you go to add new components, TCP/IP is known as a *protocol*, and file and printer sharing is known as a *service*. All of these components can be found by selecting **Microsoft** in the list of manufacturers. If you made any changes here, you'll have to restart Windows.

Part 1 (Windows NT 4.0 only)

- Double-click on the Dial-Up Networking icon in My Computer.

- If you haven't done so already, you'll be prompted to install the Dial-Up Networking components. Click **Install** at this point to have Windows copy the appropriate files from the CD.

- You'll then be asked to choose a modem or modems to use with Dial-Up Networking. If you didn't install TCP/IP during the installation (which is likely if you don't have a network adapter), you'll be asked to do so now. There aren't any settings you need to change in this window. Click **OK**.

- When the installation of Dial-Up Networking is complete, you'll have to restart your computer.

Once you've obtained the necessary information and installed the correct drivers, you can set up a connection. Connections in Windows 95 are represented by icons in the Dial-Up Networking window, each with its own set of properties. Microsoft abandoned Windows 95's object-oriented metaphor for Dial-Up Networking connections when Windows NT 4.0 was released, while adding functionality and features. For this reason, the procedure for making and using connections is different on each platform:

Part 2 (Windows 95 only)

- Double-click on My Computer and then on Dial-Up Networking.

- Double-click on the Make New Connection icon to start the wizard.

- Type the name of your connection in the first field. This can be anything, but it's recommended you type in the name of your ISP here to avoid confusion with possible future connections. Select your modem from the list below (if you have more than one), and click **Configure** to make sure your modem is configured correctly. Set the maximum speed to 57,600 for 14.4 modems and 115,200 for 28.8 modems. You might want to turn up the volume until you're sure the connection works. Make sure **Only connect at this speed** is not checked, and click **OK** when you're done.

- Click **Next**, and type in the area code and phone number given to you by your ISP to connect. If necessary, choose the country code from the list below.

- Click **Next** and then **Finish**. A new icon with the name you specified should now appear in the Dial-Up Networking window.

- Right-click on the new icon, and select **Properties** to change the settings for this connection.

- If you entered everything correctly above, you shouldn't need to change anything in this window, except for the server type. Click **Server Type** to access the Server Types window, shown in Figure 7-5.

- Turn off all options, except **Enable software compression** and **TCP/IP**. Your modem or service provider may require that you turn off **Enable software compression** as well, but for now leave it enabled.

Server Types
Type of Dial-Up Server:
PPP: Windows 95, Windows NT 3.5, Internet
Advanced options:
Log on to network
Enable software compression
Require encrypted password
Allowed network protocols:
NetBEUI
IPX/SPX Compatible
TCP/IP
TCP/IP Settings...
OK
Cancel

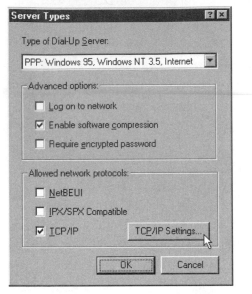

Figure 7-5: The Server Type window allows you to enter the network settings for a Dial-Up Networking connection in Windows 95

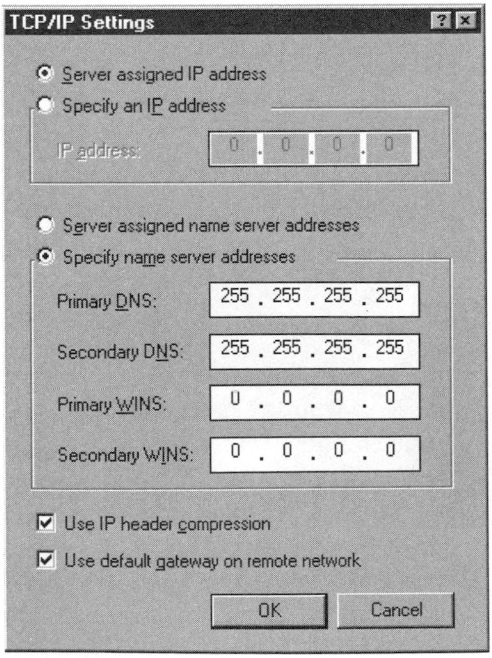

TCP/IP Settings
Server assigned IP address
Specify an IP address
IP address:
0 . 0 . 0 . 0
Server assigned name server addresses
Specify name server addresses
Primary DNS:
255 . 255 . 255 . 255
Secondary DNS:
255 . 255 . 255 . 255
Primary WINS:
0 . 0 . 0 . 0
Secondary WINS:
0 . 0 . 0 . 0
Use IP header compression
Use default gateway on remote network
OK
Cancel

Figure 7-6: The TCP/IP Settings window allows you to input your name server adresses in Windows 95 and Windows NT 4.0

- Click **TCP/IP Settings** to display a window similar to Figure 7-6. Leave all the settings as they appear, except for the name servers. Select **Specify name server addresses** and type the IP addresses of the one or two name servers given to you by your ISP in the Primary DNS and Secondary DNS fields, respectively. (DNS stands for *Domain Name Server.*)

- Click **OK** three times to close all the boxes and save your settings. Repeat the steps in Part 2 for each connection you wish to configure. If your ISP has more than one number for you to use, if you have more than one modem, or if you have more than one ISP, you'll need separate connection icons for each implementation.

- To connect, double-click on the icon. Type your username and password as given to you by your ISP; click **Save password** (if desired). If Windows 95 has trouble saving your password, see "Dial-Up Networking Refuses to Remember Passwords" later in this chapter. Note that Windows 95 will never save your password until you're successful in making a connection, so you'll have to keep entering it if you're having trouble.

- Click **Connect** to start dialing. Depending on your modem, it may take anywhere from a few seconds to over a minute to establish a connection. Once a connection is established, a timer will start keeping track of your connect time, and you can start using your Internet software. See "Software and the Internet" in the Preface for more information on obtaining free software you can use on the Internet.

Part 2 (Windows NT 4.0 only)

- Double-click on My Computer and then on Dial-Up Networking.

- Click **New** to display the window enabling you to add a new connection.

- Type a name for this connection in the **Entry Name** field. This can be anything, but it's recommended you type in the name of your ISP here to avoid confusion with possible future connections.

- Enter the area code and phone number given to you by your ISP to connect in the phone number field. Click **Alternates** to configure other phone numbers to dial if the first one fails (a nice feature not available in Windows 95).

- Select your modem from the list below (if you have more than one), and click **Configure** to make sure your modem is configured correctly. Set the maximum speed to 57,600 for 14.4 modems and 115,200 for 28.8 modems. You might want to turn off the **Disable**

modem speaker option until you're sure the connection works. Click **OK** when you're done.

- The rest of the settings for this connection are accessible by clicking on the other tabs in this window. Choose the **Server** tab, and click **TCP/IP Settings** to display the window shown in Figure 7-6 The default settings should be fine for this connection. Make sure TCP/IP is checked. Your modem or service provider may require that you turn off **Enable software compression** as well, but for now leave it enabled.

- The other tabs—**Script**, **Security**, and **X25**—are not needed except under special circumstances (see "Special Considerations," the next section). Click **OK** when you're done to return to the main Dial-Up Networking window.

- If you click **More**, you'll have access to other features, allowing you to edit, delete, or clone entries, create a shortcut for a particular entry, or change the User Preferences. All of the default User Preferences should be fine, but you may need to change them later to suit your needs.

- Click **Dial**, and enter your user name and password.

- Click **Dial** to start dialing. Depending on your modem, it may take anywhere from a few seconds to over a minute to establish a connection.

- Repeat the steps in Part 2 for each connection you wish to configure. If your ISP has more than one number for you to use, if you have more than one modem, or if you have more than one ISP, you'll need separate connections for each implementation.

- Once a connection is established, a timer will start keeping track of your connect time, and you can start using your Internet software. See "Software and the Internet" in the Preface for more information on obtaining free software you can use on the Internet.

Special Considerations

Since there are so many different kinds of connections and some ISPs don't yet support standard PPP, it can be difficult to get Windows to work with your particular circumstances. Here are some tips for nonstandard connections:

Scripting

Some connections have a complicated login procedure, requiring you to type in a series of nonstandard commands. If you're using

Windows 95, you'll need to follow the instructions in "Adding Scripting to Dial-up Networking," later in this chapter. Since Windows NT 4.0 comes with scripting functionality built in, you can access it by choosing your connection, clicking **More**, selecting **Edit Entry**, and choosing the **Script** tab. You will now be able to choose a script file on your hard disk, either that you've written, or from the collection of samples that comes with Windows. Once you've enabled scripting on your system, you'll need to contact your ISP for the proper login procedure. To determine which commands are needed in your script manually, follow these directions for Windows 95. For Windows NT 4.0, the procedure is similar.

- Double-click on the Dial-Up Networking icon in the My Computer window.

- Right-click on the connection you wish to use, and select **Properties**.

- In the Connect using portion, click **Configure**, and then click on the **Options** tab.

- Turn on the **Bring up terminal window after dialing** option, and click OK twice to close all the windows.

- Start dialing by double-clicking on the connection icon.

- After your modem has dialed, a window will appear, allowing you to type any necessary commands. Using the commands given to you by your ISP, try logging in manually. The script will enable you to automate this part of the login process.

- Write down all the prompts you see (noting all capitalization since everything is case sensitive), as well as all commands you type.

- Once you've determined your *exact* login procedure, enter your commands into the scripting utility you're using (consult the documentation of the scripting utility for the specific syntax for the commands).

- Once you have it working, you'll hopefully never need to do this again!

SLIP

Although less commonly used than PPP and not as well supported, a SLIP connection still is possible with Windows. To use SLIP (serial line Internet protocol) with Windows 95, you'll need to download the SLIP and Scripting for Dial-Up Networking add-on from Microsoft's web site. See "Software and the Internet" in the Preface for more information.

Callback

If your ISP uses a callback procedure (another machine calls your computer to connect), and you're using Windows NT 4.0, click **More** in the Dial-Up Networking window, select **Logon preferences**, choose the **Callback** tab, and enter the appropriate settings. If you're using Windows 95, and your ISP requires that you use Callback, you won't be able to use Dial-Up Networking. You'll need to install a different dialer. Trumpet Winsock for Windows 95 (see "Software and the Internet" in the Preface for more information) supports this type of connection.

Commercial services

If you use CompuServe, America Online, or another non-Internet commercial service, you might be able to use Dial-Up Networking with it as long as you have an Internet icon in Control Panel. Download the latest version of Internet Explorer if you don't have this item, or contact your service provider for specific instructions describing how to use its service with Dial-Up Networking.

Distributing a connection

Say you're an ISP and would like to send your customers a file with all of your connection information rather than spending hours on the phone walking them through the setup process. Since all of the settings for a user's connections are stored in the Registry, you can export a Registry patch (see Chapter 3 for more information) containing all of the required settings. The two types of settings you need to distribute are the installed network components (protocols and drivers) and the connection settings (phone number, name servers). This may take some doing, so be patient.

- First, create the dial-up connection you wish to distribute, following the directions at the beginning of this section.

- In Windows 95, the connection settings are stored in HKEY_CURRENT_ USER\RemoteAccess\Profile, and HKEY_CURRENT_USER\Remote- Access\Addresses. Distribute the appropriate value from the Profile key and the appropriate subkey from the Addresses key.

- In Windows NT, search your Registry for each occurrence of the word "RemoteAccess" (without a space). Distribute the appropriate value from the Profile key and the corresponding subkey from the Address key beneath it.

- When you're finished, you should have a single Registry file (*.REG), on which a user can double-click to add the connection to the system.

ISDN (Integrated Services Digital Network)

ISDN gives Internet users a connection speed of up to 128 kbps, over four times faster than the fastest analog modems available. There are two distinct types of ISDN adapters available: internal and external.

Internal adapters are treated like network adapters and therefore require the drivers included with the adapter (made especially for your version of Windows) as well as Microsoft's ISDN accelerator pack. This add-on, available on the Internet (see the Preface), allows you to use Dial-Up Networking with your ISDN adapter and may or may not be required by your adapter's software. Consult the documentation for more information.

External adapters, connected through your computer's serial port, are treated like external modems and therefore don't require the accelerator pack described above. However, you'll need a driver (available from the manufacturer) made especially for your adapter.

If you're experiencing performance problems, such as all communications halting temporarily every few minutes, try specifying a value of 576 for your MTU (Windows 95 only). See "Changing the MTU and RWIN Settings in Dial-Up Networking" later in this chapter for more information.

See "Software and the Internet" in the Preface for more information on ISDN resources.

Notes and other issues

When connecting at 112 kbps or 128 kbps, Dial-Up Networking will report only 56 kbps or 64 kbps, respectively, since that's the speed at which you're connecting on each B-channel.

Selecting an ISP

If you don't yet have an ISP, or your university or employer is about to kick you off its system, you'll need to get an account with a local Internet service provider. Here are a few things to look for:

No hourly rate

Hourly rates are a ripoff, plain and simple. Some ISPs give you a few free hours per month. Don't settle for less than 50 (they go quicker than you think). Many providers now sell a flat-rate service (no hourly charges whatsoever) for around $20 per month.

Local number

> Don't let the phone company profit from your Internet access. If you dial a local number, you can still connect to anywhere in the world, but not on your dime (see the previous tip).

Private provider

> Dealing with a small, local provider (look in the phone book) will probably mean lower rates, as well as better service and support. Unless you travel frequently and need local access around the country (or the world), forget the national providers and their proprietary software.

Troubleshooting

If your connection or any of your Internet applications don't work, or if you're experiencing poor performance, the problem could be caused by any number of things. Here are a few possibilities:

- If you were at one time using another Internet dialer (such as Trumpet Winsock), make sure you don't have any other Internet dialers in your path (specified in *AUTOEXEC.BAT*). Search your entire system for files named *WINSOCK.DLL* and delete or rename any copies that aren't dated 7/11/95 (the one that comes with Windows 95). If you can't find one dated 7/11/95, then you'll have to retrieve it from the distribution disks (the date may be different if you have a later release of Windows 95).

- It could an ISP problem. Dial the number manually with your telephone and see if you hear beeps on the other end—not an answering machine, busy signal, or Chinese restaurant.

- The information obtained from your ISP is incorrect. Make sure all your IP addresses are correct, and check your settings for typos. Make sure you hit **Add** when necessary if entering any IP addresses into the Network settings window of Control Panel.

- If your ISP doesn't support standard PPP, you might need to "add scripting to Dial-Up Networking" (covered later in this chapter). Contact your ISP's technical support for details and assistance.

- If you're trying to debug a script (get it to work), Windows 95's scripting utility has a feature that lets you watch your script execute in real time and allows you to step through it one line at a time. While Windows NT does not have this, it does have an analysis feature that allows you to view the results after a failed connection.

- Make sure your account is functioning. It can take up to several days after you subscribe before you can use your account, and be prepared for the possibility that your ISP will get your password wrong.

- Contact the phone company to see if there is a switching or routing problem (especially for ISDN customers). If you can't dial by hand, your computer can't either.

- If all else fails, contact your ISP for help. Since most users have Windows, the ISP will probably be able to diagnose and solve the problem easily. Some ISPs require special settings.

- Don't rule out hardware problems. Make sure your modem is turned on, functioning correctly, and configured correctly by using HyperTerminal to connect to the same number. If you don't use a true Windows 95 communications program, you're not testing the modem configuration! See Chapter 6, *Troubleshooting*, for additional modem troubleshooting techniques.

- If you're connecting but not at a satisfactory speed, try replacing the phone cord or wall jack. Try restarting Windows to see if that helps, and make sure there aren't any other programs running that use your modem or communications port.

- If all else fails, contact the manufacturer of your modem for technical support and possibly a driver or BIOS update.

- If things are just too slow, try specifying a value of 576 for your MTU (especially for ISDN connections). An indicator of this problem is if communications seem to halt temporarily every few minutes. See "Changing the MTU and RWIN Settings in Dial-Up Networking" later in this chapter for more information (Windows 95 only).

- Newer drivers (obtained from the manufacturer of your modem) can improve performance. Noisy phone lines can slow connections because your modem is spending more time with error correction; try replacing your phone cable, or contact the phone company to fix the problem.

- Test your throughput by transferring a binary file (text files aren't a reliable indicator, due to compression). After you've done the math, you should experience about 1.6 kilobytes/second with a 14.4 connection, 3.4 kilobytes/second with a 28.8 connection, and about 12 kilobytes/second with a 128k ISDN connection.

Coping with Dial-Up Networking

Since Dial-Up Networking is the basis for almost all Internet communication in Windows 95 and Windows NT 4.0, there are many issues and problems that can plague your system.

Bypassing the Connect To Dialog Box ●

If you use Windows 95's Dial-Up Networking, you've probably made a shortcut for your service provider by dragging the icon out of the window and onto the Desktop or **Start Menu**. Unfortunately, the Connect To box still pops up to make sure you really want to connect, as though you weren't sure when you double-clicked on the icon in the first place. If you're using Windows NT 4.0 and have made a shortcut to a connection (by clicking **More** and then **Create Shortcut**), double-clicking on the shortcut invokes dialing immediately. If you have Windows 95 OSR2, select **Settings** from the **Connection** menu in the Dial-Up Networking window, and then turn off the **Prompt for information before dialing** option. To get rid of this useless box, try the following third-party add-ons (see "Software and the Internet" in the Preface for more information):

Solution 1

- Obtain and install Dunce, which also has the ability to redial when disconnected and can launch any program when a connection has been established—freeware.

Solution 2

- Obtain and install RAS+ 95, a full-featured program that can track connect charges, manage multiple connections and phone numbers, and much more—shareware.

Solution 3

- Obtain and install RtvReco, which can also be configured to bypass other useless, repetitive dialog boxes—freeware.

Solution 4

- Obtain and install Route 1 Pro (available on the Internet at *http://www.creativelement.com/software/route1.html*). Using Route 1 Pro's scripting feature, you can launch a shortcut for the connection and have the *Type* command press the **Connect** button for you.

Adding Scripting to Dial-up Networking ●

Although Windows 95 includes support for Dial-Up Networking, allowing computers to connect to remote hosts, there is no built-in provision for scripting. Scripting may be necessary if your ISP doesn't support a common authentication protocol (PAP/SPAP/CHAP, etc.). Microsoft added this functionality in Windows NT 4.0, but some users of Windows 95 who have more complicated logon procedures won't be able to use Dial-Up Networking without a script. To add scripting capabilities to Windows 95's Dial-Up Networking, try these suggestions.

- Obtain a copy of the RoboDUN utility. See "Software and the Internet" in the Preface for more information.

- If you have the CD version of Windows 95, you might want to use the included DScript utility. To install DScript, double-click on the Add/Remove Programs icon in the Control Panel, choose the **Windows Setup** tab, click **Have Disk**, and install from the ADMIN\ APPTOOLS\DSCRIPT folder on the CD.

- If you're using Windows 95 OSR2, scripting is built in. Right-click on a connection icon, select **Properties**, and choose the **Scripting** tab.

- Microsoft's Plus Pack also has an enhanced version of DScript, which is available for download directly from Microsoft. See "Software and the Internet" in the Preface for more information.

Notes and other issues

The scripts used with this add-on to Windows 95 are the same as those used in Windows NT 4.0 (found in the **Script** tab of the Dial-Up Networking options window). In Windows NT, the script files (*.SCP*) are located in \winnt\system32\ras\. In addition to supporting the .scp scripts from Windows 95, Windows NT 4.0 also supports the *switch.inf*-style scripts from Windows NT 3.5x.

Turning On Auto-Redial in Dial-Up Networking ● ■

Auto-redial in Dial-Up Networking is turned off by default. If Dial-Up Networking isn't able to make a connection the first time, you're forced to retry manually until a connection is made. If the line is frequently busy, you'll definitely want to turn on auto-redial.

For Windows 95

- Double-click on the Dial-Up Networking icon in My Computer.

- Select **Settings** from the **Connections** menu.

- Turn on the **Redial** option, and set the desired parameters.

- Click **OK** when finished.

For Windows NT 4.0

- Double-click on the Dial-Up Networking icon in My Computer.

- Click **More** and then select **Logon preferences**.

- Choose the **Dialing** tab, and adjust the **Number of Redial Attempts**.

- Turn on the **Redial on link failure option**, and click **OK**.

Notes and other issues

To redial automatically when disconnected, try the Dunce utility. See "Software and the Internet" in the Preface and "Bypassing the Connect To Dialog Box" earlier in this chapter for more information.

To turn on auto-redial in HyperTerminal, see Appedix A, *Frequently Asked Questions*.

Using Autodial with Dial-Up Networking ● ■

The autodial feature in Windows allows you to connect to the Internet with Dial-Up Networking automatically whenever it's needed, such as when you open your World Wide Web browser or email application. You may or may not have the autodial feature on your computer, depending on which version of Internet Explorer came with your copy of Windows and whether you have an Internet icon in Control Panel. Choose one of the following situations that best suits your system, and follow the directions.

If you have Internet Explorer 3.0 or later installed

- Double-click on the Internet icon in the Control Panel. See Figure 7-7.

- Choose the **Connection** tab, and turn on the **Connect to the Internet as needed** option.

- Choose the connection to be used (if you have more than one) and if you want Windows to disconnect automatically after a period of inactivity.

- Click **OK** when finished.

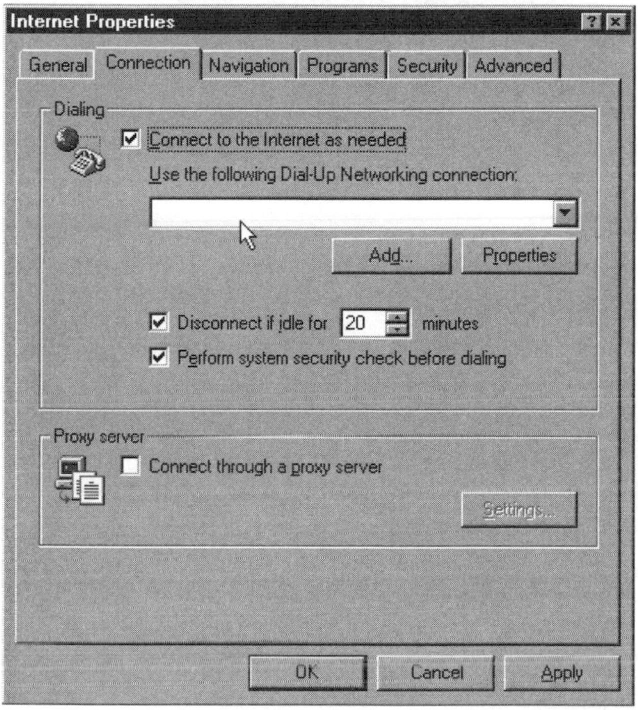

Figure 7-7: Use the Internet icon in the Control Panel to configure autodial behavior

If you have an Internet icon in Control Panel, but the only option is Use Proxy Server

If you want to download the newest version of Microsoft's Internet Explorer, see Solution 1. If not, see Solution 2 or Solution 3.

Solution 1: If you don't have an Internet icon in Control Panel

- Download and install the latest version Microsoft's Internet Explorer (see "Software and the Internet" in the Preface for more information). When you restart Windows, you'll see an Internet icon in Control Panel. Follow the directions in the first solution, assuming you've downloaded Internet Explorer 3.0 or later.

Solution 2: If you don't have an Internet icon in Control Panel

- Download and install Dunce (see "Software and the Internet" in the Preface for more information), which also has the ability to redial when disconnected and can launch any program when a connection has been established.

Solution 3: If you don't have an Internet icon in Control Panel (Windows 95 only)

- You'll need the file *url.dll*. Use the *Find: Files or Folders* command in your **Start Menu** to look for it. If you don't have it on your system, you'll need to download the Autodial Registry Patch from the Internet (see the Preface). Once you've found the file, make sure it's in your Windows\System folder.

- Open the Registry Editor (*regedit.exe*). If you're not familiar with the Registry Editor, see Chapter 3.

- Expand the branches to HKEY_LOCAL_MACHINE\System\Current-ControlSet\Services\Winsock\Autodial. Create any keys that aren't already in your Registry by selecting **New** and then **Key** from the **Edit** menu.

- Create a new string value (select **New** and then **String Value** from the **Edit** menu) called AutodialDllName32, double-click on it, and enter url.dll for its contents.

- Create a new string value called AutodialFcnName32, double-click on it, and enter AutodialHookCallback for its contents.

- Expand the branches to HKEY_CURRENT_USER\Software\Microsoft\Windows\CurrentVersion\Internet Settings. Create any keys that aren't already in your Registry by selecting **New** and then **Key** from the **Edit** menu.

- Create a new binary value called EnableAutodial, double-click on it, and enter 01,00,00,00 for its contents.

- Close the Registry Editor, and restart Windows for the change to take effect.

- To change the connection used with the autodial feature (this solution only), open the Registry Editor, expand the branches to HKEY_CURRENT_USER\RemoteAccess\, and change the value of the Internet Profile key to the name of an existing connection.

Notes and other issues

The autodial feature may not work properly for all applications. Most newer, 32-bit Winsock applications should support this functionality, however.

Some users may experience problems when connecting to the Internet using autodial, such as the modem's not being able to dial and the network's not working once the connection has been made. If this happens but Dial-Up Networking still works when you connect manually (by double-clicking on an icon in the Dial-Up Networking window), try contacting the manufacturer of your modem for an updated driver or other technical support.

Dial-Up Networking Refuses to Remember Passwords •

Many users of Windows 95 may experience some strange behavior with Dial-Up Networking, where the ability to save the dial-up password does not function. This behavior manifests itself either by disabling (graying-out) the **Save Password** checkbox in the Connect To window or by forgetting the password regardless of the checkbox setting. There are several possible causes of this behavior, and Microsoft has made a possible fix available for download on the Internet (see the Preface). Since the fix doesn't solve the problem for all users, here are several solutions that can restore Dial-Up Networking's password memory.

Solution 1

- Double-click on the Network icon in Control Panel, and choose the **Identification** tab. Although the Workgroup and Computer Description have no use in Dial-up Networking, the Computer Name should be your login (user name) for your ISP. Although this isn't always the case, it can make a difference. Furthermore, the computer name entered here is used as the default user name for all new Dial-Up Networking connections.

- Make any necessary changes, and click **OK** when finished. You'll have to restart Windows, but once you're back in, try again.

- Double-click on your connection icon. This time, your correct login will be in the **Login** field, and you should be allowed to type in your password. Remember to turn on the **Save Password** option if it's not grayed out.

- If you don't have an **Identification** tab, see Part 1 of "Installing Dial-Up Networking" earlier in this chapter, to make sure you have all the necessary network components, such as Client for Microsoft Networks installed.

Solution 2

- Try recreating the connection by opening up the Dial-Up Networking window and double-clicking on the Add New Connection icon.

Solution 3

- If you have access to Microsoft's "Knowledge Base" for Windows 95 issues, check out technical notes #Q137361 and #Q148925. See "Software and the Internet" in the Preface for more information.

Solution 4

- Double-click on the Passwords icon in the Control Panel, and choose the **User Profiles** tab. If it's not already checked, select **Users can customize their preferences...**, choose the desired options below, and click **OK**.

- Restart Windows 95 at this point. When you're asked for a username and password, leave the **password** field blank. If you're asked whether Windows 95 should remember settings for this user, answer Yes.

Solution 5

- Occasionally, your password list (a file with the .PWL extension) can get corrupted. Select **Find** and then **Files or Folders** from your **Start Menu**, look for **.PWL*, and delete any files it finds in your Windows folder. After restarting Windows, all your configured passwords should be forgotten, and Windows should allow you to start from scratch.

Solution 6

- If you have more than one connection in Dial-Up Networking and the password checkbox is turned off for at least one, it may disable all of your passwords. Make sure the checkbox is enabled for all of them. If so, try Solution 5, and then enter and save a password for each connection.

Solution 7 (if the password box is disabled)

- Open the Registry Editor (*regedit.exe*). If you're not familiar with the Registry Editor, see Chapter 3.

- Expand the branches to HKEY_LOCAL_MACHINE\SOFTWARE\Microsoft\ Windows\CurrentVersion\Network\Real Mode Net.

- If you see a value named autologon (on the right side) with a value of 00, double-click on it, and replace the value with 01 00 00 00 00.

- You'll have to restart Windows for this change to take effect.

Solution 8

*   If all else fails, you may need to use one of the scripting options mentioned in "Adding Scripting to Dial-up Networking" earlier in this chapter. With a script, you can configure Windows to enter your password regardless of the **Save Password** option.

Notes and other issues

Some users have reported this behavior only after installing Microsoft's Service Pack 1, which is supposed to alleviate this problem. If this happens, try deleting your password lists, as described in Solution 5.

Speeding Up Dial-Up Networking Initialization ● ■

Dialing up with the built-in Dial-Up Networking in Windows 95 is clean and straightforward but can seem to take an eternity. You'll notice that a connection is established long before Dial-Up Networking finishes connecting. By removing unnecessary components and turning off unneeded options, this process should be considerably faster. Feel free to try any or all of the following suggestions:

Part 1: Slim down your connections (Windows 95)

*   Double-click on the Dial-Up Networking icon in My Computer.

*   Right-click on an existing connection, and select **Properties** (you'll have to repeat this for each connection, if you have more than one).

*   Click **Server Type**, and turn off support for **NetBEUI** and **IPX/SPX** (make sure to leave TCP/IP turned on).

*   Next, turn off **Log on to network** in the same box.

*   Click **OK** and then **OK** again.

Part 1: Slim down your connections (Windows NT 4.0)

*   Double-click on the Dial-Up Networking icon in My Computer.

*   Choose an existing connection from the list, click **More** and then **Edit Entry**.

*   Choose the **Server** tab, and turn off support for **NetBEUI** and **IPX/SPX** (make sure to leave TCP/IP turned on).

*   Click **OK** and then **OK** again.

Part 2: Remove unneeded drivers (Windows 95 only)

- Double-click on the Network icon in Control Panel.

- Highlight the **Dial-Up Adapter**, and click **Properties**.

- Click on the **Bindings** tab, and turn off all options in the list other than **TCP/IP**. If there are no others, it means you've already removed them.

- Click **OK** and then **OK** again. You'll have to restart Windows for this change to take effect.

Changing the MTU and RWIN Settings in Dial-Up Networking ●

The performance of Dial-Up Networking can be modified by changing a few numbers, known as MTU and RWIN. Although this is easily accomplished in other dialers (such as the popular Trumpet Winsock), the setting isn't obvious in Windows 95's Dial-Up Networking. Note that if you don't know what these numbers mean, then you don't need to change them, and this information does not apply to you (however, see "Notes and other issues" for exceptions).

- Open the Registry Editor (*regedit.exe*). If you're not familiar with the Registry Editor, see Chapter 3.

- Expand the branches to HKEY_LOCAL_MACHINE\System\Current-ControlSet\Services\Class\NetTrans\.

- Under that branch, find a key (numbered, such as 0005) that contains "TCP/IP" assigned to the DriverDesc string value.

- Select **New** and then **String Value** from the **Edit** menu, and type MaxMTU for the name of the new value.

- Double-click on the new value, and type in the desired number; 1500 is the default. See "Notes and other issues" for sample values. If you don't know what value to use here, don't change it at all.

- Then, expand the branches to HKEY_LOCAL_MACHINE\System\ CurrentControlSet\Services\VxD\MSTCP\.

- Again, select **New** and then **String Value** from the **Edit** menu, and type DefaultRcvWindow for the name of the new value.

- Double-click on the new value, and type in the desired number. 2144 is the default. Again, if you don't know what value to use here, don't change it at all.

Notes and other issues

This will work only if you are using PPP (not SLIP) with Dial-Up Networking (not another dialer). If you are using SLIP, your MTU will be 58, regardless of the MaxMTU setting in the Registry.

If you are experiencing problems such as your Web browser stopping in the middle of a page or sudden disconnections, an MTU value of 576 might solve the problem.

Stopping Exchange from Attaching WINMAIL.DAT • ■

Since the beginning of the Internet, email has been plain text only, meaning that extended formatting (also called rich text) such as bold and italics weren't possible. With the new batch of email programs now available that support this extended formatting comes the unpleasant side effect of other recipients reading your formatted mail with an older mail reader. Microsoft Exchange (in Windows 95) and Windows Messaging (in Windows NT 4.0) attach a MIME file called *WINMAIL.DAT* that contains the extra formatting. Any mail programs that don't understand this and receive a rich-text message will either display a bunch of gibberish at the end of a message or will decode and store the *WINMAIL.DAT* file. This can be confusing for some users and irritating for everyone else, but there is a way to disable this behavior. If you use Exchange or Messaging, you won't see this file, and the message will retain its formatting. However, it can be confusing for those who don't use Exchange (the majority of the Internet population) and have no use for this file.

Step 1

- In either Microsoft Exchange or Windows Messaging, select **Options** from the **Tools** menu.

- Choose the **Services** tab, and select **Internet Mail** from the list. If Internet Mail is not listed, click **Add** to add this service to the list.

- Click **Properties**, and then **Message Format**.

- Turn off the **Use MIME when sending messages** option.

- Click **OK** and then **OK** again.

Step 2

- Double-click on the name of each recipient in your Address Book.

- Turn off the option that reads **Always send to this recipient in Microsoft rich-text format**.

- This option needs to be set for each recipient of a message. If even one has this turned on, all recipients will still get the attachment.

Notes and other issues

Either of these methods should work for most users, but sometimes nothing seems to work. If you plan on sending lots of Internet email, seriously consider using a mail program more suited to the task, such as the freely available Eudora Lite. See "Software and the Internet" in the Preface.

A bug in Exchange may cause line breaks to be replaced with equal signs when rich-text mail is disabled.

Just a note for computer fanatics out there: email on the now-defunct NeXTstep system also supported rich text as well as plain text, but the designers of NeXT included a button in plain view to allow the user to choose between NeXT mail, and non-NeXT mail (plain text).

See "Coping with Microsoft Exchange and Windows Messaging" later in this chapter for more information, including what to do about the equals signs that appear at the end of messages.

Forcing Internet Explorer to Use the Clients You Want ● ■

Although Internet Explorer is a Web browser generally designed to display World Wide Web documents, it also supports links (as do other browsers) to email addresses, ftp sites, Telnet addresses, and news groups. If you don't use Exchange (or Windows Messaging, if you're using Windows NT 4.0), it may be important to have Internet Explorer use a different mail program (a.k.a. client) whenever you click on a `mailto:` link, for example. Configuring Internet Explorer to use custom clients isn't obvious, but it is possible if the specific clients support such a configuration. Here's how to configure your own client, using the Telnet application included with Windows 95 and Windows NT as an example.

Internet Explorer 2.0 and earlier

- Open the My Computer window, select **Options** from the **View** menu, and choose the **File Types** tab.
- Click on **URL:Telnet Protocol**, and click **Edit**. Although we're using Telnet for this example, you can change any of the URL: file types in the same way.
- Select **Open** from the list of Actions, and click **Edit** again.

- Click **Browse**, and choose the desired program. The default program for the Telnet protocol is *telnet.exe*, located in the Windows folder in Windows 95, and the Windows\System32 folder in Windows NT 4.0.

- When finished, close each window by clicking **OK**.

Internet Explorer 3.0 and later

- Select **Options** from Internet Explorer's **View** menu, and choose the **Programs** tab. In the Mail and News section, select the desired programs for Mail and News from the respective lists.

- If the program you wish to use is not listed here, you may be able to add the program by editing the Registry. To do so, open the Registry Editor (*regedit.exe*). If you're not familiar with the Registry Editor, see Chapter 3.

- Expand the branches to HKEY_LOCAL_MACHINE\SOFTWARE\ Clients\mail or HKEY_LOCAL_MACHINE\SOFTWARE\Clients\news, depending on which client you're trying to configure.

- The syntax can be complex. Use the existing entries in conjunction with your program's documentation to add your program to the Registry. Note that not all programs can be used in this way. Contact the manufacturer of the client software you wish to use for more information.

- Close the Registry Editor and restart Windows for the change to take effect. To configure programs to work with protocols other than mail and news, refer to "Internet Explorer 2.0 and Earlier," the previous section.

Notes and other issues

In order for this to work, the program must support specific command line parameters or DDE conversations. Refer to the other program's documentation, or contact the software manufacturer for more information. Not all programs can be used in this way.

More recent versions of Eudora (the lite version is freely available; see "Software and the Internet" in the Preface for more information) can automatically configure themselves to work with Internet Explorer.

If you're a user of Netscape Navigator, the process is different. You can easily change the program used for Telnet or "view source" in the options screen, but replacing the mail or news client is impossible in Netscape if you're not using software designed especially for the task. Qualcomm's Eudora Pro 3.0 supports Netscape mail.

You may be able to use the Runmail utility to configure Internet Explorer to work with one of your clients. See "Software and the Internet" in the Preface for more information.

Coping with Microsoft Exchange and Windows Messaging ● ■

Microsoft Exchange and Windows Messaging are the mail programs that come with Windows 95 and Windows NT 4.0, respectively. Both programs, while free, are also quite limited. What follows is a list of issues and solutions for the many bugs and annoyances that have sprung up. For the solutions that require third-party software, see "Software and the Internet" in the Preface for more information.

Use a signature

A signature is a small text file automatically appended to every message you send. For example, a signature can have your name, email, address, and company name, which can save you the task of typing the information in manually every time. To use a signature with Exchange, you'll need a third-party add-on. Try either Widgets for Microsoft Exchange or the Internet Idioms utility.

Turn off the WINMAIl.DAT attachment

See "Stopping Exchange from attaching *WINMAIL.DAT*" earlier in this chapter for a way to turn off rich-text email.

Remove extraneous equals signs

Once you've figured out how to turn off rich text in Exchange (see previous tip), you now see equals signs at the end of each line. To fix this bug in Exchange, select **Options** from the **Tools** menu in Exchange or Messaging. Choose the **Services** tab, and select **Internet Mail** from the list. If Internet Mail is not listed, click **Add** to add this service to the list. Click **Properties**, and then **Message Format**. Click **Character Set** and change the selection from ISO-8859-2 to US ASCII. Click **OK** and then **OK** again when finished.

Make a shortcut to the address book

The Inbox icon is provided as a shortcut to the inbox in Exchange and Messaging, but there's no shortcut for the address book. To create one, first create a shortcut to *exchng32.exe* (it's the same for Exchange or Messaging). Then right-click on the shortcut, select **Properties**, choose the **Shortcut** tab, and add a space and then / a to the end of the text in the **Target** field.

Change font of incoming mail

> Make it more readable by changing the font; obtain and install the Internet Idioms utility.

Quote sender's message in reply

> Most other mail programs allow you to quote someone's message when sending a reply with the > character. To add this functionality to Exchange, obtain and install the **MailQuote** utility.

Notes and other issues

You may have noticed any of the following additional issues. Some of these bugs have been fixed by Microsoft in recent updates; other issues can be resolved with the Widgets for Microsoft Exchange utility.

- Exchange incorrectly stores negative time zone (east of Greenwich).

- Some users report that Exchange spontaneously and randomly deletes messages.

- Occasionally, blank messages are sent, or the same message is sent multiple times.

- Exchange hangs if the connection failed when repeatedly dialing to auto-check email.

- Exchange isn't compatible with the phonebook in Schedule+.

- Fax cover pages are sometimes unavailable.

- Word 7 Email template won't work when sending email from a MAPI-compatible application.

Rather than putting up with the limitations and problems with this software, you may be better off switching to a third-party application. Eudora is highly recommended, and the Lite version is free on the Internet.

A

Frequently Asked Questions

No matter how good an index is, it still may be hard to find the information you need. From the thousands of email messages received in response to the Windows95 Annoyances web site (see Chapter 1, *So You're Stuck with Windows*, for details), I've found the most frequently asked questions and organized them here.

Explorer, the Desktop, and the Start Menu

Q: *Why don't folders remember their position, sort order, or icon size?*

A: Windows supposedly remembers all this information for the past 26 windows you open, although this feature has never worked very well. See "Forcing Windows to Remember Explorer Settings" in Chapter 2, *Customizing Your System*, for more information. Yes, your folders are part of Explorer, even if you aren't using the tree view entitled "Exploring."

Q: *How do I move the taskbar and the Start Menu?*

A: Grab a blank portion of the taskbar with the mouse and drag it to any of the four sides of your screen. You can also grab the edge of the taskbar and stretch it to make it larger or smaller. If you start doing this and find that you can't see the taskbar anymore, you've probably shrunk it down too far. As for moving the **Start Menu** button from one end of the taskbar to the other, it's not possible—bad news for left-handed users.

Q: *How do I change icons of folders so they don't all look alike?*

A: You can't. However, you can make a shortcut to a specific folder and give the shortcut any icon you like (right-click on it, select **Properties**, choose the **Shortcut** tab, and click **Change Icon**). You can also change the yellow folder icon used by all folders. See "Changing the Icons of System Objects" in Chapter 4, *Advanced Customization Techniques*.

Q: *How do I hide the text from the icons on my Desktop? I want "naked" icons.*

A: The only way to do this is to rename the various icons on your Desktop to have spaces for titles. Since a shortcut can't have a space for a title, you can use one or more blank characters. Use the Character Map utility, choose MS Sans Serif (or whatever font you've chosen for Desktop items), select the blank character (#160), and paste it into the filename. If you have more than one shortcut, use a different number of blank characters (one space, two spaces, etc.). See "Renaming the Recycle Bin" and "Getting Rid of the My Computer Icon" in Chapter 4 for more information.

Q: *Can I change the folder used by Explorer in Start Menu's context menu?*

A: No. By right-clicking on the **Start Menu**, you are telling Windows that you want to explore in the **Start Menu** folder. This yields the same result as right-clicking on any folder and clicking **Explore**. Any other behavior would be inconsistent with the object-oriented paradigm. A more effective way of starting Explorer is to place it in the top level of the **Start Menu**. You can also configure My Computer to open Explorer. See "Customizing My Computer" in Chapter 4. For more information, see "Force Explorer to Start with the Folder You Want" in Chapter 2.

Q: *How do I display the date in the tray (next to the clock)?*

A: Hold your mouse cursor over the time display for more than a second, and the date will appear temporarily. To add the date to the tray permanently, you'll need the TrayDate utility. See "Software and the Internet" in the Preface for information.

Q: *How do I change the font used in Explorer?*

A: Right-click on the Desktop, choose Properties, and choose the **Appearance** tab. Choose **Icon** from the list of Items, and select the desired font name and size. This font, while used to display the caption of Desktop icons, will also be used in Explorer.

Q: *How do I make the text background on Desktop icons transparent?*

A: If you are using a solid background, this isn't a problem. However, if you are using wallpaper or a Desktop pattern, all your text will be placed on a rectangle the same color as your original Desktop color. To eliminate this, obtain and install the Disappear utility. See "Software and the Internet" in the Preface. While it's not possible to do it without a third-party utility, there are a few tricks you can implement. Your best bet is to make your Desktop color the same as the background of the wallpaper image you're using. Right-click on the Desktop, choose **Properties**, and choose the **Appearance** tab. Choose **Desktop** from the list of Items, and choose a color that most closely matches your wallpapcr.

Q: *How do I show hidden files (such as MSDOS.SYS)?*

A: Open My Computer, and select **Options** from the **View** menu. Click on the **View** tab, choose **Show all files**, and press **OK**.

    Note: There is currently no way to choose which files to hide. The mentality behind hiding .DLL files remains a mystery.

Q: *How do I unhide a file?*

A: In DOS or a DOS Window, type `ATTRIB -S -H filename` to turn off the hidden attributes (replace the minus signs with plus signs to turn them back on). See Appendix B, *MS-DOS Crash Course*, for more information.

    In Windows, right-click on the file icon, and select **Properties**. Windows will allow you to turn on or off all attributes, except for the "System" tag (known as "S" to ATTRIB).

    Both of these settings can also be changed with the old Windows 3.1 file manager (*WINFILE.EXE*).

Q: *Help! I've lost a file, and I can't find it!*

A: It may have been inadvertently saved or moved to your Fonts folder. Explorer will see font files only in that folder; even Find won't be able to find it. Try using the command prompt or the old Windows 3.1 File Manager (*WINFILE.EXE*) to locate and move the file.

Q: *How do I see my file associations?*

A: Open My Computer, select **Options** from the **View** menu, and choose the **File Types** tab. To learn more about file types, see Chapter 3, *The Registry*.

Q: *Why won't Explorer let me format a floppy?*

A: If you've ever tried to format a floppy (or any drive for that matter) while in Explorer, you've undoubtedly seen the message "Windows cannot format this drive. Quit utilities or other programs that are using this drive, and make sure that no window is displaying the contents of the drive. Then try formatting again."

Here's what's happening. Even though Explorer may be the only program running, you are trying to access your floppy drive with two programs: the Explorer window and the format program. (If you read the error message carefully, it says this as well.)

To get around it, select a different drive in Explorer with the left mouse button, and then right-click on the drive you wish to format, and select **Format** from the context menu. This way, you won't be trying to format a floppy that's having its contents viewed at the same time. Calling this a bug isn't exactly accurate, but then again, someone at Microsoft should've caught this one and done something about it.

✱ Q: *Why can't I open documents with spaces in the filenames?*

A: The problem is the way the file type is configured in the Registry. See "Understanding File Types" in Chapter 3 and "Customizing Context Menus" in Chapter 4 for more information. Clue: You need quotes around those command lines.

System Configuration

Q: *How do I add or remove sound events from Control Panel?*

A: You can remove unwanted sound events by editing the Registry (using *REGEDIT.EXE*) by removing the respective keys from HKEY_CURRENT_ USER\AppEvents\EventLabels and HKEY_CURRENT_ USER\AppEvents\Schemes\Apps\.Default. If that doesn't work, look for unwanted entries in the [Sounds] section of your *WIN.INI* file. There's no actual need to do this, except to reduce the clutter in the Sounds applet of Control Panel. However, you can't add new events and expect them to be integrated into the operating system without using third-party software made especially for this purpose.

Q: *How do I change aspects of the Shut Down options screen?*

A: The **Shut Down** options screen allows you to specify whether you want to shut down your computer, restart, log on as a different user, or restart in MS-DOS mode. Short of using a hex editor to edit the code in *explorer.exe*, there's no way to remove unwanted entries from this dialog box. The only optional entry, **Close all programs and log on as a different user,** is automatically installed if you have any network drivers installed (including Dial-Up Networking). The only way to remove it is to remove any installed network drivers.

Q: *How do I stop a program from running whenever I start Windows 95?*

A: A program can be started automatically at bootup if a shortcut to the program is in your Startup folder (which is inside your **Start Menu** folder).

Older programs might still install themselves in your *WIN.INI* file (on the same line that starts with "LOAD="). Use a plain text editor, such as Notepad, to edit this file.

Some drivers can also display errant messages and are loaded from your Registry (do a search to find them) and in your *SYSTEM.INI* file. Use a plain text editor, such as Notepad, to edit this file.

Also, programs may be specified in your Registry, in the following locations:

```
HKEY_LOCAL_MACHINE\SOFTWARE\Microsoft\Windows\CurrentVersion\Run
HKEY_LOCAL-MACHINE\SOFTWARE\Microsoft\Windows\CurrentVersion\RunOnce
HKEY_LOCAL_MACHINE\SOFTWARE\Microsoft\Windows\CurrentVersion\RunServices
HKEY_LOCAL_MACHINE\SOFTWARE\Microsoft\Windows\CurrentVersion\
RunServicesOnce
HKEY_LOCAL_MACHINE\SOFTWARE\Microsoft\Windows\CurrentVersion\
ShellExtensions\Approved
HKEY_LOCAL-MACHINE\SOFTWARE\Microsoft\Windows\CurrentVersion\
ShellExtensions\Approved
```

Programs notorious for putting things in these places include backup utilities that automatically load their useless scheduler programs and the software that comes with older versions of Microsoft mice and keyboards.

Q: *How do I know if Windows is using a specific file?*

A: Check the date of the file (right-click on it and select **Properties**). If it's recent, it's most likely being used.

If the file is large and you want to know if you can delete it, try renaming it or moving it to another directory to see if everything still works before you delete it.

No, you shouldn't delete your swap file (*win386.swp, 386spart.par,* or *Pagefile.sys*), although if you do, it will be recreated when you restart Windows.

Q: *Why can't I start Windows 95 when I boot from a floppy?*

A: When you use Windows 95 to make a startup or "boot" diskette, it isn't complete. Copy the file *MSDOS.SYS* from the root directory of your hard disk onto the floppy, and reboot. This file tells DOS where your Windows 95 directory is located and will enable it to start.

Q: *How do I find out what version (a.k.a. "Build") of Windows I have?*

A: Open a DOS Window and type `ver`, or double-click on the System icon in Control Panel and choose the **General** tab. The final release of Windows 95 is build 950, and the final release of Windows NT 4.0 Workstation is build 1189. If you've installed the service packs for Windows 95 or Windows NT 4.0, the builds are 950a and 1381, respectively. If you have the Windows 95 OSR2 (see Chapter 1), the build number is 1111, or 950b (if you're using System Properties in Control Panel).

Q: *How do I get my mouse to work in DOS programs?*

A: You have to load the DOS mouse driver to use the mouse in DOS. Type `MOUSE` at the command prompt to load the driver once or add it to *AUTOEXEC.BAT* to load it every time.

     You can also use *DOSSTART.BAT* (saved in your Windows directory) instead of *AUTOEXEC.BAT* if you don't want this driver loaded all the time. Note: the following caveats do apply to this solution; certain limitations prevent environment variables to be used effectively, and *DOSSTART.BAT* isn't used at all with the command prompt shortcut found in your **Start Menu**.

Q: *How do I get HyperTerminal to redial when busy?*

A: Download and install the newest version of HyperTerminal, Personal Edition. See "Software and the Internet" in the Preface for more information.

Q: *How do I choose my own extensions in WordPad?*

A: To stop WordPad from appending .TXT to your filenames, enclose the desired filename in quotation marks.

Q: *How do I remove unwanted programs from the Open With list?*

A: These are all the applications you have configured in your file types. Remove any unwanted file types, and the associated applications will disappear from this list. It may not be sufficient to remove some stubborn applications in this way. If an application remains, remove all references to it in your Registry as well as in your *WIN.INI* file, or run the program's uninstall utility.

Q: *How do I store files on floppies that are too large to fit?*

A: Use the PKZip 2.04g utility, along with the -& parameter to compress the data and span it across as many floppies as necessary. See "How do I format DMF (1.7 MB) diskettes?" later in this appendix for another solution.

Q: *How do I remove old keyboard shortcuts (hotkeys) for programs?*

A: Keyboard shortcuts that you may have created for applications remain even if the application has been removed from the system. This seems to be a bug in Windows 95, and there is not yet a solution.

Q: *How do I set an application's default directory?*

A: Use this procedure to configure where an application saves its files (i.e., where your WWW browser saves its downloads). Note that some applications may not function if you do this, so make sure to back up the shortcut before continuing. Right-click on the shortcut to the application, and select **Properties**. Choose the **Shortcut** tab, and specify the desired directory in the field labeled **Start In**.

Q: *How do I sort by extension in Explorer?*

A: In Windows 95, files are classified by their file type, which is one step beyond the file extension. However, there are circumstances where it is advantageous to sort by file extension, and not file type. Although sorting by file type and by extension yields similar results, they are not identical. A temporary although impractical solution to this limitation is to rename all your file types to mirror the extension names (such as **.TXT* = "TXT file," **.WPD* = "WPD file"). As of yet, there is no way to sort the files in Explorer by the actual extension.

Q: *How do I get WordPad to save .WRI files?*

A: The new replacement for Write is WordPad, the scaled-down version of the over-rated Microsoft Word. WordPad can, in fact, read .WRI files (Write's native format), although WordPad cannot save .WRI files. The only way to save .WRI files is to use Word 7.0. What's even stranger is that the previous version of Word wasn't able to read or save .WRI files! I suppose this is Microsoft's way of phasing out the Write format. The only apparent solution is not to use .WRI files anymore. Note: If you own Windows 3.x, you can still use the old version of *Write.exe* (which Windows 95 overwrites), which can open and save Write files.

Q: *How do I set the default sort order for use with the DOS dir command?*

A: The *dir* command is used to display the contents of the current directory in the command prompt. Using a text editor such as Notepad, include the following line in your *AUTOEXEC.BAT* file:

```
SET DIRCMD=/O:xxx /A
```

where xxx can be any or all of the following letters, in order by preference: **N** to sort by name, **E** for extension, **S** for size, **D** for date, **G** to group directories first, **A** by last access date (earliest first). Prelude any letter with a minus sign to reverse the order. Some examples include */O:EN* to sort by extension and then name, */O:-D* to sort by reverse date, and */O:SAG* to sort by size and last access date, grouping directories first. Type DIR /? to see all the possible options.

Q: *What's the best way to install Windows 95?*

A: If you don't already have it, buy the CD version if you have a CD drive. There is no reason to get the floppy version unless you have no CD drive. If you have the time, it is best to install on a clean machine, rather than over your old installation of Windows 3.x. Here's how to do it:

- Remove all drivers from *CONFIG.SYS* and *AUTOEXEC.BAT*, except the ones for your CD-ROM drive.

- Install Windows 95 into a new directory.

- When finished, remove *CONFIG.SYS* and *AUTOEXEC.BAT* altogether, so that Windows 95 will install native 32-bit drivers for your CD-ROM drive. See "Do I Still need *CONFIG.SYS* and *AUTOEXEC.BAT?*" in Chapter 6, *Troubleshooting*, for more information.

Since Windows NT 4.0 doesn't use your *CONFIG.SYS* or *AUTOEXEC.BAT* files at all, you don't have to worry about them when installing NT.

Q: *How do I install, remove, or reinstall one of the components that came with Windows?*

A: Unfortunately, it's sometimes necessary to reinstall Windows. However, if you only need to install, remove, or reinstall one of the Windows components, just double-click on the Add/Remove Programs icon in Control Panel, and choose the **Windows Setup** tab.

Q: *How do I uninstall Windows?*

A: For many users, the uninstall feature that comes with Windows 95 either doesn't work that well or doesn't work at all. Since Windows 95 installs a new file system in addition to all the program files, it is recommended that you reformat your hard disk to remove Windows 95 completely.

As for Windows NT 4.0, there is no included uninstall utility, so you'll need to reformat your drive completely, especially if you've installed the NTFS (the NT file system), which isn't compatible with DOS or Windows 95.

Q: *How do I change screen resolution without rebooting?*

A: When changing the resolution or color depth of your display, Windows 95 usually wants to restart the computer. However, you can install a small utility that allows you to change resolution on the fly. Windows NT 4.0 has this functionality built in, as do many specialized video drivers (available from the manufacturer of your video card).

To add this functionality to Windows 95, obtain and install the QuickRes utility. See "Software and the Internet" in the Preface for more information.

If you frequently switch screen resolutions, try EzDesk (also available on the Internet), which can save your Desktop layout for each resolution.

Q: *How do I use CAB files?*

A: When using a complex operating system with hundreds of support files like Windows, once in a while you'll need to get one of the files off the distribution diskettes. Microsoft's new applications are all distributed in .CAB (Cabinet) files, which contain all of the compressed distribution files (similar to .ZIP files—see "Windows Basics" in Chapter 1).

To extract files from the Cabinet files, obtain and install the CabView utility. See "Software and the Internet" in the Preface for more information. This utility turns CAB files into virtual folders. Just double-click on a CAB file icon, and a folder will appear, allowing you to extract the desired file by dragging it out of the window.

Currently there's no way to create CAB files, unless you happen to work at Microsoft.

You'll also notice that CAB files can be quite large. In order to fit the 1.7 megabyte variety onto a standard floppy diskette, you'll need a DMF format utility (see the next topic).

Q: *How do I format DMF (1.7 MB) Diskettes?*

A: Most of Microsoft's new products are shipping on their new DMF (distribution media format) disks. This new format can hold about 1.7 megabytes (compared with 1.44 for normally formatted floppies). Although neither Explorer nor the *Format* command allows you to create these disks, the following third-party programs are able to format and/or duplicate these disks:

*   Norton Navigator for Windows 95 (commercially available). Use the Format command in the Norton File Manager.

*   WinImage 2.2 (shareware, available for download from the Internet; see Preface). Choose **Format Disk** from the **Disk** menu, and then select either **DMF (cluster 1024)** or **DMF (cluster 2048)**.

*   Other freeware or shareware programs capable of creating DMF diskettes include FDFO, Disk Duplicator v5.0, and CopyQM 3.20.

Generally CAB files are used in conjunction with this new format (see the previous topic)

Q: *Why do even the smallest files take up so much disk space?*

A: Now that new, large hard disks (1 GB and larger) are so affordable, more users are being faced with this problem. This occurs when you have your entire hard disk in one partition (rather than having it split up into several small partitions). What's worse is that all the tiny shortcuts used by Windows 95 and other Microsoft products can create megabytes of wasted disk space.

The problem is slack space, or the amount of disk space that is wasted by having a large cluster size. For example, if a 300-byte file is stored on a disk with a cluster size of 4,096 bytes, there will be 3,796 bytes of slack space that can't be used for any other files. You can see how much space is allocated to a file by typing DIR /v at the command prompt.

Here's how it works: for drives of 16 MB to 128 MB in size, the cluster size is 2 kB. Thereafter, drives up to 256 MB in size have a cluster size of 4 kB; drives up to 512 MB have a cluster size of 8 kB; drives up to 1 gB have a cluster size of 16 kB; drives up to 2 GB have a cluster size of 32 kB; and so on. In other words, if you have a 1.5 GB hard drive, each file less than 32 kB is taking up the full 32,768 bytes. A 33 kB file would take up 65,536 bytes, and so on.

While this problem inflicts drives formatted with FAT (file allocation table), drives formatted with FAT32 (available in Windows 95 OSR2;

see Chapter 1) or NTFS (available in Windows NT) are much more efficient.

For more information, see "Cluster Size and Slack Space" in Appendix C.

Q: *How do I increase the memory in my system without spending so much money?*

A: A series of RAMdoubler programs have recently hit the market, but there is substantial evidence that these programs accomplish absolutely nothing. Besides, you can buy another 8 or 16 megabytes of memory for the price of one of these programs, so what's the point? If you have old memory that won't fit in your computer but is fast enough, you can get SIMM expanders, which allow you to put 30-pin SIMMs in 72-pin slots, as well as put four SIMMs in a single slot. Note that the price of RAM has dropped substantially recently, so upgrading the RAM in your system isn't nearly as expensive as it used to be.

Q: *What do I do if an important application doesn't work with or crashes Windows 95?*

A: Contact the manufacturer of your software for a bug fix (usually free) or an upgrade (usually expensive).

Q: *What do I do if my BIOS is causing a problem with Windows 95?*

A: Many problems with newer and older computers alike are caused by a buggy or incompatible BIOS in your system. The BIOS controls many of the basic operations of your computer, such as your keyboard, text display, floppy and hard drives, and ports. You can upgrade the BIOS in an older computers by replacing the BIOS chip. Contact the manufacturer of your motherboard for details. If you have a newer Pentium motherboard, you may be able to upgrade your bios with software. See "Software and the Internet" in the Preface for more information.

Q: *Why does my CD-ROM drive work in Windows 95, but not when I restart in DOS mode to run my favorite antique DOS game?*

A: When Windows 95 isn't running, neither are any of the drivers. You'll have to install the appropriate drivers for all of your devices into ancient files called *AUTOEXEC.BAT* and *CONFIG.SYS*. Follow the instructions that come with each device to do so.

Q: *How do I get a specific DOS game won't run under Windows 95?*

A: Make sure you have enough conventional memory. If not, try to free some up. Try turning off your Soundblaster-type sound effects. If that works, there's your problem. Your game might not run under Windows 95. You might want to use a startup menu to give yourself easy access. See "Getting DOS Games to Work" in Chapter 6 for more information.

Q: *When I choose Shut Down from the Start Menu, my computer hangs at the Please Wait screen.*

A: Most likely, one or more of the Windows 95 device drivers is not allowing itself to be unloaded. Check to see if all of your devices are compatible with Windows 95, and contact the manufacturers of the various devices for the most recent drivers. Try hitting Enter when it hangs to "wake it up."

Try holding Shift while clicking **OK** in the Shut Down dialog box in Windows 95. This might allow you to shut down faster and bypass whatever is causing your system to hang.

This can also happen if the sound file for the Shutdown event becomes corrupted. Double-click on the Sounds icon in the Control Panel and remove or change the sound event for shutdown.

Q: *When I choose Shut Down from the Start Menu, my computer restarts instead of shutting down.*

A: If you've customized your shutdown screens, it could be caused by a problem with one of the files. A buggy driver that won't allow itself to be unloaded can also cause this. Older mouse drivers are notorious for this behavior.

Networking

Q: *How do I resolve Dial-Up Networking problems (WINSOCK.DLL conflicts)?*

A: This manifests itself in messages like "This program is making an invalid dynamic link call to a .DLL file" and in behavior such as WWW browsers not connecting. See the "Software Issues" in Chapter 6, *Troubleshooting*.

Q: *How do I get my Fonts folder to work like it's supposed to, rather that just like an ordinary folder?*

A: Microsoft's TweakUI PowerToy allows you to fix a broken fonts folder. See "Software and the Internet" in the Preface for more information.

Q: *When I change a simple setting, such as my clock style or screen colors, Windows 95 forgets those settings when I restart!*

A: This type of problem is usually caused by your not being "logged in" to your system. Select **Shut Down** from the **Start Menu**, choose **Close all Windows and log on as a different user**, and click **OK**. When you've logged back on (just hit Enter if you don't want to enter a password), Windows should start remembering your settings.

If that doesn't work, double-click on the Network icon in the Control Panel, and choose the **Identification** tab. Make sure all of the fields are filled in correctly (even if you're not on a network), click **OK**, and restart your computer. If that doesn't work, you're most likely experiencing a bug in Windows 95.

Q: *How do I get Windows 95 to save my password when I try to connect to the Internet?*

A: See "Dial-Up Networking Refuses to Remember Passwords" in Chapter 7.

Q: *How do I stop Windows 95 from altering floppy disks?*

A: You probably don't know it, but Windows 95 will change the contents of any floppy inserted into a Windows 95 system. This is to update the file system on the floppy to accept long filenames, but it can have disastrous effects on your valuable data. Diskettes affected include some older versions of MS-DOS startup diskettes, many copy-protected programs, and software that inspects the validity of the diskette before installing. In particular, the place being changed is the OEM-ID of a disk, offset 3 in the boot sector. To prevent Windows 95 from altering your floppies, the solution is quite simple. Just write-protect any floppies before putting them into a Windows 95 machine.

Q: *What do I do with "unknown" devices in Device Manager?*

A: This means that Windows 95 has detected a device for which it has no driver. Go over the other devices in your system, see if you have any hardware that isn't listed, and then contact the manufacturer of the missing devices for the appropriate drivers. Note that sometimes the Device Manager lists devices that either don't exist or exist but don't need drivers.

Q: *How do I fix the Details view in Explorer?*

A: If you see only partial information or no information at all when trying to use the Details view in Explorer, odds are the columns are messed up. Use your mouse to resize them by moving the arrow until it changes to a horizontal resize arrow between the column headings. Then click down, and drag the columns until you can see all the information.

If you click on the column headings themselves, the window will sort accordingly. Double-clicking the column separators will automatically adjust the column widths so that all the information is displayed.

If you don't see any columns, they've all been squeezed to the left. Take your mouse, and move it slowly around the upper-left portion of the window until the double arrow (for resizing) appears.

Q: *Windows 95 keeps deleting my applications!*

A: A few users have reported that Windows 95 has deleted entire applications (directories and all!) without warning. I personally have had WordPerfect for Windows deleted four times by Windows 95. Microsoft has no explanation, although Microsoft products seem to be immune to this spontaneous deletion.

A possible solution is to turn off support for long filenames (which Microsoft calls "enabling the Windows 3.1 file system"). At the command prompt, type `scandskw /o` to remove long filenames and all extended file attributes from the disk. Then, run the Registry Editor (see Chapter 3, *The Registry*, for more information), expand the branches to `Hkey_Local_Machine\System\CurrentControlSet\Control\FileSystem`, and change the value of Win31FileSystem from `0` to `1`. You'll have to restart your computer for this change to take effect. This may cause other problems, so be very careful using this solution.

Back up often!

Q: *What do I do when the Windows 95 Desktop won't accept dropped files?*

A: Sometimes, and for no apparent reason, Windows 95 will display a "no" cursor (circle with a line through it) whenever you try to drag-drop a file onto the Desktop, move an icon from one part of the Desktop to another, or drop something into the recycle bin. If this happens, the best way to fix it is to restart Explorer. See "Refreshing the Desktop Without Restarting Windows" in Chapter 2, *Customizing Your System*.

Q: *What do I do if I hate Microsoft Exchange or Windows Messaging?*

A: The email and fax program that comes with Windows 95 and Windows NT 4.0, respectively, is quite limited, compared to other software available for the task. The advantage for some users is the global inbox, which stores both incoming faxes and email messages. If you can cope with the gross inconsistencies of this design, you might be able to put up with this program. However, other email software, like the freely available Eudora Lite (see "Software and the Internet" in the Preface for more information), is much more suitable for sending and receiving Internet email. As for using your fax, try the software that came with your fax/modem (as long as it's designed especially for Windows 95 or Windows NT, whichever is applicable). Additionally, third-party commercial software is available for both services that far outperforms Exchange and Messaging—necessary if you use either service extensively.

Q: *How do I share a UNIX resource as a network drive over Dial-Up Networking?*

A: Although the differences between the Windows file system and that of UNIX computers is substantial, and the Dial-Up Networking connection is limited in this regard, you can share remote UNIX resources with Dial-Up Networking with special third-party software. Obtain and install Samba. See "Software and the Internet" in the Preface for more information.

Q: *Why doesn't Autodial always work?*

A: If you've configured Windows to connect to the Internet automatically when you open your Web browser or email program, you may find that the connection doesn't always work. This seems to be a compatibility problem with Dial-Up Networking and certain types of software. It might also be caused by your modem or modem software. Contact the manufacturer of your modem for technical support, and refer to "Installing Dial-Up Networking" in Chapter 7 to make sure your system is configured correctly. If you can't get it to work, you'll have to dial manually (double-click on your connection icon in Dial-Up Networking before starting your browser). If you don't have Autodial installed, see "Using Autodial with Dial-Up Networking" in Chapter 7.

Q: *How do I stop Dial-Up Networking from being launched every time I open my browser?*

A: You've turned on Windows' Autodial feature. To turn it off, Double-click on the Internet icon in the Control Panel, and turn off the **Use Autodial** option. If you don't have the Internet icon, see "Using Autodial with Dial-Up Networking" in Chapter 7.

Q: *How do I stop Internet Explorer from loading a "home page"?*

A: Right-click on the shortcut for Internet Explorer, and select **Properties**. If you're using the Internet icon on your Desktop, you need to create a new shortcut. You can remove the Internet icon (see Chapter 1), and replace it with your own shortcut, if you wish.

In the Properties window, choose the **Shortcut** tab, and add -nohome to the text in the **Target** field (with a space separating beforehand), so that it looks something like this:

```
iexplorer.exe -nohome
```

This may cause problems with Internet Explorer 3.0. Subsequent releases may or may not fix the bug.

Q: *Why can't I get the direct-cable connection to work?*

A: There are many things that can cause conflict with direct-cable connection, such as your mouse, modem, or any other serial devices. Faulty cables, loose plugs, or other running software may also cause problems. However, if you've gotten rid of the network neighborhood icon (see Chapter 4, *Advanced Customization Techiques*), you may have to put it back in order to use direct-cable connection.

Q: *Why don't the new 32-bit Internet applications work on my system?*

A: Let me guess: you've downloaded the newest version of Netscape Navigator, for example, and thought it would be a good idea to get the 32-bit version since you're using Windows 95 or Windows NT. Now, to your dismay, it doesn't work at all. The problem is that although you now have a 32-bit operating system that will run 32-bit applications, you're probably still using a 16-bit dialer (such as Trumpet Winsock). The solution is to switch to a 32-bit dialer, such as Dial-Up Networking, the dialer that comes with Windows 95 and Windows NT 4.0. See "Installing Dial-Up Networking" in Chapter 7, *Networking*, for complete instructions.

Q: *Which software should I use with the Internet?*

A: There are a lot of things you can do on the Internet, and you'll most likely need a different program for each one. Some programs handle more than one of these tasks, but more often than not, they don't do as good a job as programs designed exclusively for the task. A good example is Netscape Navigator (called "Communicator" in version 4.0 and later). Netscape is by far the best World Wide Web browser available, but its included email, newsgroup, and FTP clients aren't as good as other individual programs. The following software, all available for free download on the Internet, should allow you accomplish any given task (see the *Glossary* for details):

- Netscape Navigator/Communicator—World Wide Web browser

- Eudora Light—Email

- WS_FTP32—FTP (file transfer protocol)

- Telnet—Telnet (included in Windows 95 and Windows NT 4.0)

- Free Agent—Newsgroups

Other clients are available for more specific needs, such as IRC (Internet Relay Chat), audio and video conferencing, ping, finger, and whois. Depending on your needs and budget, you'll need to choose one that's right for you. The above applications should serve most (if not all) of your needs.

Q: *How do I share Dial-Up Networking over a local area network?*

A: There's no support for sharing modems across a local area network (LAN) in Windows, meaning that you can't facilitate Internet access to other machines on an LAN simply by dialing up with a single machine. However, since the fax components of fax/modems are treated like printers, they can be shared over an LAN as easily as any printer (see "Setting up a Workgroup" in Chapter 7). However, since Windows has no built-in provision for sharing a modem and the TCP/IP protocol used with Internet connections can't be transmitted over a workgroup, a third-party solution is required. In order to share Dial-Up Networking over a network, you need to obtain and install WinGate, a third-party utility available for download on the Internet (see Preface). WinGate configures the computer with the modem as a gateway for the other computers on the LAN. This means you'll have to reconfigure your Winsock software on the other computers, assuming that the software supports it. Although this means the process isn't entirely painless, it does work relatively well with most software, including most Web browsers.

B

MS-DOS Crash Course

Many solutions in this book require that you type commands into a DOS Window. If you don't quite have a grasp on this concept, here's a crash course on MS-DOS (short for Microsoft Disk Operating System). DOS has been included with PCs since the IBM PCs in the early 1980s, and even the newest PCs still use it to some extent. DOS was the PC operating system used before Microsoft Windows became the standard and still has some use today. All versions of Windows from 1.0 to 3.11 relied on DOS. Windows was thought of only as an extension, as one needed to load DOS before starting Windows. Windows 95 is still based somewhat on MS-DOS for compatibility with the vast majority of available software and hardware products, but does a good job of hiding this dependence. Microsoft has made Windows NT 4.0 completely independent of MS-DOS, but still makes available the command prompt for those who need the functionality.

Rather than unloading Windows to access the command prompt, you can simply load another command prompt while remaining in Windows. This is often referred to as a DOS Box or DOS Window. If you don't have a command prompt item in your **Start Menu**, you can use the **Start Menu**'s *Run* command to execute command.com. You'll see a window that looks like the one shown in Figure B-1. The cursor indicates the command line (where commands are typed), and the prompt usually shows the current working directory (here, C:\Windows).

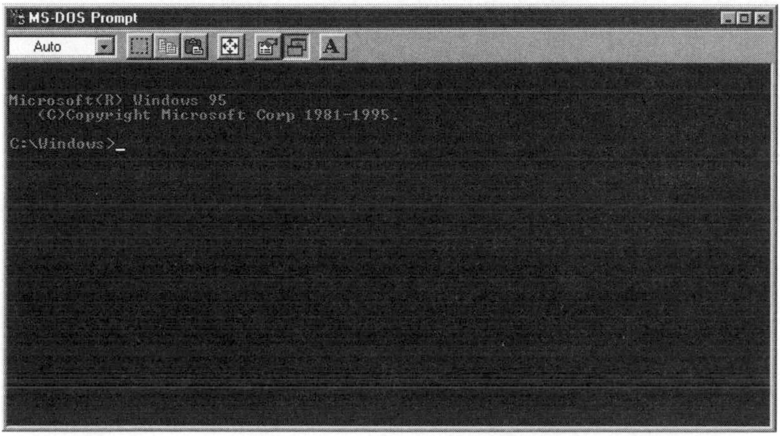

Figure B-1: The command prompt is used to complete some of the solutions in this book.

To run programs in a DOS box, type the name of the program at the command line (also called the C prompt because it usually looks like C:\>) and press Enter. You should know the following basic DOS commands to be able to complete the solutions in this book. The commands are in uppercase, and the parameters (the information you supply to the command) are in lowercase. If there is more than one parameter, each is separated by a space.

CD foldername

Changes the working directory to *foldername*. If the prompt indicates you are in *C:\Windows*, and you want to run a DOS program located in *C:\Files*, type CD C:\FILES.

DIR

Displays a listing of all the files and directories in the current working directory. Use CD to change to a different directory. Type DIR C:\FILES to display the contents of C:\Files without using the CD command. Type DIR /? for additional options.

ATTRIB filename

Changes the attributes (also called properties) of a file. In Explorer, you can right-click on a file or group of files to change the attributes (R for *read only*, S for *system*, A for *archive*, and H for *hidden*). ATTRIB is the DOS counterpart to this functionality. In addition, ATTRIB lets you change the S attribute—something Explorer doesn't let you do. Here are some examples:

- ATTRIB +H MYFILE.TXT—This turns *on* the "H" parameter for the file *myfile.txt*.

- ATTRIB -R "ANOTHER FILE.DOC"—This turns off the "R" parameter for the file another *file.doc* (note the quotes used because of the space in the filename).

- Type ATTRIB /? for additional options.

COPY filename destination

Copies a file to another directory or drive, specified as *destination*. This is the same as dragging and dropping files in Explorer, except that the keyboard is used instead of the mouse. For example, to copy the file *myfile.txt* (located in the current working directory) to your floppy drive, type COPY MYFILE.TXT A:\.

MOVE filename destination

The same as COPY, except that the file is moved instead of copied.

REN oldfilename newfilename

Renames a file to *newfilename*. This is especially useful, as you can use the *ren* command to rename more than one file once—something Explorer doesn't let you do. For example, to rename *myfile.txt* to *herfile.txt*, type REN MYFILE.TXT HERFILE.TXT. To change the extensions of all the files in the current working directory from .TXT to .DOC, type REN *.TXT *.DOC.

DEL filename

Deletes a file. For example, to delete the file *myfile.txt*, type DEL MYFILE.TXT. This is not the same as deleting a file in Windows, as the file will *not* be stored in the Recycle Bin.

EXIT

Closes the command prompt window. This command has no effect if Windows isn't running. In most situations, you can just click the **close** button [x] at the upper right corner of the Window, but the Exit command is safer.

C

Glossary

Following is a brief collection of terms used throughout the book. These cover hardware, software, the Internet, and many things in between. For more complete definitions, check out O'Reilly & Associates' *Dictionary of PC Hardware and Data Communications Terms* by Mitchell Shnier. The book is also available free on the World Wide Web at *http://www.ora.com/ reference/dictionary/*.

ActiveX	A new term (for the purposes of marketing), synonymous with OCX, or a Windows custom control that uses OLE (object linking and embedding). ActiveX controls can be used in Internet Explorer and several Windows software development environments, including Visual Basic 4.0 and later. See also *custom control, OLE*.
Address	A unique name identifying the recipient or originator of transmitted data. This can be an email address, a World Wide Web address, an address in your computer's memory or bus, or a network address. Problems occur when two things (hardware or software) try to use the same address. For example, a word processor will store your document in a particular memory address while you have it open.

An address can also be the location of a document or file on the Internet, such as *http://www.creativelement.com/*, or an email address, such as *book@creativelement.com*. There are IP addresses, such as 204.247.136.39, and ethernet addresses for hardware attached to an LAN.

Alias   A nickname. In UNIX and some varieties of DOS, an alias is a short word used to carry out a long command. On a network, an alias is an easy-to-remember name for a resource, such as a drive or printer.

Anonymous FTP   A method of using FTP without a password. Anyone who wishes to make files publicly available can allow users to use FTP by specifying anonymous for the user name, and their email address for the password. See also *FTP*.

Applet   A small application. For example, each of the windows that appear when you double-click on an icon in Control Panel are considered Applets; although they are small applications by themselves, they require a larger application (Control Panel) to operate them.

Application   Any program on your hard disk. An application usually has its own directory and can be started by clicking on its icon in the **Start Menu**. Most applications have their own window.

Archive   A collection of software or files. Many public archives exist on the Internet, that allow anyone to download (retrieve) files. A personal archive would be where a single user stores files for infrequent access.

Bandwidth   A frequency, measured in hertz (Hz), defined as the difference between the lowest and highest frequencies of a transmission. A larger bandwidth (a greater difference) means that more data can be transmitted in a shorter amount of time. Metaphorically, bandwidth can be represented as a garden hose: a larger-diameter hose can handle a greater flow of water.

BBS	Short for bulletin board system. This generally takes the form of a computer accessible to the outside world to other computers by telephone (modem) connections. Members of a BBS can call up and gain access to file and information archives, share email, chat, and leave messages. Originally used for hobbyists and support centers for large companies, BBSs are losing popularity to the Internet.
BIOS	Short for basic input-output system. This is a chip (or set of chips) in your computer that controls how your computer communicates with some of the basic hardware components in your system, such as the keyboard, floppy drive, and hard disk. In newer computers, the BIOS supports Plug & Play. A buggy or incompatible BIOS is a common cause of problems in Windows. See Chapter 6 for more information.
Boot	The process of starting up a computer. See *reboot.*
Browser	A Winsock client (software) used to navigate the World Wide Web. Netscape, Mosaic, and Internet Explorer are examples.
Browsing	The act of looking for something on a network—for example, browsing a World Wide Web site by looking through a few Web pages or browsing the Network Neighborhood to see which disk resources are shared on a network.
Buffer	The use of part of your computer's memory to relieve the burden on a specific component, such as the keyboard or printer. For example, if you press all of the keys on your keyboard at once (on a slow computer), the letters would appear on the screen slower than you've typed them.

Since the computer isn't able to process keys that quickly, they keys you have pressed are stored in a buffer and fed to the computer at a slower rate it can handle. In this way, your keystrokes aren't lost. Note that your computer will beep if the buffer is full, telling you keys pressed thereafter will be forgotten. Similar to cache.

Bug

An error in software that causes it to work improperly or not at all. This term comes from an occurrence when an actual bug made a nest in an early hard-wired (without software) computer, causing it to malfunction.

Button

A 3D control on the screen that looks as if it's pushed in when you click on it. This is different from an icon, although buttons can contain icons. Buttons usually get a single left-click, while icons get a double-click.

Byte

The smallest unit of storage on a disk or in memory. For example, in a document created by a word processor, each character takes up at least 1 byte. See also *gigabyte*; *kilobyte*; and *megabyte*.

Cache

The use of part of your computer's memory to improve the performance of a specific component, such as the hard disk, CD-ROM drive, or even processor. By storing recently accessed information in a disk cache, for example, your computer can respond faster because it is accessing memory instead of the slower hard disk. (Pronounced "cash.") Similar to buffer.

Character

A letter, number, or symbol—anything that can be typed from the keyboard.

Client

(1) An application used over a Winsock connection, such as an email program or a World Wide Web Browser. (2) A computer (hardware) on a network that isn't a server.

Cluster Size	The smallest amount of hard disk space a file can occupy. Floppies have a cluster size of 512 bytes, and hard disks can have a cluster size ranging from 1 kilobyte to 32 kilobytes (sometimes even more). The larger the partition, the larger the cluster size. See also *slack space*.
CMOS	A small bit of memory used by your computer to store certain settings while it's turned off, such as the type of hard disk installed. You can typically change the CMOS settings by pressing a certain keystroke (such as Del or Esc) during the system boot.
Command Prompt	One of the simplest ways to control a computer. The user runs applications and performs other activities by typing commands at a prompt. UNIX and DOS are examples of command prompts.
Context Menu	The menu that appears when you right-click on an object, such as a folder or a file. It's called a context menu because the items in the menu depend on what's being clicked. The menu is appropriate to the context.
Control	An element of the user interface, such as an icon, a button, or a window.
Cooperative Multitasking	A type of multitasking where the operating system assigns an equal amount of processor cycles to each application, regardless of how much power it actually needs. Preemptive multitasking (used in Windows 95 and Windows NT) is more efficient and powerful than the cooperative multitasking found in Windows 3.x.
CPU	Central processing unit—another name for the processor.

Custom Control   A modular add-on used to help build an applica-
                          tion. The add-on may implement a customized
                          user-interface control (such as a grid, enhanced
                          push button, or fancy dial), provide Internet
                          connectivity, or add other functionality to a
                          program. Some custom control files have the file-
                          name extension .VBX or .OCX. Newer OLE-
                          compatible custom controls, called ActiveX, are
                          used by World Wide Web browsers to enhance
                          web pages. See also *ActiveX*; *DLL*; and *OLE*.

Cyberspace   An annoying and hackneyed term loosely refer-
                          ring to the virtual world one enters when
                          connected to the Internet or other large
                          computer network.

Database   A collection of information stored in an orga-
                          nized fashion, suitable for updating and
                          viewing the information contained within
                          frequently and easily. A database application is
                          required to access the information in a
                          database.

DDE   Short for dynamic data exchange. The method
                          by which different applications can communi-
                          cate with each other. For example, installation
                          programs use DDE to communicate with your
                          Start Menu (or the Program Manager in
                          Windows 3.x) to add new program icons. See
                          also *OLE*.

Default   An original factory setting. For example, the
                          taskbar in Windows 95 and Windows NT 4.0 is
                          located at the bottom of the screen by default,
                          but you can move it to any side of the screen
                          by dragging it with the mouse.

Defragment   Using the Disk Defragmenter application, you
                          can fix all the files on your hard disk that have
                          become fragmented. When many files become
                          fragmented, your hard disk performance is
                          slower, and the danger of file corruption is
                          greater, so it is a good idea to defragment
                          often. This is also known as optimizing your
                          hard disk.

Desktop	The blank area on your screen behind all the windows. The Windows Desktop is really a directory on the hard disk and can hold icons. Right-click on the Desktop to change its many properties.
Dial-Up Networking	The feature built into Windows 95 and Windows NT 4.0 allowing one to connect to the Internet or other remote computer network using standard phone lines. See also *PPP*; *SLIP*.
Directory	A container for files. It can have any name, but always has a yellow folder for its icon. Every directory has its own icon, into which other icons can be dropped.
Disk	A storage device used to hold files and directories. There are hard disks and floppy disks.
Diskette	Another name for floppy disk.
DLL	Short for Dynamic Link Library; files with this extension are used when creating Windows applications. DLL files allow multiple applications to "share" code; a .DLL file that contains the functionality to play a video clip on the screen may be used by many applications to perform that action, eliminating the need for each application to handle it individually.
DNS	Short for Domain Name Service. Specific computers (nameservers) on the Internet are designed to assist some computers with connecting to other computers. Nameservers use a database of all domains on the Internet to allow connections to hosts referred to by their easier-to-remember host names rather than their numerical IP addresses.
Document	The file you create in an application (e.g., a letter written in a word processor). Every document has its own icon.

Domain	A subset of a network such as an Internet domain name, or an NT security domain. It's usually the suffix of a site address on the Internet, such as *creativelement.com*. The address of a company's home page on the World Wide Web usually begins with *www.* followed by the domain name. Example: *www.creativelement.com*. Email addresses are formed by combining a user's login with the domain name, separated by the @ symbol. Example: *book@creativelement.com*.
DOS	Disk Operating System. The first operating system available for the PC platform. Easily recognized by the C:\> prompt. See also *Command Prompt*.
Download	Retrieve a file over a network or modem connection from a remote computer. When you download a file from the Internet, you are copying a file from another computer onto your own hard disk. See also *Upload*.
Driver	A piece of software that assists your computer in using a specific device, such as a printer or scanner. Buggy drivers cause the majority of problems with a computer. See also Chapter 6.
Email	A method of sending and receiving personal messages over a network, such as the Internet. Windows 95 and Windows NT 4.0 come with Exchange and Windows Messaging, respectively, two poorly regarded examples of Internet email client software.
Explorer	The interface for Windows 95 and Windows NT 4.0. This includes the folders in My Computer and the items in the task bar, as well as the window with the tree view.
Extension	The part of a filename that follows the period. This allows Windows to determine what type a file is. For example, a file with the .TXT extension tells Windows that it is a text file. Extensions are hidden by default in Windows 95.

FAQ

Short for frequently asked questions. A collection of questions and answers commonly used in World Wide Web sites, newsgroups, and other discussion forums. This book is based on *Windows95 Annoyances*, a web site structured around the popular Frequently Asked Questions paradigm.

File

Files contain data, whether it's a document you've written or an application used to create the document. Every file has its own icon. Files are stored in folders.

Finger

A very old way of looking up someone's email address on the Internet. Assuming a user's Internet Service Provider supports it, fingering a user on the Internet displays the last time the person logged in and whether he or she has any mail to be read. There also may be special information displayed if the user has set up a Plan file. In Windows 95, you need a finger client (software) to use this feature of the Internet. Windows NT 4.0 comes with a finger utility.

Firmware

Software stored in a certain device's ROM, used to control the device. This software is often user upgradable, meaning that the device can be upgraded by downloading a software "patch" rather than opening the computer and replacing the unit. Older units allow firmware upgrades by replacing ROM chips; while not as convenient as downloading a patch, it is certainly better than replacing the entire device. See also Chapter 6.

Floppy Disk

This is an inexpensive, removable disk that has a much lower capacity and speed than a hard disk. Its capacity can be measured in kilobytes or megabytes.

Folder

Interchangeable with directory, although *folder* is a newer term.

Fragmented	Broken up into pieces. Imagine if you saved a file to your hard disk and then saved another right after it. When you go to add more to the first file and then save it again, it no longer can fit in the space allotted and must be split apart. When many files become fragmented, hard disk performance is slower, and the danger of file corruption is greater. To fix fragmented files, you must defragment your hard disk.
FTP	File transfer protocol. A method of transferring files from one computer to another across the Internet. You need FTP client software to use FTP. Windows 95 and Windows NT 4.0 come with a simple DOS-based FTP client, *Ftp.exe*, but most web browsers support FTP (as in *ftp:// ftp.creativelement.com/*). Anonymous FTP is the most common use of FTP.
GB	An abbreviation for gigabyte.
Gigabyte	One billion bytes, or more precisely, 1,024 mega-bytes (1,073,741,824 bytes). Different definitions of this term cause discrepancies between different manufacturers and applications.
Gopher	An older version of the World Wide Web, but its structure is a more rigid menu system, and it doesn't have any graphics. If you'd like to play with Gopher, try a Veronica Search.
GUI	Short for graphical user interface. A type of user interface that uses graphics (such as icons and windows) to control the computer. Windows uses a GUI.
Hard Disk	A disk permanently connected to your computer; it has a much higher capacity and speed than a floppy disk. Its capacity is measured in megabytes and can be divided into several partitions.
Hardware	A general term used to describe the equipment that makes up and is connected to your computer. To the beginner, software is what-ever you see on the screen, and hardware is everything you can touch.

Hex	Traditionally a prefix meaning six (6), but also a numerical base (base 16) by which computer code is written. Unlike a text editor such as Notepad, a hex editor allows a user to edit binary files.
Hidden	A property of a file. Hidden files cannot normally be seen in Explorer or from the DOS prompt unless the Show All Files option (select **Options** from Explorer's **View** menu) is turned on. Right-click on a file and select **Properties**, or use the *Attrib DOS* command to turn on or off the "hidden" attribute of any file.
Host	A server on the Internet that contains a file, web page, or other data. Using an appropriate client application, you can retrieve information from a host.
Hypertext	An enhancement to rich text that allows certain words or images in an electronic document (such as a Windows Help file or web page) to be linked to other information. For example, you use hypertext when you click on a green, underlined word or phrase in a help file to go to another part of the help file. See also *rich text*.
Icon	The little pictures that you see on the screen, usually representing folders and files. Icons can be dragged onto other icons, onto applications, and into folders. Icons usually get a double-click; buttons get a single left-click.
Interface	The method by which you control anything. The screen is the interface to your computer, just as a dashboard is the interface to your car and a doorknob is the interface to a door. See also *user interface*.

Internet	A term used incorrectly to describe the World Wide Web. The Internet is a Wide Area Network, and a superset of the World Wide Web. Originally connecting a few universities and the government, it was designed to provide a network that could withstand a war because of its decentralized structure. See also *email*, *ftp*, and *telnet*.
Interrupt	A method by which a piece of hardware communicates with the processor. It's called interrupt because the device (such as a sound card) interrupts the computer to carry out a function (such as playing a sound). See also *IRQ*; Chapter 6.
IRQ	Short for interrupt request line. A number used to describe an interrupt. An IRQ can be any number from 0 to 15, inclusive. IRQ problems occur because two pieces of hardware try to use the same IRQ. See also *interrupt*; Chapter 6.
ISDN	Short for Integrated Services Digital Network. A newer type of digital telephone service, as opposed to the analog POTS (plain old telephone service). ISDN adapters can facilitate much faster connections than analog modems (what most telephone customers use). Around for nearly a decade, ISDN is only now gaining popularity as an inexpensive, high-speed connection to the Internet. To use ISDN, you must have an ISDN adapter, ISDN service from your phone company, and an ISDN account through your local Internet Service Provider.
ISP	Short for internet service provider. These are the folks who bill you for access to the Internet. This can be a large organization, such as America Online or CompuServe, or a small, local provider. If you have free Internet access through a university, the university is your ISP. Tip: Look for an ISP that doesn't charge by the hour! See also *POP*.
KB	Abbreviation for kilobyte.

Kilobyte	One thousand bytes, or more precisely, 1,024 bytes.
LAN	Local Area Network. A specific type of network, usually implying that all of the components (computers, printers, etc.) are close together geographically.
Local	Used to describe a computer or resource directly in front of the user, as opposed to remote from the user.
Lost Chains	Pieces of files that are no longer being used but are still taking up disk space. Use Scandisk (see Chapter 5, *Maximizing Performance*) to clean up your lost chains and delete them. If you convert them to files, they will have the .CHK extension. These files will be useless to you unless you know how to retrieve your data from them.
Macro	A feature used to reduce a series of steps to a single keystroke or mouse click. Most applications come with a macro facility that, by using a VCR metaphor, allows you to record a series of keystrokes and mouse clicks to be played back later.
Marketing	The only way a company with a customer satisfaction rating as low as Microsoft's could be so successful.
MB	Abbreviation for megabyte.
Megabyte	One million bytes, or more precisely, 1,024 kilobytes (totaling 1,048,576 bytes).
Memory	Also known as RAM, this is what allows your applications to run. The more memory you have, the more windows you can have open and the more applications you can run simultaneously. Memory, while not the same as disk space, is also measured in bytes, kilobytes, and megabytes.

Menu	A list of things that an application does. In Windows, nearly every application has a menu along the top of its window, usually containing the items **File**, **Edit**, **View**, and **Help**. When clicked, additional subordinate menu items are displayed.
Modem	Short for modulator-demodulator. A piece of hardware that allows your computer to make connections to other computers over a standard phone line. Dial-Up Networking uses your modem to connect to the Internet.
MRU	While this isn't actually a formal computer term, it is a sequence that is frequently seen in the Registry (see Chapter 4, *Advanced Customization Techniques*). It stands for "most recently used" and generally titles a recorded history of actions. For example, every time you use the **Start Menu**'s *run* command, it records what you've typed and presents it in a list for quick access the next time it's used. This is an MRU list.
Multitasking	The method by which more than one application runs simultaneously. See also *cooperative multitasking*, *multithreading*, and *preemptive multitasking*.
Multithreading	The method by which an operating system is able to run different parts of the same application simultaneously. See also *multitasking*.
Network	What you get when you connect two or more computers together. The Internet is a type of network. The terms LAN (local area network) and WAN (wide area network) imply the geographic scope of the network.
Object	A general term used to describe almost everything on the screen. In a stricter sense, objects are used in an object-oriented design.

Object-Oriented	An overused term, originally used to describe an advanced method of computer programming. For example, the interface in Windows 95 and Windows NT 4.0 is considered to be sort of object-oriented, because files and most of the controls are treated as strict objects, each having its own property sheet.
OLE	Short for object linking and embedding. A method by which applications can share information. Basically, it allows you to cut something from one application and paste it into another, and then edit the object in place. This second-rate technology (invented and pushed by Microsoft) has been known to cause Pentium-class systems to behave like 286s, is responsible for erratic drag-drop behavior, and is completely outclassed by competing technologies such as OpenDoc. See also *DDE, marketing.*
Operating System	The software used to control a computer and run applications. Windows, DOS, and UNIX are all examples of operating systems.
Partition	A division of a hard disk. For example, a 500-megabyte hard disk can be divided into two 250-megabyte partitions. Smaller partitions can be used to organize files and reduce the cluster size.
Patch	A small piece of software used to update an large piece of software. For example, software companies often make patches available for download on the Internet, so that users can easily, quickly, and inexpensively update their software to the newest version. It's much easier to download a small file containing only the differences between the old and new versions, rather than the entire new version of the software. Patches are used to upgrade applications, operating systems, firmware, and drivers; also known as updaters.

Ping	From Navy terminology, used to find out if a machine on the Internet exists and is responding. To use this feature, open a DOS window while you're connected, and type `ping www.creativelement.com` (or any other server). Ping will send small pieces of information to the machine; you know if the server is "up" if you get a response.
Plain Text	A property of text where no additional formatting (bold, italics, graphics) is used. It's important to understand the distinction between plain text and rich text. When you're editing a configuration file used by some applications (a file with the .INI extension) or sending email to someone using an older email application, you must use plain text. The use of any additional formatting may cause compatibility problems. Plain text uses less storage space than rich text.
POP	Short for Point Of Presence or Post Office Protocol, two entirely different terms both relating to the Internet. A point of presence is basically a local phone number, installed by your Internet service provider (ISP), you can use to connect to the Internet. It's best to have a point of presence in close proximity to avoid long-distance phone charges. The post office protocol (usually known as POP3) is the language your email program uses when talking with your ISP to retrieve your incoming email.
PPP	Short for Point-to-Point Protocol; the protocol (language) used by Dial-Up Networking to connect to a remote network, such as the Internet. Most Internet service providers support PPP, but some older services support only serial-line Internet protocol (SLIP). Both PPP and SLIP use standard phone lines to "fool" your computer into thinking that it's connected directly to the Internet, which allows the use of network clients such as web browsers and email programs. See also *Dial-Up Networking*; *Protocol*; *SLIP*.

Preemptive Multitasking	A type of multitasking where the operating system assigns processor cycles to applications depending on how much power they need. Preemptive multitasking is used in Windows 95 and Windows NT 4.0 and is better than the less efficient cooperative multitasking found in Windows 3.1. However, only 32-bit applications can take advantage of this feature.
Processor	The chip in your computer that does all the calculations. For Windows 95 users, it's based on Intel's x86 architecture, which includes the 386, 486, and Pentium series. Windows NT 4.0 supports a wider variety of processors, including more than one simultaneous chip in the same computer. Also referred to as the CPU.
Protocol	A formal set of conventions used to complete a task. Standards in the computer industry are established when companies agree on protocols for various forms of communication. For example, your email program uses POP (the post office protocol) to retrieve email from your account on the Internet. Your computer uses a specific protocol to communicate with your printer to ensure that your printouts look as expected.
RAM	Short for random access memory. This is the main type of memory in your computer. See also *ROM*.
RAS	Short for remote access service. A general term to describe the type of connection attained when one computer "dials into" another one. For example, the Dial-Up Networking included in Windows 95 and Windows NT 4.0 is a type of RAS.
Reboot	The process of restarting your computer. If you turn it off and then on again, or use the reset button on the front of your computer, it's called a cold boot. If you hold Ctrl and Alt while pressing Del, it's called a warm boot. See also *boot*.

Registry   A complicated database of settings for use in
                                 Windows 95 and Windows NT 4.0. You can
                                 edit these settings with the Registry Editor,
                                 REGEDIT.EXE. The Registry is stored in two
                                 files in your Windows directory, *USER.DAT* and
                                 SYSTEM.DAT. See Chapter 3 for more
                                 information.

Remote   Used to describe another computer or resource
                                 over a network or modem connection, other
                                 than your own. Since remote literally means
                                 "far away," it generally (but not always)
                                 involves physical distance. See also *local*.

Rich Text   A property of text that signifies advanced
                                 formatting, such as bold, italic, multiple colors
                                 and fonts, and graphics. Newer email applica-
                                 tions use rich text in email messages rather
                                 than just plain text. All word processors work
                                 with rich text. See also *hypertext; plain text*.

ROM   Short for read-only memory. A type of storage
                                 or memory that can only be read, not written
                                 to. A CD-ROM is an example of a ROM
                                 storage. See also *RAM*.

Root Directory   The top-level directory in the tree. For drive C,
                                 the root directory is signified by a single back-
                                 slash: C:\.

Server   A computer on a network that handles a
                                 specific function for the rest of the network.
                                 For example, a print server can allow all the
                                 computers on a local area network to use a
                                 printer. A World Wide Web server contains
                                 pages that are sent to other computers on the
                                 Internet for viewing. Also referred to as a host.
                                 In a client-server environment, the server
                                 machines handle certain functions on the
                                 network, while the client machines allow users
                                 to control those functions and access informa-
                                 tion on the network.

Shortcut	A small file that allows you to put an icon for an application in a directory other than the one containing the application. You can also make shortcuts to folders and files. Useful places for shortcuts are the Desktop and the **Start Menu**. You can tell a shortcut from other icons by the curved arrow in the lower-left corner. For those users familiar with UNIX, this is similar to a symbolic link.
SIMM	Short for single inline memory module. A SIMM is a small circuit board that holds memory chips. Rather than installing individual chips to increase your system's memory, you install SIMMs, which are much easier to install and remove. Nearly all newer computers (those capable of running Windows) use SIMMs.
16-Bit	In reference to Windows applications, a method by which an application uses your computer's memory and communicates with other applications. Sixteen-bit (sometimes called Legacy) applications lack several features found in their 32-bit counterparts.
Slack Space	The amount of disk space wasted by having a large cluster size. For example, if a 300-byte file is stored on a disk with a cluster size of 4,096 bytes, there will be 3,796 bytes of slack space that can't be used for any other files. You can see how much space is allocated to a file by typing DIR /v at the command prompt.
SLIP	Short for serial-line Internet protocol. An older protocol (language) used by Internet dialers to connect to a remote network, such as the Internet. Most Internet service providers support the newer point-to-point protocol (PPP), but some older services support only serial-line Internet protocol. Both PPP and SLIP use standard phone lines to "fool" your computer into thinking that it's connected directly to the Internet, which allows the use of network clients such as Web browsers and email programs. See also *Dial-Up Networking*, *PPP*, *Protocol*.

Software	A general term to describe the programs that can be used on a computer, such as applications, drivers, and operating systems. To the beginner, software is whatever you see on the screen, and hardware is everything you can touch.
Start Menu	The menu that appears when you click the button labeled **Start** at the bottom of your screen, on the taskbar.
Swap File	A file on your hard disk called *Win386.swp* that Windows 95 uses to store information when you run out of memory. In Windows NT 4.0, the file is called *Pagefile.sys*. Since a hard disk is slower than memory, a system without a lot of RAM will run out of memory sooner, requiring heavier use of the swap file, thereby resulting in slower performance. If you've upgraded from Windows 3.x, the old filename for the swap file (*386spart.par*) may be preserved. See also Chapter 5.
Task	Any program currently running on your computer. You can switch between tasks with the taskbar or by pressing Alt-Tab on the keyboard.
Taskbar	The bar along the bottom of your screen containing the **Start Menu** and a button for each running task.
TCP/IP	The combination of two protocols, Transmission Control Protocol and Internet Protocol, that are used to allow a computer to communicate over the Internet. On one end of the connection, TCP breaks apart information to be transmitted; on the other end, TCP puts it back together and checks it for errors. IP is the method by which the actual pieces of information are transferred from one computer to another across the Internet.

Telnet	A method of connecting to other computers on the Internet. You need a Telnet client (software) and an appropriate account to use Telnet. Windows 95 and Windows NT 4.0 both come with a simple Telnet client, *Telnet.exe*.
32-Bit	In reference to Windows applications, a method by which an application uses your computer's memory and communicates with other applications. Thirty-two-bit applications typically embody several features not found in their 16-bit counterparts, such as long filenames, preemptive multitasking, and multithreading.
Titlebar	The stripe across the top of a window containing the title of the application in the window. You can move a window by dragging its titlebar.
Tray	The small indented area on your taskbar that holds the clock by default. See also Chapter 2, *Customizing Your System*, for more information.
Tree	A graphical diagram used to display the hierarchical structure of the directories on a disk. The Windows Explorer allows the disk to be viewed in this fashion.
UNIX	The primary operating system used on the Internet. It is the networking counterpart to DOS, as it also is based on a command prompt.
Updater	A user-friendly synonym for patch.
Upload	To send a file over a network or modem connection to a remote computer. When you upload a file to the Internet, you are copying a file from your hard disk onto another computer. See also *download*.
User Interface	The interface to your computer—a combination of controls used to perform any operation. See also *Command Prompt/*; *GUI*.

Version	Most computer products (both software and hardware) go through several stages during the course of their development. For example, the first release of a word processing application would be known as version 1.0. Any minor changes or additions to the product would be released as version 1.1 or 1.2. A bug fix might be released as version 1.21 or 1.24. A major revision usually means a larger jump, such as version 2.0. Once the developers get tired of incrementing the version number, they often start over at 1.0, while appending "Pro" to the product's name. This signifies that the product is so much better than the original that it deserves a "professional" connotation.
WAN	Wide area network. A specific type of network, usually implying that all of the components (computers, servers, etc.) are far apart (geographically). Because of the proximity between components, the connections are usually serial (i.e., modems, ISDN adapters, T1, T3). The Internet is the ultimate WAN.
Window	A rectangular box containing an application, part of an application, a message, or a folder. This concept is the basis for the user interface in Windows.
Winsock	Short for Windows Sockets. This is the language the computer speaks when it's connected to the Internet. Dial-Up Networking is the winsock support built into Windows 95 and Windows NT 4.0. Once you've connected Windows to the Internet, you can use Winsock clients (software).
Winsock Client	See *client* (software).
Workgroup	A type of LAN. The computers that make up a workgroup tend to share the responsibilities equally, as opposed to a client-server relationship.
World Wide Web	The subset of the Internet you used to access this page. Netscape, Internet Explorer, and Mosaic are examples of browsers used to navigate the World Wide Web (WWW).

D

Contents of MSDOS.SYS File

When you install Windows 95, the file *MSDOS.SYS* is created in the root directory of your boot drive (usually C:\). While this file was a system file in previous versions of MS-DOS, it's now a text file used to store various settings for Windows 95 initialization.

To edit this file, you need to unhide it by typing the following command from the command prompt:

```
attrib -r -s -h c:\msdos.sys
```

You can then edit the file with a plain text editor, such as Notepad. The layout of the file is the same for standard Windows initialization (*.INI) files. See Chapter 4, *Advanced Customization Techniques*, for details.

The file consists of settings divided into two sections: [Paths], which lists the locations for certain Windows 95 files, and [Options], which allows you to customize the boot process. Any settings not already found in your *MSDOS.SYS* file can be manually inserted.

The [Paths] section can contain the following settings:

HostWinBootDrv={Root of Boot Drive}
> Default: C
>
> Purpose: Specifies the drive letter of the boot drive.

WinBootDir={Windows Directory}
> *Default:* Windows directory specified during Setup (usually *C:\Windows*)
>
> *Purpose:* Specifies the location of the required startup files.

WinDir={Windows Directory}

Default: Windows directory specified during Setup (should be the same as WinBootDir)

Purpose: Specifies the location of Windows 95.

The [Options] section can contain the following settings:

BootDelay={Seconds}

Default: 2

Purpose: Specifies the amount of time to display the "Starting Windows" message before continuing to boot Windows 95.

BootFailSafe={Boolean}

Default: 0

Purpose: A setting of 1 forces your computer to boot in safe mode.

BootGUI={Boolean}

Default: 1

Purpose: A setting of 1 forces the loading of the GUI (graphical user interface), more commonly known as Windows 95. A setting of 0 (zero) will allow you to boot directly into MS-DOS (see Chapter 3, *The Registry*, for more information).

BootKeys={Boolean}

Default: 1

Purpose: A setting of 1 allows you to use the function key to choose from the various boot options (see "Creating a Startup Menu" in Chapter 6, *Troubleshooting*). A setting of 0 (zero) disables these function keys.

Note: A setting of BootKeys=0 overrides the BootDelay setting.

BootMenu={Boolean}

Default: 0

Purpose: A setting of 1 enables the Startup menu (see "Creating a Startup Menu" in Chapter 6). A setting of 0 (zero) means that you must press F8 when Starting Windows appears to display the Startup menu.

BootMenuDefault={Number}

Default: 1

Purpose: This setting is automatically set to 4 (safe mode) if your system hangs when trying to load Windows 95. Use this setting to set the default menu item. See "Creating a Startup Menu" in Chapter 6 for all possible menu choices.

BootMenuDelay={Number}

   Default: 30

   Purpose: This setting is used to set the number of seconds your system will pause on the Startup menu (see "Creating a Startup Menu" in Chapter 6). If the number of seconds counts down to 0 without user intervention, the option specified in BootMenuDefault is activated.

BootMulti={Boolean}

   Default: 0

   Purpose: A setting of 0 (zero) disables the **multiboot** option, meaning that you will not be allowed to boot your previous operating system even if your system is set up to do so. A setting of 1 allows you to boot your previous operating system with the F4 and F8 keys.

   Note: This setting is set to 0 by default to avoid problems encountered by loading certain programs intended for earlier versions of MS-DOS.

BootWarn={Boolean}

   Default: 1

   Purpose: A setting of 0 disables the safe mode warning message at boot time as well as the startup menu (see "Creating a Startup Menu" in Chapter 6).

BootWin={Boolean}

   Default: 1

   Purpose: A setting of 1 forces Windows 95 to load at startup. A setting of 0 (zero) disables Windows 95 as your default operating system, allowing you to load MS-DOS version 5.x or 6.

   NOTE: Pressing F4 during startup changes this setting temporarily only if BootMulti=1. (For example, pressing F4 with a setting of 0 forces Windows 95 to load.)

DisableLog={Boolean}

   Default: 0

   Purpose: A setting of 0 (zero) disables creation of the bootlog.txt file during startup.

DoubleBuffer={Boolean}

   Default: 0

   Purpose: A setting of 1 enables double-buffering for disk controllers that need it (for example, some older SCSI controllers). A setting of 2 forces double-buffering regardless of whether the controller needs it.

A setting of 0 (zero) disables double-buffering. Don't change this setting unless your controller specifically requires it.

DBLSpace={Boolean}
  Default: 1

  Purpose: A setting of 1 allows the automatic loading of the *DBLSPACE.BIN* file if the DoubleSpace disk compression utility is in use. A setting of 0 prevents this program from loading and may make any DoubleSpace'd drives inaccessible.

DRVSpace={Boolean}
  Default: 1

  Purpose: A setting of 1 allows the automatic loading of the *DRVS-PACE.BIN* file if the DriveSpace disk compression utility is in use. A setting of 0 prevents this program from loading and may make any DriveSpace'd drives inaccessible.

LoadTop={Boolean}
  Default: 1

  Purpose: A setting of 0 (zero) prevents Windows 95 from loading *COMMAND.COM* or *DRVSPACE.BIN/DBLSPACE.BIN* at the top of conventional memory (the first 640 K). If you are having problems with software that may be making assumptions about the available memory, try setting this to 0. Otherwise leave it alone.

Logo={Boolean}
  Default: 1

  Purpose: A setting of 1 forces the ugly Windows 95 logo to appear while Windows 95 is loading. A setting of 0 (zero) prevents the animated logo from being displayed, which can have the added benefit of avoiding incompatibilities with certain third-party memory managers. See Chapter 2 for information on customizing the startup logo.

Network={Boolean}
  Default: 0

  Purpose: A setting of 1 means that network drivers have been installed, and that the "Start Windows, bypassing startup files, with network support" option should appear in the Windows 95 Startup menu (see "Creating a Startup Menu" in Chapter 6).

The *MSDOS.SYS* file also has a section that contains seemingly useless information. This information is necessary to support programs that expect the *MSDOS.SYS* file to be at least 1024 bytes in length. For example, if an antivirus program detects that the *MSDOS.SYS* file is less than 1024 bytes, it may assume that the *MSDOS.SYS* file is infected with a virus. If you delete the *MSDOS.SYS* file your computer will not start. The following statement, followed by a series of Xs, appears in the *MSDOS.SYS* file:

```
;The following lines are required for compatibility with other
                        programs.
;Do not remove them (MSDOS.SYS needs to be >1024 bytes).
```

Since each line begins with a semicolon, the lines are not read by the system.

Index

About the Author

David A. Karp is the chief executive officer of Creative Element, a freelance Internet consulting and graphics design firm in the San Francisco Bay area. His specialties include user-interface design and computer-based training; he currently consults with clients on web site production and software. David, who has a degree in mechanical engineering from the University of California at Berkeley, has written for a number of magazines, most recently for Windows Sources.

He created the Windows95 Annoyances web site, upon which this book is based. This critically acclaimed technical resource is devoted to both supporting and criticizing Microsoft's popular new operating system.

Colophon

The animal on the cover of Windows Annoyances is a Surinam Toad (Pipa Pipa). Surinam Toads are entirely aquatic, never venturing onto land from the dark, muddy South American rivers where they dwell. Adapted to life in a constantly murky environment, the eyes of the Surinam Toad are little more than small dark spots on its evenly brown body. Adult toads are about six inches long with a broad, flat, almost rectangular appearance. They have large, heavily webbed hind feet and small sensory feelers on their front feet and around their mouths. The use these feelers to aid in the search for food along the muddy river bottom. Once a morsel is located, the toad uses its front feet to stir up the water and swish the food into its gaping, toungeless mouth. It will consume anything it can swallow, dead or alive.

Surinam toads are remarkable even among the several other similar species of aquatic frogs. Rather than depositing her eggs in a secluded location and leaving their fate to chance, the female toad relies on the male to direct the fertilized eggs onto the softened skin of her back. Over the course of several hours the skin swells and completely envelopes the eggs. Here the young remain for several months until metamorphosis is complete, emerging as tiny, fully developed toads.

More Titles from O'Reilly

Windows

Inside the Windows 95 Registry

By Ron Petrusha
1st Edition August1996
594 pages, includes diskette
ISBN 1-56592-170-4

This book covers remote registry access, differences between the Win95 and NT registries, and registry backup. You'll also find a thorough examination of the role that the registry plays in OLE, coverage of undocumented registry services, and more. Petrusha shows programmers how to access the Win95 registry from Win32, Win16, and DOS programs, in C and Visual Basic. VxD sample code is also included. The book includes a diskette with registry tools such as REGSPY, a program that shows exactly how Windows applications, libraries, and drivers use settings in the registry.

Windows NT in a Nutshell

By Eric Pearce
1st Edition June 1997 (est.)
342 pages, ISBN 1-56592-251-4

Anybody who installs Windows NT, creates a user, or adds a printer is an NT system administrator (whether they realize it or not). This book organizes NT's complex 4.0 GUI interface, dialog boxes, and multitude of DOS-shell commands into an easy-to-use quick reference for anybody who uses or manages an NT system. It features a new tagged callout approach to documenting the GUI as well as real-life examples of command usage and strategies for problem solving, with an emphasis on networking. Windows NT in a Nutshell will be as useful to the single-system home user as it will be to the administrator of a 1,000-node corporate network.

Inside the Windows 95 File System

By Stan Mitchell
1st Edition May 1997
400 pages, ISBN 1-56592-200-X

This book details the Windows 95 File System, as well as the new opportunities and challenges it brings developers. Over the course of the book, the author progressively strips away the layers of the Win95 File System, which reside in a component named Installable File System Manager or IFSMgr, providing the reader with information crucial for effective File System development. Its "hands-on" approach will help developers become better equipped to make design decisions using the new Win95 File System features.

Windows Annoyances

By David A. Karp
1st Edition June 1997
300 pages (est.), ISBN 1-56592-266-2

Windows Annoyances, a comprehensive resource for intermediate to advanced users of Windows 95 and NT 4.0, details step-by-step how to customize your Win95/NT operating system through an extensive collection of tips, tricks, and workarounds.

You'll learn how to customize every aspect of these systems, far beyond the intentions of Microsoft. An entire chapter on the registry explains how to back up, repair, compress, and transfer portions of the registry for personal customization. Win95 users will discover how Plug and Play, the technology that makes Win95 so hardware-compatible, can save time and improve the way you interact with your computer. You'll also learn how to benefit from the new 32-bit software and hardware drivers that support such features as improved multitasking and long filenames.

How to stay in touch with O'Reilly

1. Visit Our Award-Winning Site

http://www.ora.com/

★"Top 100 Sites on the Web" —*PC Magazine*
★"Top 5% Web sites" —*Point Communications*
★"3-Star site" —*The McKinley Group*

Our web site contains a library of comprehensive product information (including book excerpts and tables of contents), downloadable software, background articles, interviews with technology leaders, links to relevant sites, book cover art, and more. File us in your Bookmarks or Hotlist!

2. Join Our Email Mailing Lists

New Product Releases

To receive automatic email with brief descriptions of all new O'Reilly products as they are released, send email to:
listproc@online.ora.com
Put the following information in the first line of your message (*not* in the Subject field):
subscribe ora-news "Your Name" of "Your Organization" (for example: subscribe ora-news Kris Webber of Fine Enterprises)

O'Reilly Events

If you'd also like us to send information about trade show events, special promotions, and other O'Reilly events, send email to:
listproc@online.ora.com
Put the following information in the first line of your message (*not* in the Subject field):
subscribe ora-events "Your Name" of "Your Organization"

3. Get Examples from Our Books via FTP

There are two ways to access an archive of example files from our books:

Regular FTP

- ftp to:
  ftp.ora.com
  (login: anonymous
  password: your email address)
- Point your web browser to:
  ftp://ftp.ora.com/

FTPMAIL

- Send an email message to:
  ftpmail@online.ora.com
  (Write "help" in the message body)

4. Visit Our Gopher Site

- Connect your gopher to:
  gopher.ora.com

- Point your web browser to:
  gopher://gopher.ora.com/

- Telnet to:
  gopher.ora.com
  login: gopher

5. Contact Us via Email

order@ora.com
To place a book or software order online. Good for North American and international customers.

subscriptions@ora.com
To place an order for any of our newsletters or periodicals.

books@ora.com
General questions about any of our books.

software@ora.com
For general questions and product information about our software. Check out O'Reilly Software Online at **http://software.ora.com/** for software and technical support information. Registered O'Reilly software users send your questions to:
website-support@ora.com

cs@ora.com
For answers to problems regarding your order or our products.

booktech@ora.com
For book content technical questions or corrections.

proposals@ora.com
To submit new book or software proposals to our editors and product managers.

international@ora.com
For information about our international distributors or translation queries. For a list of our distributors outside of North America check out:
http://www.ora.com/www/order/country.html

O'Reilly & Associates, Inc.
101 Morris Street, Sebastopol, CA 95472 USA
TEL 707-829-0515 or 800-998-9938
(6am to 5pm PST)
FAX 707-829-0104

O'REILLY™

Titles from O'Reilly

Please note that upcoming titles are displayed in italic.

WEB PROGRAMMING
Apache: The Definitive Guide
Building Your Own Web
 Conferences
Building Your Own Website
Building Your Own Win-CGI
 Programs
CGI Programming for the World
 Wide Web
Designing for the Web
HTML: The Definitive Guide
JavaScript: The Definitive Guide,
 2nd Ed.
Learning Perl
Programming Perl, 2nd Ed.
Mastering Regular Expressions
WebMaster in a Nutshell
Web Security & Commerce
*Web Client Programming with
 Perl*
World Wide Web Journal

USING THE INTERNET
Smileys
The Future Does Not Compute
The Whole Internet User's Guide
 & Catalog
The Whole Internet for Win 95
Using Email Effectively
Bandits on the Information
 Superhighway

JAVA SERIES
Exploring Java
Java AWT Reference
Java Fundamental Classes
 Reference
Java in a Nutshell
Java Language Reference
Java Network Programming
Java Threads
Java Virtual Machine

SOFTWARE
WebSite™ 1.1
WebSite Professional™
Building Your Own Web
 Conferences
WebBoard™
PolyForm™
Statisphere™

SONGLINE GUIDES
NetActivism   NetResearch
Net Law   NetSuccess
NetLearning   NetTravel
Net Lessons

SYSTEM ADMINISTRATION
Building Internet Firewalls
Computer Crime: A
 Crimefighter's Handbook
Computer Security Basics
DNS and BIND, 2nd Ed.
Essential System Administration,
 2nd Ed.
Getting Connected: The Internet
 at 56K and Up
*Internet Server Administration
 with Windows NT*
Linux Network Administrator's
 Guide
Managing Internet Information
 Services
Managing NFS and NIS
Networking Personal Computers
 with TCP/IP
Practical UNIX & Internet
 Security, 2nd Ed.
PGP: Pretty Good Privacy
sendmail, 2nd Ed.
sendmail Desktop Reference
System Performance Tuning
TCP/IP Network Administration
termcap & terminfo
Using & Managing UUCP
Volume 8: X Window System
 Administrator's Guide
Web Security & Commerce

UNIX
Exploring Expect
Learning VBScript
Learning GNU Emacs, 2nd Ed.
Learning the bash Shell
Learning the Korn Shell
Learning the UNIX Operating
 System
Learning the vi Editor
Linux in a Nutshell
Making TeX Work
Linux Multimedia Guide
Running Linux, 2nd Ed.
SCO UNIX in a Nutshell
sed & awk, 2nd Edition
Tcl/Tk Tools
UNIX in a Nutshell: System V
 Edition
UNIX Power Tools
Using csh & tcsh
When You Can't Find Your UNIX
 System Administrator
Writing GNU Emacs Extensions

WEB REVIEW STUDIO SERIES
Gif Animation Studio
Shockwave Studio

WINDOWS
Dictionary of PC Hardware and
 Data Communications Terms
Inside the Windows 95 Registry
Inside the Windows 95 File
 System
Windows Annoyances
*Windows NT File System
 Internals*
Windows NT in a Nutshell

PROGRAMMING
Advanced Oracle PL/SQL
 Programming
Applying RCS and SCCS
C++: The Core Language
Checking C Programs with lint
DCE Security Programming
Distributing Applications Across
 DCE & Windows NT
Encyclopedia of Graphics File
 Formats, 2nd Ed.
Guide to Writing DCE
 Applications
lex & yacc
Managing Projects with make
Mastering Oracle Power Objects
Oracle Design: The Definitive
 Guide
Oracle Performance Tuning, 2nd
 Ed.
Oracle PL/SQL Programming
Porting UNIX Software
POSIX Programmer's Guide
POSIX.4: Programming for the
 Real World
Power Programming with RPC
Practical C Programming
Practical C++ Programming
Programming Python
Programming with curses
Programming with GNU Software
Pthreads Programming
Software Portability with imake,
 2nd Ed.
Understanding DCE
Understanding Japanese
 Information Processing
UNIX Systems Programming for
 SVR4

BERKELEY 4.4 SOFTWARE DISTRIBUTION
4.4BSD System Manager's
 Manual
4.4BSD User's Reference Manual
4.4BSD User's Supplementary
 Documents

4.4BSD Programmer's Reference
 Manual
4.4BSD Programmer's
 Supplementary Documents
X Programming
Vol. 0: X Protocol Reference
 Manual
Vol. 1: Xlib Programming
 Manual
Vol. 2: Xlib Reference Manual
Vol. 3M: X Window System User's
 Guide, Motif Edition
Vol. 4M: X Toolkit Intrinsics
 Programming Manual, Motif
 Edition
Vol. 5: X Toolkit Intrinsics
 Reference Manual
Vol. 6A: Motif Programming
 Manual
Vol. 6B: Motif Reference Manual
Vol. 6C: Motif Tools
Vol. 8 : X Window System
 Administrator's Guide
Programmer's Supplement for
 Release 6
X User Tools
The X Window System in a
 Nutshell

CAREER & BUSINESS
Building a Successful Software
 Business
The Computer User's Survival
 Guide
Love Your Job!
Electronic Publishing on CD-
 ROM

TRAVEL
Travelers' Tales: Brazil
Travelers' Tales: Food
Travelers' Tales: France
Travelers' Tales: Gutsy Women
Travelers' Tales: India
Travelers' Tales: Mexico
Travelers' Tales: Paris
Travelers' Tales: San Francisco
Travelers' Tales: Spain
Travelers' Tales: Thailand
Travelers' Tales: A Woman's
 World

O'REILLY™

TO ORDER: **800-998-9938** • **order@ora.com** • **http://www.ora.com/**
OUR PRODUCTS ARE AVAILABLE AT A BOOKSTORE OR SOFTWARE STORE NEAR YOU.
FOR INFORMATION: **800-998-9938** • **707-829-0515** • **info@ora.com**

International Distributors

UK, Europe, Middle East and Northern Africa (except France, Germany, Switzerland, & Austria)

INQUIRIES
International Thomson
Publishing Europe
Berkshire House
168-173 High Holborn
London WC1V 7AA, UK
Tel: 44-171-497-1422
Fax: 44-171-497-1426
Email: itpint@itps.co.uk

ORDERS
International Thomson
Publishing Services, Ltd.
Cheriton House, North Way
Andover, Hampshire SP10 5BE,
United Kingdom
Tel: 44-264-342-832 (UK)
Tel: 44-264-342-806
   (outside UK)
Fax: 44-264-364418 (UK)
Fax: 44-264-342761 (outside
UK)
UK & Eire orders:
itpuk@itps.co.uk
International orders:
itpint@itps.co.uk

France

Editions Eyrolles
61 bd Saint-Germain
75240 Paris Cedex 05
France
Fax: 33-01-44-41-11-44

FRENCH LANGUAGE BOOKS
All countries except Canada
Tel: 33-01-44-41-46-16
Email: geodif@eyrolles.com

ENGLISH LANGUAGE BOOKS
Tel: 33-01-44-41-11-87
Email:
distribution@eyrolles.com

Australia

WoodsLane Pty. Ltd.
7/5 Vuko Place, Warriewood
NSW 2102
P.O. Box 935,
Mona Vale NSW 2103
Australia
Tel: 61-2-9970-5111
Fax: 61-2-9970-5002
Email: info@woodslane.com.au

Germany, Switzerland, and Austria

INQUIRIES
O'Reilly Verlag
Balthasarstr. 81
D-50670 Köln
Germany
Tel: 49-221-97-31-60-0
Fax: 49-221-97-31-60-8
Email: anfragen@oreilly.de

ORDERS
International Thomson
Publishing
Königswinterer Straße 418
53227 Bonn, Germany
Tel: 49-228-97024 0
Fax: 49-228-441342
Email: order@oreilly.de

Asia (except Japan & India)

INQUIRIES
International Thomson
Publishing Asia
60 Albert Street #15-01
Albert Complex
Singapore 189969
Tel: 65-336-6411
Fax: 65-336-7411

ORDERS
Telephone: 65-336-6411
Fax: 65-334-1617
thomson@signet.com.sg

New Zealand

WoodsLane New Zealand Ltd.
21 Cooks Street (P.O. Box 575)
Wanganui, New Zealand
Tel: 64-6-347-6543
Fax: 64-6-345-4840
Email: info@woodslane.com.au

Japan

O'Reilly Japan, Inc.
Kiyoshige Building 2F
12-Banchi, Sanei-cho
Shinjuku-ku
Tokyo 160 Japan
Tel: 81-3-3356-5227
Fax: 81-3-3356-5261
Email: kenji@ora.com

India

Computer Bookshop (India)
PVT. LTD.
190 Dr. D.N. Road, Fort
Bombay 400 001 India
Tel: 91-22-207-0989
Fax: 91-22-262-3551
Email:
cbsbom@giasbm01.vsnl.net.in

The Americas

O'Reilly & Associates, Inc.
101 Morris Street
Sebastopol, CA 95472 U.S.A.
Tel: 707-829-0515
Tel: 800-998-9938 (U.S. &
Canada)
Fax: 707-829-0104
Email: order@ora.com

Southern Africa

International Thomson
Publishing Southern Africa
Building 18, Constantia Park
240 Old Pretoria Road
P.O. Box 2459
Halfway House, 1685 South
Africa
Tel: 27-11-805-4819
Fax: 27-11-805-3648

O'REILLY™

O'REILLY™

O'Reilly & Associates, Inc.
101 Morris Street
Sebastopol, CA 95472-9902
1-800-998-9938

Visit us online at:
http://www.ora.com/
orders@ora.com

O'REILLY WOULD LIKE TO HEAR FROM YOU

Which book did this card come from?

_____

Where did you buy this book?
- ❏ Bookstore   ❏ Computer Store
- ❏ Direct from O'Reilly   ❏ Class/seminar
- ❏ Bundled with hardware/software
- ❏ Other _____

What operating system do you use?
- ❏ UNIX   ❏ Macintosh
- ❏ Windows NT   ❏ PC(Windows/DOS)
- ❏ Other _____

What is your job description?
- ❏ System Administrator   ❏ Programmer
- ❏ Network Administrator   ❏ Educator/Teacher
- ❏ Web Developer
- ❏ Other _____

❏ Please send me O'Reilly's catalog, containing
a complete listing of O'Reilly books and
software.

Name _____ Company/Organization _____

Address _____

City _____ State _____ Zip/Postal Code _____ Country _____

Telephone _____ Internet or other email address (specify network) _____

Nineteenth century wood engraving
of a bear from the O'Reilly &
Associates Nutshell Handbook®
Using & Managing UUCP.

POST CARD

BUSINESS REPLY MAIL

FIRST CLASS MAIL   PERMIT NO. 80   SEBASTOPOL, CA

Postage will be paid by addressee

O'Reilly & Associates, Inc.
101 Morris Street
Sebastopol, CA 95472-9902